T0326654

A bibliography of

higher education in Canada

Supplement 1981/Supplément 1981

Bibliographie de

l'enseignement supérieur au Canada

Etudes sur l'Histoire d'Enseignement Supérieur au Canada/Studies in the History of Higher Education in Canada. Sponsored by the Association of Universities and Colleges of Canada, with financial support from the Carnegie Corporation of New York

1. Robin S. Harris and Arthur Tremblay
   A bibliography of higher education in Canada

2. W.P. Thompson
   Graduate education in the sciences in Canadian universities

3. Robin S. Harris
   A bibliography of higher education in Canada: supplement 1965

4. D.C. Masters
   Protestant church colleges in Canada: a history

5. Robin S. Harris
   A bibliography of higher education in Canada: supplement 1971

6. Laurence K. Shook
   Catholic post-secondary education in English-speaking Canada A History

7. Robin S. Harris
   A history of higher education in Canada 1663-1960

8. Robin S. Harris, Marcel de Grandpré, Hazel Roberts and Hugh L. Smith
   A bibliography of higher education in Canada: supplement 1981

A Bibliography of higher education in Canada

Supplement 1981/Supplément 1981

Bibliographie de l'enseignement supérieur au Canada

ROBIN S. HARRIS
MARCEL DE GRANDPRÉ
HAZEL ROBERTS
HUGH L. SMITH

University of Toronto Press
Toronto   Buffalo   London

©University of Toronto Press 1981
Reprinted in paperback 2017
ISBN 978-0-8020-2440-4 (cloth)
ISBN 978-1-4875-9142-7 (paper)

Canadian cataloguing in publication data

Harris, Robin S., 1919-

A bibliography of higher education in Canada : supplement 1981 = Bibliographie de l'enseignement supérieur
au Canada : supplément 1981

(Studies in the history of higher education in Canada,
ISSN 0081-7988 ; 8 = Etudes sur l'histoire d'enseignement
supérieur au Canada, ISSN 0081-7988 ; 8)

Text in English and French.

ISBN 978-0-8020-2440-4 (bound)   ISBN 978-1-4875-9142-7 (pbk.)

1. Education, Higher - Canada - Bibliography. I. Title.
II. Title: Bibliographie de l'enseignement supérieur au
Canada. III. Series: Studies in the history of higher
education in Canada ; 8.

Z5815.C311372 1981   016.37871   C81-095081-2E

FOREWORD

The fourth volume in this bibliographic series, in addition to being a valuable research tool, gives a scholar's-eye-view of a decade of transition -- from the uninhibited growth of the sixties to the uncertainties of the eighties.

It was a decade of major provincial studies of postsecondary systems -- and the Angers, the Graham, the Oliver, the Worth and the Wright Reports - as well as national studies. It saw publication of Robin Harris' mammoth History of Higher Education in Canada. It was a period which coincided with the first decade of the Canadian Society for the Study of Higher Education, a learned society dedicated to an examination of the objectives, achievements and character of Canadian post-secondary education.

That continuing examination will be supported and stimulated by the publication of this, the most ambitious of the bibliographies. Scholars, whether working within the half-dozen graduate programmes established during the decade, or as members of departments of economics, history, philosophy, psychology, sociology and others with a major interest in post-secondary education, or in government agencies, owe another major debt to Professor Harris and his colleagues. They will pay for it, no doubt, by adding their titles to the bibliographic record of the new decade.

The Canadian Society for the Study of Higher Education, in saluting the compilers, also thanks the Carnegie Corporation of New York and the Social Sciences and Humanities Research Council of Canada for contributions that made this publication possible.

Jeffrey Holmes,
President,
Canadian Society for the
Study of Higher Education

AVANT-PROPOS

Le quatrième volume de cette série bibliographique est non seulement un précieux instrument de recherche mais aussi un apperçu érudit d'une décennie de changements, de la croissance incontrôlée des années soixante à l'incertitude des années quatre-vingt.

D'importantes études des systèmes d'éducation postsecondaire tant au niveau provincial - les rapports Anger, Graham, Oliver, Worth et Wright - que national ont été faites au cours de ces dix années. Au cours de cette période, Robin Harris a aussi publié son gigantesque History of Higher Education in Canada. La première décennie de la Société canadienne pour l'étude de l'enseignement supérieur, société savante vouée à l'examen des objectifs, des réalisations et des caractéristiques de l'éducation post-secondaire au Canada, a coïncidé avec cette époque.

La poursuite de cet examen sera soutenue et stimulée par cette publication, la plus ambitieuse des bibliographies. Les chercheurs, qu'ils oeuvrent à l'intérieur de la demi-douzaine de programmes au niveau des études supérieures établis au cours de cette décennie, qu'ils soient membres de facultés ou de départements d'économie, d'histoire, de philosophie, de psychologie, de sociologie ou d'autres s'intéressant à l'éducation post-secondaire, ou qu'ils fassent partie d'organismes gouvernementaux, sont à nouveau en dette envers le professeur Harris et ses collègues. Sans doute la rembourseront-ils en ajoutant leurs publications à la liste bibliographique de la nouvelle décennie.

La Société canadienne pour l'étude de l'enseignement supérieur, en saluant les compilateurs, désire aussi remercier la Carnegie Corporation de New York et le Conseil de recherches en sciences humaines du Canada pour leurs contributions qui ont rendu cette publication possible.

Jeffrey Holmes,
Président,
Société canadienne pour
l'étude de l'enseignement
supérieur

CONTENTS

II NON-DEGREE GRANTING INSTITUTIONS/ETABLISSEMENTS QUI NE CONFERENT PAS DE GRADE

INTRODUCTION

The 1981 Supplement to A Biliography of Higher Education in Canada closely resembles its 1971 predecessor both in the number of entries (approximately 3,500) and the arrangement for classifying them. A comparison of the tables of contents of the two volumes will reveal a) that about a dozen categories have been dropped in Sections 1 (history and organization), 2 (current trends and problems) and 3 (curriculum and teaching) and that Part III (Agencies and Government Departments) has been eliminated; and b) that about the same number of categories have been added in Part I. Part II (non-degree granting institutions) remains unchanged.

The omissions reflect the editors' failure to identify a sufficient number of significant entries to warrant their continuance in this volume, the most revealing of these being "The University and the Church"; the evidence simply is that this topic ceased to be discussed in the 1970's. It must be emphasized, however, that the omission of a category indicates in only two instances the cessation of activity; Notre Dame University of Nelson, B.C. no longer exists, and the changes in the educational system of the Province of Québec have resulted in the disappearance of la faculté des arts as an undergraduate division in the francophone universities. Despite its not being listed, Sainte-Anne continues to exist, and there continues to be activity in the fields of archaeology, Byzantine studies and the other humanities specializations that are not presented in this volume. Almost without exception, the agencies and government departments listed under Part III of the 1971 Supplement continue to function and to publish as will be apparent from an examination of such sections as "The University and the State." The change here is entirely in the interests of conserving space.

There are some changes in Section 1 as the result of the renaming of institutions (Concordia University, Nova Scotia University of Technology, Wilfrid Laurier University). The establishment of a second university in Saskatchewan has necessitated the addition of a category for the universities of that province. The considerable interest during the 1970's in providing locally for the higher education of residents of the Northwest Territories and the Yukon has led to the introduction of "The University of the North." The very great interest that has been apparent throughout the decade in the question of who goes to university and who does not has encouraged the editors to introduce in Section 2 the category Accessibility to Higher Education, as distinct from Admissions (Section 4) under which this topic had previously been listed. Parallel interest in Canadian studies, much of it stimulated by the Symons Report, has resulted in the addition of this topic to Section 3. The introduction of collective bargaining, perhaps the most significant of all the changes in higher education that have occurred during 1970's, explains the introduction of a new category in Section 6.

The relatively small number of changes in the organization of a bibliography which in effect covers the ten-year period 1971-1980 is in striking contrast to the situation in 1971 when major changes were required. The reasons for these changes were described in the Introduction to the 1971 Supplement to which the reader is respectfully referred. The period 1965-1970 was one of remarkable change in Canadian post-secondary education which necessitated fundamental rearrangement of the material. In contrast, the 1970's have proved to be a generally stable period. The problems have been continuing rather than new.

A considerable number of the entries in the 1981 Supplement have appeared earlier in issues of the Canadian Journal of Higher Education and its predecessor Stoa from 1971 to 1980 as "Select Bibliography of Higher Education in Canada." Such items constituted perhaps one half of the entries which the editors had compiled for each issue. The present list includes most of the missing items as well as the much larger number which were identified after a systematic search of the literature. The Select Bibliography used the 1971 Supplement categorization at the outset but introduced the new categories referred to above as the decade advanced.

The number of journals examined for the 1981 Supplement is approximately 200, substantially less than the over 250 consulted in 1971. This reflects no decline in the number of relevant journals, a phenomenon noted in the Introduction to the 1971 Supplement as of considerable significance in the development of post-secondary education in Canada during the 1965-70 period. Rather it is due to greater selectivity on the part of the editors in deciding which journals to search systematically. As the asterisks in the list of journals testify, over 60 new publications have been examined.

In the assembling of the material for this volume the editors have been assisted by Monique Richard of Université de Montréal and Robert Clark and Sheila Dutton of the University of Toronto; their contribution has been substantial. The editors also wish to recognize the work of Vera Baker and her colleagues in the Department of Secretarial Services of the University of Toronto, of Ronald Schoeffel and his colleagues at the University of Toronto Press, and of Daniel Lang, formerly editor of the Canadian Journal of Higher Education and his assistant, Margaret MacKay in preparing the manuscript for publication. Finally, they wish to acknowledge the financial support provided by the Association of Universities and Colleges of Canada and the Canadian Society for the Study of Higher Education and indirectly by the Carnegie Corporation of New York and the Social Sciences and Humanities Research Council of Canada which has made this publication possible.

R.S. Harris
M. de Grandpré
H. Roberts
H. Smith

INTRODUCTION

Le Supplément 1981 de la Bibliographie de l'enseignement supérieur au Canada est semblable à celui de 1971 à la fois par le nombre des références (environ 3,500) et par leur classement. Si l'on compare la table des matières des deux volumes, on constate: a. qu'on a supprimé une douzaine de divisions dans les Sections 1 (Histoire et organisation), 2 (Orientations et problèmes actuels) et 3 (Programmes d'études et méthodes d'enseignement), ainsi que la Troisième partie (Organismes et départements gouvernementaux) au complet; b. qu'on a ajouté à la Première partie (Universités et Collèges qui confèrent des grades) autant de divisions qu'on en a supprimé. La Deuxième partie (Etablissements qui ne confèrent pas de grades) demeure inchangée.

Les divisions supprimées ne contenaient plus assez de références pour justifier leur maintien. Par exemple, "L'Université et l'Eglise" n'a plus fait l'objet d'études depuis 1970. Dans deux autres cas, il s'agit de la disparition d'institutions: Notre Dame University of Nelson, B.C., et d'autre part la faculté des Arts des universités francophones, par suite des changements dans le système scolaire du Québec. Malgré son omission à son titre, le Collège Sainte-Anne continue d'exister et on y est toujours actif dans les domaines de l'archéologie, des études byzantines et des autres secteurs spécialisés des humanités qui ne sont pas présentés dans ce livre. Presque sans exception, les organismes et ministères des gouvernements groupés dans le Supplément 1971 continuent d'exister et de publier comme on peut le constater à l'examen de divisions comme "L'Université et l'Etat". Le changement a pour but de prendre moins d'espace.

Certaines modifications dan la Première partie proviennent du changement de nom des institutions (Concordia University, Nova Scotia University of Technology, Wilfrid Laurier University). La fondation d'une seconde université en Saskatchewan a entraîné une addition pour cette province. L'intérêt porté dans les années 1970 aux services d'enseignement supérieur pour la population des Territoires du Nord Ouest et du Yukon a fait ajouter "The University of the Canadian North". L'intérêt remarquable porté au cours de la décennie au problème de "l'accès à l'université" a fait introduire ce sujet dans la Section 2 à part du titre "Admission" (Section 4) où il était compris jusque-là. L'intérêt attaché, comme en témoigne le Rapport Symons, aux "Etudes candiennes" a fait ajouter ce titre à la Section 3. L'apparition des "négociations collectives"·(peut-être le changement le plus significantif dans l'enseignement supérieur dans les années 1970) explique l'introduction de ce thème dans la Section 6.

Ce nombre relativement petit de changements dans l'organisation de la bibliographie contraste avec les modifications majeures qu'il avait fallu introduire dans celle de 1971. Le lecteur peut trouver dans l'introduction du Supplément 1971 les raisons de ces changements. Les années 1965-1970 avaient produit dans l'enseignement postsecondaire au Canada des

changements si importants qu'il avait fallu faire des modifications
fondamentales dans le classement des sujets. Au contraire, les années 1970
ont été une période de stabilité générale. Les mêmes problèmes ont continué
à se poser, sans qu'il en apparaisse de nouveaux.

Une proportion considerable des références du Supplément 1981 ont
déjà paru de 1971 à 1980 dans La revue canadienne d'enseignement supérieur
et dans Stoa, qui l'a précédée, sous le titre de "Bibliographie choisie sur
l'enseignement supérieur au Canada". Les auteurs publiaient dans la revue
environ la moitié des fiches qu'ils avaient établies. Ils y ajoutent
maintenant la plupart des références omises alors et, à la suite d'une
recherche systematique, un bon nombre d'autres. La "Bibliographie choisie"
a suivi le plan du Supplément 1971 en y introduisant, à mesure que la
nécessité s'en faisait sentir, les modifications énumérées plus haut.

Les revues dépouillées dans le Supplément 1981 sont au nombre
d'environ 200, substantiellement moins que les 250 de 1971. Le nombre des
revues pertinentes s'est maintenu. Le Supplément 1971 signalait combien
leur action avait favorisé le développement de l'enseignement supérieur au
Canada dans les années 1965 à 1970. Il a fallu sélectionner davantage.
L'astérisque dans la liste des revues indique quand même l'addition de 60
revues nouvelles.

Les auteurs ont reçu dans la compilation de ce volume l'aide de
Monique Richard à l'université de Montréal et, à l'Université de Toronto,
celle de Robert Clark et de Sheila Dutton. Leur apport a été important.
Les auteurs désirent aussi signaler le travail de Vera Baker et des ses
collègues du département des services de secrétariat à l'Université de
Toronto, de University of Toronto Press, ainsi que celui de Daniel
Lang, ancien rédacteur-en-chef de La Revue canadienne d'enseignement
supérieur au Canada, et de son assistante, Margaret MacKay, dans la
préparation du manuscrit pour la publication. Ils désirent enfin exprimer
leur reconnaissance pour l'aide financière de l'Association des Universités
et Collèges du Canada, de la Société canadienne pour l'étude de l'enseignement supérieur et, indirectement, de la Carnegie Corporation, de New York,
ainsi que du Conseil canadien de recherche en sciences sociales et dans les
humanités. Sans leur aide cette publication était impossible.

R.S. Harris
M. de Grandpré
H. Roberts
H. Smith

SOURCES

I: BIBLIOGRAPHIES

Association of Universities and Colleges of Canada/Association des Universités et Collèges du Canada.

1961-80   Select bibliography of higher education in Canada/Bibliographie
          sélective sur l'enseignement superieur. Compiled by H.J. Roberts
          et al. Quarterly.

1975-80   Inventory of research into higher education in Canada/Inventaire
          des recherches sur l'enseignement superieure au Canada. Edited by
          J.F. Houwing and A.M. Kristjanson. Annual.

1979-80   An index to Canadian university newspapers/Index des journaux uni-
          versitaires canadiens. By M.J. van den Bergh. Quarterly.

1979   Council of University Presidents conference on excellence, June 6,
          1979: some references. Compiled by D. Michaud. 43 p.

1980   Faculty collective bargaining in Canadian universities/La négocia-
          tion collective chez les professeurs des universités canadiennes,
          1974-1979. Compiled by H.J. Roberts. 44 p.

Canadian Education Association

1969-80   Directory of education studies in Canada/Annuaire d'études en
          education au Canada. Annual.

Canadian Historical Review

1970-80   "Recent publications relating to Canada". In each issue.

National Library of Canada

1960-80   Canadian theses/Thèses canadienne. Irregular.

1978-80   Canadiana, Part II: Theses in microform/Microcopies de thèses.
          Monthly.

Auster, E. Reference sources on Canadian education : an annotated biblio-
          graphy. Toronto, Ontario Institute for Studies in Education, 1978.
          114 p.

Hogan, B.E. "A current bibliography of Canadian church history. Can. Catholic Hist. Assoc. Report 44 (June 1977), 111-144.

Mallea, J.R. and E.C. Shea. Multiculturalism and education: a select bibliography. Toronto: Ontario Institute for Studies in Education, 1979. 290 p.

Rochais, G. Bibliographie annotée de l'énseignement supérieur au Québec, I: Les universités 1968-1978. Montréal: commission d'étude sur les universités, Gouvernement du Québec, 1979. 400 p.

Rochais, G. et C. Locas. Bibliograpie annotée de l'énseignement supérieur au Québec, II: La formation de maîtres. Montréal: Commission d'étude sur les universités, Gouvernement du Québec, 1980. 120 p.

Roland, C. and P. Potter. An annotated bibliography of Canadian medical periodicals 1826-1975. Toronto: Hannah Institute for the History of Medicine, 1979. 77 p.

II CANADIAN JOURNALS: PERIODIQUES CANADIENS

The journals have been searched for the years indicated, but in a small number of cases particular issues could not be examined. Journals not included in the 1971 Supplement to a Bibliography of Higher Education in Canada are indicated by an asterisk. Two asterisks beside a date indicate the cessation of publication of the journal.

Abbreviation	Title	Dates
*Acadiensis	Acadiensis	1971-78
Act. Econ.	Actualité Economique	1970-80
Act. Nat.	Action Nationale	1970-78
*Act. péd.	Actualités pédagogiques	1967-72**
*Act. univ.	Action universitaire	1970-78
Agr.	Agriculture	1970-80
*Alberta Hist.	Alberta History	1975-80
Alta. Jour. Educ. Res.	Alberta Journal of Education Research	1970-80
*Am. Rev. Can. Studies	American Review of Canadian Studies	1971-80
Anthrop. Jour. Canada	Anthropological Journal of Canada	1968-80
*Antigonish Rev.	Antigonish Review	1970-80
Arch. Concept	Architecture Concept	1970-78
*Archivaria	Archivaria Supersedes Can. Archivist	1975-80
Atlantic Advocate	Atlantic Advocate	1970-80
*Atlantis	Atlantis	1975-80
AUCC Proc.	Association of Universities and Colleges of Canada Proceedings	1970-80
Bien-être	Bien-être Social Canadien Superseded by Digest Sociale	1971-73**
*B.C. Perspectives	B.C. Perspectives	1972-80
*B.C. Studies	B.C. Studies	1970-80
*Bull. Hist. Medicine	Bulletin of the History of Medicine	1970-78
Bull. Inf. Cath.	Bulletin des Infirmières Catholiques	1969-76**
*Bull. United Church	Bulletin of the United Church of Canada	1969-77
Bus. Quart.	Business Quarterly	1970-80
*CACUL Newsletter	Canadian Association of College and University Libraries Newsletter	1970-80
*Cah. can musique	Cahiers Canadiens de Musique	1970-76**
Cah. Dix	Cahiers des Dix	1970-76
Cah. géog	Cahiers de géographie de Québec	1970-78
Cah. hist	Cahiers d'Histoire	1969-77
Cah. Nursing	Cahiers du Nursing Canadien	1970-78
*Cah. Québec	Cahiers de l'Université du Québec	1969-73**
Can. Admin.	Canadian Administrator	1971-80

*Can-Am. Rev. Hungarian Studies	Canadian-American Review of Hungarian Studies	1974-78
*Can. Archivist	Canadian Archivist <u>Superseded by</u> Archivaria	1970-74**
Can. Arch.	Canadian Architect	1970-80
Can. Bar Assoc. Jour.	Canadian Bar Association Journal	1970-73**
Can. Bar. Rev.	Canadian Bar Review	1970-80
Can. Bus.	Canadian Business	1970-78
Can. Chartered Accountant	Canadian Chartered Accountant <u>Superseded by</u> Chartered Accountant	1970-73
Can. Cath. Hist. Assoc. A.R.	Canadian Catholic Historical Association Annual Report	1970-77
*Can. Cath. Hist. Assoc. S.S.	Canadian Catholic Historical Association Study Session	1970-79
Can. Counsellor	Canadian Counsellor	1970-80
Can. Dent. Assoc. Jour.	Canadian Dental Association Journal	1970-78
Can. Ethnic Studies	Canadian Ethnic Studies	1970-78
Can. Family Physician	Canadian Family Psysician	1970-78
Can. Forum	Canadian Forum	1970-80
Can. Geog. Jour.	Canadian Geographic Journal	1970-80
Can. H.P.E.R. Jour.	Canadian Association for Health Physical Education and Recreation Journal	1969-80
Can. Hist. Assoc. Papers	Canadian Historical Association Papers	1970-80
Can. Hist. Rev.	Canadian Historical Review	1970-80
Can. Home Econ. Jour.	Canadian Home Economics Journal	1970-80
*Can. International Educ.	Canadian and International Education <u>Supersedes</u> Comp. Inter. Educ. Soc.	1972-80
Can. Jewish Outlook	Canadian Jewish Outlook	1970-80
Can. Jour. African Studies	Canadian Journal of African Studies	1970-80
Can. Journ. Behav. Science	Canadian Journal of Behavioural Science	1970-80
Can. Jour. Econ.	Canadian Journal of Economics	1970-80
*Can. Jour. Educ.	Canadian Journal of Education	1976-80
*Can. Jour. Higher Educ.	Canadian Journal of Higher Education <u>Supersedes</u> Stoa	1975-80
*Can. Jour. Hist. Soc. Sci.	Canadian Journal of History and Social Science	1970-74**
*Can. Jour. Sport. Phys. Educ.	Canadian Journal of History of Sport and Physical Education	1970-80
*Can. Jour. Information Sci.	Canadian Journal of Information Sciences	1976-78
Can. Jour. Linguistics	Canadian Journal of Linguistics	1970-80
Can. Jour. Occ. Therapy	Canadian Journal of Occupational Therapy	1970-80
Can. Jour. Political Sci.	Canadian Journal of Political Science	1970-80

*Can. Jour. Political Social Theory	Canadian Journal of Political and Social Theory	1977-80
Can. Jour. Psych.	Canadian Journal of Psychology	1970-80
Can. Jour. Public Health	Canadian Journal of Public Health	1974-80
*Can. Jour. Soc. Work Educ.	Canadian Journal of Social Work Education	1974-78
*Can. Jour. Sociology	Canadian Journal of Sociology	1975-80
Can. Jour. Theology	Canadian Journal of Theology	1970**
*Can. Jour. Univ. Cont. Educ.	Canadian Journal of University Continuing Education	1974-80
Can. Library Jour.	Canadian Library Journal	1970-80
Can. Lit.	Canadian Literature	1970-80
Can. Med. Assoc. Jour.	Canadian Medical Association Journal	1970-80
*Can. Mental Health	Canadian Mental Health	1970-78
Can. Mod. Lang. Rev.	Canadian Modern Language Review	1970-80
Can. Museum Assoc. Gaz.	Canadian Museum Association Gazette	1970-80
Can. Music Educ.	Canadian Music Educator	1970-80
Can. Nurse	Canadian Nurse	1970-80
Can. Pharm. Jour.	Canadian Pharmaceutical Journal	1970-80
Can. Physiotherapy	Canadian Physiotherapy Association Journal Superseded by Physiotherapy Canada	1970-72**
Can. Psych. Assoc. Jour.	Canadian Psychiatric Association Journal	1964-80
Can. Psych. Rev.	Canadian Psychological Review Supersedes Can. Psych.	1975-78
Can. Psych.	Canadian Psychologist Superseded by Can. Psych. Rev.	1970-74**
Can. Public Admin.	Canadian Public Administration	1970-80
*Can. Public Policy	Canadian Public Policy	1975-80
Can. Research	Canadian Research Supersedes Can. R. and D.	1975-80
Can. R. and D.	Canadian Research and Development Superseded by Can. Research	1970-74**
Can. Rev. Amer.Studies	Canadian Review of American Studies	1971-80
Can. Rev. Soc. Anthrop.	Canadian Review of Sociology and Anthropology	1970-80
Can. Slav. Papers	Canadian Slavonic Papers	1970-79
Can. Slav. Studies	Canadian Slavonic Studies	1970-78
Can. Speech Jour.	Canadian Speech Communication Jour.	1970-76
*Can. Student Services Jour.	Canadian Association of University Student Personnel Services Journal	1966-70**
*Can. Tax Jour.	Canadian Tax Journal	1970-80
Can. Univ. & College	Canadian University and College	1970-73**
Can. Vet. Jour.	Canadian Veterinary Journal	1970-80
CAUT Bull. ACPU	Canadian Association of University Teachers Bulletin/Bulletin de l'Association Canadienne des Professeurs d'Université	1970-80

Chartered Accountant	Chartered Accountant Supersedes Can.	
	Chartered Accountant	1973–80
Chitty's Law Jour.	Chitty's Law Journal	1970–80
*College Canada	College Canada	1976–80
Comm. Jour.	Commerce Journal	1970–78
*Community Planning Rev.	Community Planning Review	1970–77
*Comp. Inter. Educ. Soc.	Comparative and International Educational Society of Canada Papers Superseded by Can. International Educ.	1970–72**
Continuous Learning	Continuous Learning	1970**
Convergence	Convergence	1968–80
Culture	Culture	1970**
*Dal. Law Jour.	Dalhousie Law Journal	1973–80
Dalhousie Rev.	Dalhousie Review	1970–80
Dialogue	Dialogue	1970–78
Digest Sociale	Digest Sociale Supersedes Bien-Être	1974–78
Education Canada	Education Canada	1970–78
*Educ. et Soc.	Education et Société	1970–75**
*Educ. Québec	Education Québec	1970–79
Eng. Jour.	Engineering Journal	1970–80
English Quart.	English Quarterly	1970–78
*English Studies in Canada	English Studies in Canada	1975–80
Etudes Lit.	Etudes Littéraire	1970–78
Etudes Slav.	Etudes Slaves et Est-européenes	1970–76
Executive	Executive	1970–78
*Feliciter	Feliciter	1970–80
For. Chron.	Forestry Chronicle	1970–78
Fôr.-Cons.	Forêt-Conservation	1970–80
*Forum	Forum	1970–80
Hist. Kingston	Historical Kingston	1972–78
*Histoire Soc.	Histoire Sociale	1970–80
Humanities Assoc. Rev.	Humanities Association Review	1975–80
Ing.	L'Ingenieur	1970–80
Inst. Prof. Librarians Ont. Q.	Institute of Professional Librarian of Ontario Quarterly	1970–76**
Infirmier Can.	Infirmier Canadienne	1970–80
*Interchange	Interchange	1970–80
*International Jour.	International Journal	1970–80
*Jour. A.C.C.C.	Journal of the Association of Canadian Community Colleges	1977–80
Jour. Musicales	Journal des Jeunesses Musicales du Canada	1970–71
*Jour. Can. Art Hist.	Journal of Canadian Art History	1974–79
Jour. Can. Studies	Journal of Canadian Studies	1970–80
Jour. Educ. (N.S.)	Journal of Education Department of Education, Halifax, Nova Scotia	1970–80
*Jour. Educ. Vanc.	Journal of Education of the Faculty of Education: Vancouver	1973–75**

Jour. Educ. Thought	Journal of Educational Thought	1970-80
Jour. Can. Church Hist. Soc.	Journal of the Canadian Church Historical Society	1970-80
*Jour. Hist. Med.	Journal of the History of Medicine & Related Sciences	1970-80
*Jour. Social Issues	Journal of Social Issues	1970-80
Lakehead Univ. Rev.	Lakehead University Review	1970-80
*Laurentian Univ. Rev.	Laurentian University Review	1970-80
Lib. Assoc. Alta. Bull.	Library Association of Alberta Bulletin	1970-80
Liberté	Liberté	1970-78
Maintenant	Maintenant	1970-74**
*Malahat Rev.	Malahat Review	1970-80
*Man in the Northeast	Man in the Northeast	1971-80
Man. Jour. Educ.	Manitoba Journal of Education	1970-78
Man. Law Jour.	Manitoba Law Journal	1970-80
McGill Jour. Educ.	McGill Journal of Education	1970-78
Mém. S.R.C.	Mémoires de la Société Royale du Canada	1970-80
Modern Med. Canada	Modern Medicine in Canada	1970-80
*Mouvement	Mouvement	1966-76**
Nat. Can.	Naturaliste Canadien	1970-80
*Newfoundland Quart.	Newfoundland Quarterly	1970-78
*Nova Scotia Hist. Quart.	Nova Scotia Historical Quarterly	1971-78
*Ont. Geog.	Ontario Geography	1970-78
Ont. Hist.	Ontario History	1970-80
Ont. Lib. Rev.	Ontario Library Review	1970-78
Ont. Med. Rev.	Ontario Medical Review	1970-80
Ont. Psych.	Ontario Psychologist	1970-80
*Opinion Canada	Opinion Canada	1972-78
*Optimum	Optimum	1973-80
Orbit	Orbit	1970-80
Osgoode Law Jour.	Osgood Hall Law Journal	1970-80
Our Generation	Our Generation	1970-80
Perf. Arts. Can.	Performing Arts in Canada	1970-80
Pharm.	Le Pharmacien	1970-78
Phoenix	Phoenix	1970-80
Physics in Canada	Physics in Canada	1972-80
Physiotherapy Can.	Physiotherapy Canada Superseded Can. Physiotherapy	1972-80
Prospectives	Prospectives	1978-80
*Quart Can. Studies	Quarterly of Canadian Studies	1972-80
*Québec Sci.	Québec Science	1969-80
Queen's Quart.	Queen's Quarterly	1970-80
Recherches Soc.	Recherches Sociographiques	1970-78
*Records Management Quart.	Records Management Quarterly	1970-80
Relations	Relations	1970-80
Relations Ind.	Relations Industrielles	1970-78

*Rev. AUPELF	Revue de l'AUPELF	1970-78
Rev. Barreau	Revue du Barreau	1970-80
*Rev. Can. d'ens. Sup.	Revue Canadien de l'Enseignement Supérieur	1975-80
*Rev. Can. comportement	Revue Canadienne des Sciences du Comportement	1970-78
*Rev. Sci. Educ.	Revue des Sciences de l'Education	1969-72
Rev. Desjardines	Revue Desjardines	1970-78
Rev. Géog. Montréal	Revue de Géographie de Montréal	1970-77
Rev. Hist.	Revue d'Histoire de l'Amérique Française	1970-80
Rev. Notariat	Revue du Notariat	1970-80
Rev. Scolaire	Revue Scolaire	1970-78
Rev. Univ. Ottawa	Revue de l'Université d'Ottawa	1970-80
Royal Astron. Jour.	Royal Astronomical Society of Canada Journal	1970-80
*Saguenayensis	Saguenayensis	1970-78
Sask. Hist.	Saskatchewan History	1970-80
Sask. Lib.	Saskatchewan Library	1972-76**
Schol. Pub.	Scholarly Publishing	1970-80
*School Guidance Worker	School Guidance Worker	1970-80
*School Progress	School Progress	1970-73**
*Science Dimension	Science Dimension	1970-80
Science et Esprit	Science et Esprit	1970-80
Science Forum	Science Forum	1970-80
*Seminar	Seminar	1965-78
Serv. Soc.	Service Sociale	1970-78
*Soc. Can. Eglise Cath.	Société Canadienne d'histoire de l'Eglise Catholique, Sessions d'étude	1970-78
*Soc. Hist.	Social History	1970-80
Soc. Worker	Social Worker	1974-80
Society/Société	Society/Société	1977-78
*Soc. Rev.	Sociological Review	1970-80
*Sociologie et Sociétés	Sociologie et Sociétés	1969-80
*Stoa	Stoa Superseded by Can. Jour.Higher Ed./Rev. Can. d'ens. Sup.	1971-74**
*Studies in Religion	Studies in Religion	1971-80
*Teacher Educ.	Teacher Education	1968-80
Thémis	Revue Juridique Thémis	1970-80
This Magazine	This Magazine is about Schools	1970-80
Trans. R.S.C.	Transactions of the Royal Society of Canada	1970-80
UBC Law Rev.	UBC Law Review	1970-80
Union Méd.	Union Médicale	1970-80
UNB Law Jour.	UNB Law School Journal	1970-80
Univ. Aff./Aff. univ.	University Affairs/Affaires universitaire	1970-80
Univ. Toronto Law Jour.	University of Toronto Journal	1970-80
Univ. Tor. Quart.	University of Toronto Quarterly	1970-80

Vie Médicale   La Vie Médicale au Canada <u>Supersedes</u>
                       Laval Médicale   1970-80

1.   History and Organization/Histoire et organization

A. GENERAL/GENERALITES

1969 Epstein, M. "Sir William Macdonald, benefactor of education." M.A.
thesis, McGill Univ. 1969.

McDougall, E.A. "Towards the establishment of a Church of Scotland
university in the Canadas." Bulletin of the United Church of Canada
21 (1969-70) 3-27.

1970 Giroux-Masse, T. "La Constitution canadienne et l'éducation dans une
société moderne." Thémis 5 (1970) 367-398.

Harris, R.S. "Higher education in Australia and Canada: a comparative
study." Comp. Inter. Educ. Soc. Papers 1970, 13-31.

Penfield, W. "The University" and "L'Université" in Second thoughts:
science, the arts and the spirit." Toronto: McClelland & Stewart,
(1970) p.14-23 and 136-146.

Wilson, H.T. "Continentalism and Canadian higher education." Can.
Rev. of American Studies (Fall 1970) 89-99.

Zsigmond, Z.E. and C.J. Wenaas, Enrolment in Educational Institutions
by Province, 1951-52 to 1980-81. Ottawa: Queen's Printer, 1970. 306
p. (Economic Council of Canada Staff Study No. 25).

1971 Burn, B. "Higher education in Canada" in Higher education in nine
countries. Edited by B. Burn, New York: McGraw-Hill, 1971. p.91-122.

Charland, T. "La démission du Dr Meilleur comme surintendant de
l'éducation (1855)." Rev. Hist. 24 (mars 1971) 513-515.

Meltz, N.M. Patterns of university education in Ontario, Canada and
the United States by field of study, 1950-51 to 1980-81. Toronto: U
of T Press, 1971. 39 p.

Shook, L.K. Catholic Post-Secondary Education in English-Speaking
Canada: a History. Toronto: U. of T. Press, 1971. 457 p.

1972 Bissell, C. T. "Canada" in J.A. Perkins, ed. Higher Education: from
Autonomy to Systems (New York: International Council for Educational
Development, 1972) p 175-184.

Picard, R. "L'université aussi." Educ. et Soc. 3 (sept. 1972)18-19.

Simoneau, R. "Doctrines universitaires et systèmes universitaires:
une étude de cas. Recherches soc. 13 (sept.-déc. 1972) 365-380.

1973 Lebel, M. "Influences américaines sur les universités canadiennes."
Mém. S.R.C. 1973. 43-63.

Canada, Statistics Canada, Education, Science and Culture Division.
Education in Canada: a Statistical Review for the Period 1960-61 to
1970-71. Ottawa: Information Canada, 1973. 613 p.

Hunt, P. "Commentary: toward the totalitarian university." Jour. Can.
Studies 8 (Feb. 1973) 57-64.

Schaafsma, J. "An econometric study of the demand for higher education in Canada." Ph.D. thesis, Univ. of Toronto, 1973.

1974 Aucoin, P. and R. Treach, "The Ministry of State for Science and
Technology." Can. Public Admin. 17 (fall 1974) 461-481.

Bergen, J.J. "A comparative analysis--Councils of Ministers of Education in Canada and West Germany." Alta. Jour. Educ. Res. 20 (Dec.
1974) 293-304.

Chaiton, A. "The History of the National Council of Education of
Canada." M.A. thesis, Univ. of Toronto, 1974.

Cook R. "The professor and the prophet of unrest." Trans. R.S.C.
1974. 227-250.

Daoust, G. et P. Bélanger, L'université dans une société éducative.
Montréal: Les Presses de l'Université de Montréal, 1974. 246 p.

Gayfer, M. An overview of Canadian education. Toronto: Can. Educ.
Assoc. 1974. 40 p.

Harris, R.S. "The Universities of Canada." Commonwealth Universities
Yearbook 1974 (London: Assoc. of Commonwealth Univs.). 768-782 (arti-
cle appears with annual revision in subsequent yearbooks to 1980).

Patterson, R.S., J.W. Chalmers and J.W. Friesen, Profiles of Canadian
educators (M. Bourgeoys, T. McCulloch, J. Strachan, E. Ryerson, M.
d'Avray, et al). Toronto: D.C. Heath, 1974. 409 p.

Pilkington, G. "A History of the National Conference of Canadian
Universities, 1911-1961." Ph.D. Thesis, Univ. of Toronto, 1974.

1974 Munroe, D. The organization and administration of education in
Canada. Ottawa: Information Canada, 1974. 219 p.

Stamp, R.M. "Canadian universities and Canadian identity." Can.
International Educ. 3 (June 1974) 17-34.

1975   Alexander, D. "Canadian Higher Education—a review of the Graham Royal Commission." Dalhousie Rev. 55 (autumn 1975) 491-504.

Larose, W. "The struggle for a federal office of education for Canada." M.A. thesis, McGill Univ. 1975.

1976   Canadian universities, a statistical summary/Universités canadiennes, sommaire statistique. Prepared by Statistics Canada in co-operation with the Association of Universities and Colleges of Canada/Préparé par Statistique Canada en collaboration avec l'Association des Universités et Collèges du Canada. Ottawa, Ont., Statistics Canada, 1976. 118p.

1976   Cook, G.L. "Alfred Fitzpatrick and the foundation of Frontier College." Canada 3 (June 1976) 15-39.

Harris, R.S. A history of higher education in Canada 1663-1960. Toronto: U. of T. Press, 1976. 715 p.

Masters, D.C. "The Scottish tradition in higher education," in The Scottish tradition in Canada. Edited by W.S. Reid, Toronto, McClelland and Stewart, 1976. p.248-272.

Organization for Economic Cooperation and Development. Reviews of national policies for education: Canada. Paris: OECD, 1976. 264 p.

Shortt, S.E.D. The search for an ideal: six Canadian intellectuals and their convictions in an age of transition. 1890-1930. Toronto: U. of T. Press, 1976. 216 p.

Stokes, L.D. "Canada and an academic refugee from Nazi Germany: the case of Gerhard Herzberg." Can. Hist. Rev. 57 (1976) 150-160.

Wojciechowski, J.A. "Universities and Canadian culture." Rev. Univ. Ottawa 2 (avril-juin 1976) 169-179.

1977   Cook, T.G. "The thought and public career of Sir George Parkin, 1846-1922." Ph.D. thesis, Queen's Univ. 1977.

Côté, F. "... la plus grande menace—c'est la violence sociale à l'intérieur." Univ. aff./Aff.univ. 18(Sept. 1977) 7.

Splete, A. "U.S. university deeply involved in Canada-U.S. relations." Univ. aff./Aff. univ. 18(Sept. 1977) 8.

Sullivan, N. "Canada needs 'fewer and better universities'." Univ. aff./Aff. univ. 18(Sept. 1977) 4-6.

1978 From the sixties to the eighties: a statistical portrait of Canadian higher education. Prepared by Max von Zur-Muehlen (et al) for the Congress of the Universities of the Commonwealth, Vancouver, B.C., 1978. Ottawa, Statistics Canada, 1978. 111 p.

Horn, M. "Academics and Canadian social and economic policy in the depression and war years." Jour. Can. Studies 13 (1978) 3-10.

Ostry, B. The cultural connection: an essay on culture and government policy in Canada. Toronto: McClelland & Stewart, 1978. 218 p.

Sheffield, E.F. et al. Systems of higher education: Canada. New York: International Council for Educational Development, 1978. 219 p.

Stamp, R.M. "Canadian high schools in the 1920's and 1930's: the social challenge to the academic tradition." Hist. Papers (1978) 76-93.

1979 Blauer, M. "A functional analysis of post-secondary commissions" in Issues in Higher Education. Edited by A. Gregor and K. Watson. Winnipeg: Univ. of Manitoba, 1979. p.45-54.

Gregor A. "The re-alignment of post-secondary education systems in Canada." Can. Jour. Higher Educ. 9, 2 (1979) 35-49.

Naimark, A. "Post-secondary commissions" in Issues in higher education. Ed. by A. Gregor and K. Wilson. Winnipeg: Univ. of Manitoba, 1979. p.29-44.

Sheffield, E.F., H.J. Nash and H. Hamm-Brucher. "The OECD review and higher education." Can. Jour. Higher Education. 9,2 (1979) 1-18.

Axelrod, P. "Business aid to Canadian universities 1957-1965." Interchange. 11.1 (1980).

1980 Grayson, J. and L. Grayson. "Canadian literary and other elites: the historical and institutional bases of shared realities." Can. Rev. Soc. Anthrop. 17, 4 (1980) 338-356.

Jarrell, R.A. and N.R. Ball, eds. Science, Technology and Canadian history/les sciences, la technologie et l'histoire canadienne. Waterloo: Wilfred Laurier University Press, 1980. 246 p.

Von Zur-Muehlen, M. and J-.A. Belliveau. Three decades of full-time Canadian university teachers: a statistical portrait. Ottawa: the authors 1980. 295 p.

Leslie, P.N. Canadian universities 1980 and beyond: enrolment, structural change and finance. Ottawa: Assoc. Univs. Colleges of Canada, 1980. 446 p.

B. THE ATLANTIC PROVINCES/LES PROVINCES ATLANTIQUES

1968 Kitchen, H.W. Universal education in the Atlantic provinces: the next decade. Halifax: Atlantic Development Board, 1968. 49 p.

1969 Crean, J.G., M.F. Ferguson and H.J. Somers. Higher education in the Atlantic provinces for the 1970's: a study prepared under the auspices of the Association of Atlantic Universities for the Maritime Union Study. Halifax: Assoc. of Atlantic Univs. 121 p.

1972 An outline for the proposed Maritime Provinces Higher Education Commission. Charlottetown, PEI: Council of Maritime Premiers, 1972. McCreath, P. "Current developments in education in Atlantic Canada." Can. Forum 51 (Oct.-Nov. 1972) 70-72.

1973 Macnutt, W.S. "The universities of the Maritimes - a glance backward." Dalhousie Rev. 53 (Autumn 1973) 431-448.

1975 Maritime Provinces Higher Education Commission. Annual report/Rapport annuel 1974/75 - . Fredericton, N.B.: Council of Maritime Premiers, MPHEC, 1975 - .

1976 Maritime Provinces Higher Education Commission. Higher Education in the Maritimes: an Overview. Fredericton: the Commission, 1976. 40 p.

1978 Maritime Provinces Higher Education Commission. Balancing needs and resources: evolving three years regional planning for higher education in the Maritime Provinces/Equilibre entre les besoins et les ressources: planification trienniale dévelopante au niveau de la région pour l'enseignement superiéur dans les Provinces Maritimes. Fredericton: MPHEC, 1978. 42, 52 p.

1979 Maritime Provinces Higher Education Commission. Issues in the eighties: evolving three year regional planning for higher education in the Maritime Provinces 1979-80 to 1981-82/Les perspectives des années quatre-vingt: planification triennale dévelopante au niveau de la région pour l'enseignement superieur dans les Provinces Maritimes 1979-80 à 1981-82. Fredericton: MPHEC, 1979. 66, 72 p.

1980 Maritime Provinces Higher Education Commission/Commission de l'enseignement supeéieur des provinces maritime. Planning for the 80's. Evolving three year regional planning for higher Education in the Maritime Province 1980-81 to 1982-83./Planification pour les années 80. Planification triennale développante au niveau de la région pour l'enseignement superieur dans les provinces maritimes 1980-81 à 1982-83. Fredericton, N.B.: M.P.H.E.C./CESPM. 1980. 66p./p. 68.

Maritime Provinces Higher Education Commission/Commission de l'enseignement superieur des provinces maritimes. Student aid for The eighties: report of the study of financial aid to Maritime students/ l'aide dux étudiants dans les années 1980: rapport de l'étude sur l'aide financière aux étudiants des provinces maritimes. Fredericton, N.B.: MPHEC/CESPM, 1980. 124 p./p. 128.

Watkins, L. "Halifax, Dartmouth area: one of the three biggest marine science centres in Western hemisphere." Can. Geog. Jour. 100, 5 (1980) 12-23.

MEMORIAL UNIVERSITY OF NEWFOUNDLAND

1971 Frecker, G.A. "Address on the occasion of his installation (as chancellor)" MUN Gazette 4 (Oct. 1971) 3-6.

1974 Gleason, M. "Harbor Grace, Cow Head, Nain - the extension service reaches out." Univ. aff./Aff. univ. 15 (May 1974) 2-4.

1974 Halpert, H. and N.V. Rosenberg. "Folklore work at Memorial University." Can. Forum 53 (Mar.1974) 31-32.

Morgan, M.O. "Installation Address (as President)." MUN Gazette 6 (Apr. 1974) 4-7.

1975 Bellows, G.R. "The foundation of Memorial University College 1919 - 1925." Newfoundland Quart. 71 (Summer 1975) 5-9.

1976 Memorial University Report of Task Force on University Priorities. St. John's: the University, 1976. 309 p.

Newett, J. "History of School of Nursing." MUN Gazette 9 (29 Oct 1976) 1-2.

Rowe, F.W. Education and culture in Newfoundland. Toronto: McGraw-Hill Ryerson, 1976. 225 p.

1977 "Educational Television Centre: ten years service to the University and the province." MUN Gazette 9 (1 Apr. 1977) 5-8.

Gleason, M. "C.A.R.E. examines M.U.M.'s extension projects." Univ. aff./Aff. univ. 18 (Dec. 1977) 6-7.

1979 Coish, C. "The Health Sciences Centre." Atlantic Advocate 69 (Feb. 1979) 10-11, 15-17.

1980 Sullivan, A.M. "A successful academic upgrading programme: follow-up over five years." Can. Jour. Higher Educ. 10, 2 (1980) 85-102.

UNIVERSITY OF PRINCE EDWARD ISLAND

1971   Shook, L.K.   "St. Dunstan's University" in Catholic post-secondary education in English-speaking Canada. Toronto: U. of T. Press, 1971. p.35-56.

1972   Brehaut, W.   Teacher education in Prince Edward Island.   Toronto: O.I.S.E., 1972. 58 p.

1975   Howell, D.G.   Report of a study of the establishment of a school of veterinary medicine in the Atlantic region.   Fredericton: Maritime Provinces Higher Education Commission, 1975.   45 p.

University of Prince Edward Island, Senate Committee on Objectives. Towards a university community: goals in perspective. Charlottetown: the University, 1975.

1976   Callbeck, L.   "PEI's university: a story of progress."   Atlantic Advocate 66, 10 (1976) 56-59.

1977   University of Prince Edward Island, Senate Research Committee. University of Prince Edward Island: research and related activities 1969-1976.   Charlottetown: the University, 1977.

THE UNIVERSITIES OF NOVA SCOTIA/
LES UNIVERSITES DE LA NOUVELLE-ECOSSE

1966   Rimmington, G.T.   "The founding of universities in Nova Scotia." Dalhousie Rev.   46 (1966) 319-337.

1972   Leffe, J.   "An early attempt at university consolidation in Nova Scotia."   Nova Scotia Hist. Quart.   2 (Fall 1972).

1973   Healy, D.   "The University of Halifax 1875-1881."   Dalhousie Rev. 53 (Spring 1973) 39-56.

1974   Nova Scotia.   Royal Commission on Education, Public Services and Provincial-Municipal Relations.   Report.   Vol. 111, 1974, Education. Halifax: Queen's Printer.

1975   Graham, J.F.   "An introduction to the Nova Scotia Royal Commission." Can. Public Policy 1 (Summer 1975) 345-354.

1977   Deveau, D.   "L'université et le développement socio-culturel en Acadie."   Act. Nat. (nov.-déc. 1977) 257-273.

ACADIA UNIVERSITY

1968   Balloch, A.E.   "Founders' Day address." Acadia Bull. (Feb. 1968) 5-7.

Beveridge, J.M.K.   "The functions and responsibilities of a university." Acadia Bull. (Feb. 1968) 14-15, 18.

1973   "The changing scene at Acadia: interview with the President." Acadia Bull. (Summer 1973) 1-4.

1975   Perkin, J.R.C., ed.   Undoing of Babel. Toronto: McClelland & Stewart, 1975.   128 p.   (Includes memoir of Watson Kirkconnell by J.M.K. Beveridge).

DALHOUSIE UNIVERSITY/UNIVERSITY OF KING'S COLLEGE

1970   "Dal plans transition year for disadvantaged students." Univ. Aff./ Aff.univ. 11 (May 1970) 7.

1972   Baird, F.   "A missionary educator: Dr. Thomas McCulloch." Dalhousie Rev.   52 (Winter 1972-73) 611-617.

1976   Perkyns, D.   "How Dalhousie became the centre of Halifax's cultural life."   Performing Arts in Canada 13 (Spring 1976) 29-31.

Shortt, S.E.D. "Archibald MacMechan: romantic idealist" in The search for an ideal: six Canadian intellectuals and their convictions in an age of transition 1890-1950. Toronto: U. of T. Press, 1976. p. 40-57.

1977   Ritchie, C.   An Appetite for Life: the education of a young diarist 1924-1927.   Toronto: Macmillan.   192 p.

1978   Bishop, R.L.   "Joseph Leverett and the King's College observatory." R. Astron.Soc. Jour.   72 (June 1978) 138-148.

1979   "The Atlantic Regional Laboratory – a quarter century of research." Science Dimension 9(5) 12-19.

Montgomery, L.M.   "A girl's place at Dalousie College, 1986." Atlantis 5.1 (1979) 146-153.

Waite, P.B.   "Playing at universities: Dalhousie and the sectarian struggles in Nova Scotia."   Higher Education in Canada: historical perspectives.   Monographs in Education II.   Winnipeg: Univ. of Manitoba, 1979.   p. 67-81.

Willis, J.   A History of Dalhousie Law School.   Toronto: U. of T. Press, 1979.   302 p.

1980   DeMont, J.   "Dal's new athletic centre."   <u>Atlantic Advocate</u> (Oct. 1980) 38, 40, 43.

Page, F.H.   "William Lyall in his setting."   <u>Dalhousie Rev.</u>   60 1 (Spring 1980) 49-66.

MOUNT SAINT VINCENT

1971   Shook, L.K.   "Mount Saint Vincent" in <u>Catholic post-secondary education in English-speaking Canada</u>.   Toronto: U. of T. Press, 1971.   p. 96-102.

NOVA SCOTIA COLLEGE OF ART AND DESIGN 1980

Pierre, G.   "Nova Scotia College of Art and Design makes historic move."   <u>Univ. Aff./Aff. univ.</u> 21, 2 (1980) 20-21.

ST. FRANCIS XAVIER UNIVERSITY

1969   Crean, J.G., M.F. Ferguson and H.J. Somers.
<u>Higher education in the Atlantic Provinces for the 1970's: a study prepared under the auspices of the Association of Atlantic Universities for the Maritime Union Study</u>.   Halifax: Assoc. of Atlantic Univs.   121 p.

1971   Laidlaw, A.F. ed.   <u>The Man from Margaree: writings and speeches of M.M. Coady, educator/reformer/priest</u>.   Toronto: McClelland & Stewart. 1971.   218 p.

Shook, L.K.   "St. Francis Xavier University" in <u>Catholic post-secondary education in English-speaking Canada</u>.   Toronto: U. of T. Press, 1971. p.75-95.

1974   Fossien, R.F.   "Moses M. Coady and adult education in the Maritimes." M.A. thesis, Univ. of Alberta. 1974.

ST. MARY'S UNIVERSITY

1971   Shook, L.K. "St. Mary's University" in <u>Catholic post-secondary education in English-speaking Canada</u>.   Toronto: U. of T. Press, 1971. p.57-74.

1972   Fotheringham, G.H.   "A comparison of two small Maritime universities with differing religious backgrounds: Saint Mary's University and Mount Allison University."   M.A. thesis, St. Mary's Univ. 1972.

TECHNICAL UNIVERSITY OF NOVA SCOTIA 1980

    Shore, V. "Technical University of Nova Scotia: a place on the move." Univ. Aff./Aff. univ. 21, 7 (1980) 2-3.

THE UNIVERSITIES OF NEW BRUNSWICK/
LES UNIVERSITES DE NOUVEAU-BRUNSWICK

1972 Flexibility for the 70's: a report to the Government on the resources required for the development of higher education in New Brunswick. Fredericton: Higher Education Commission, 1972. 64 p.

1973 McCready, D.J. "Federal education grants, 1945-1967: economic development in New Brunswick." Ph.D. thesis, Univ. of Alberta, 1973.

1974 New Brunswick Higher Education Commission. Perspective: a report to Government on operating and capital assistance to universities and colleges in New Brunswick. Fredericton: The Commission, 1974. 44 p.

1975 Crandell, E. "They meant it when they said a university for Saint John." Atlantic Advocate 68 (Sept. 1977) 30-32.

    Maritime Provinces Higher Education Commission. Report of the committee on higher education in the French sector of New Brunswick. Fredericton: the Commission, 1975. 84 p.

1977 Maritime Provinces Higher Education Commission. In process: three year regional planning for higher education in the Maritime Provinces. Fredericton: the Commission, 1977. 63 p.

UNIVERSITE DE MONCTON

1963 Cormier C. "Une nouvelle université de langue française dans l'Est du Canada." Revue de l'AUPELF 1 (fév. 1963) 9-11.

1966 Cadieux, J. "Le problème du bilinguisme à l'Université de Moncton (Canada). Revue de l'AUPELF 4 (fév. 1966) 52-54.

1970 "University sets up research council." Science Forum. 3 (June 1970) 29.

1971 Commission de la planification académique de l'Université de Moncton. Rapport. Moncton: Univ. de Moncton, 1971. 624 p.

1974 Bourque, E.-P. "une étude sur les mortalités scolaires à l'Université de Moncton pour les années académiques 1970-71, 1971-72." M.A. thesis, Université de Moncton, 1974.

Cleason, T.P. et P. Dumas, "Perspectives sociales des étudiants de l'Université de Moncton." Rev. Univ. Moncton. 7 (jan. 1974) 43-48.

1975 Cormier, C. L'Université de Moncton: historique. Moncton: Centre d'études acadiennes, Univ. de Moncton, 1975. 404 p.

1976 Ayling, V. "New man at the helm of Moncton University." Atlantic Advocate 66 (8) 54-55.

MOUNT ALLISON UNIVERSITY

1954 Fraser, R. This is our heritage. (Founder's Day address) Sackville: Mount Allison Univ., 1954. 4 p.

1955 McKiel, H.W. Builders of Mount Allison. (Founder's Day address) Sackville: Mount Allison Univ. 6 p.

1972 Fotheringham, G.H. "A comparison of two small Maritime universities with differing religious backgrounds: Saint Mary's University and Mount Allison University." M.A. thesis, St. Mary's Univ. 1972.

1973 Daley, H. "Introducing Mount Allison." Can. Library Jour. 30 (Jan.-Feb. 1973) 9-13.

1980 Feltmate, P. "Mount Alleson in the forefront of women's education." Atlantic Advocate (Dec. 1980) 32-34.

UNIVERSITY OF NEW BRUNSWICK

1967 Wade, S. and H. Lloyd. Behind the hill. Fredericton: Univ. of New Brunswick, 1967. 222 p.

1968 Cattley, R.E.D. Honoris Causa, the effervescences of a university orator. Fredericton: Univ. of New Brunswick, 1968. 158 p.

1970 Fraser, J.A. By force of circumstance: a history of St. Thomas University. Fredericton: Miramichi Press, 1970. 125 p.

1971 Shook, L.K. "St. Thomas University" in Catholic post-secondary education in English-speaking Canada. Toronto: U. of T. Press, 1971. p. 113-123.

1973 Jarrell, R.A. "Science education at the University of New Brunswick in the nineteenth century." Acadiensis 11 (Spring 1973) 55-79.

1974 Hamilton, W.B. "Marshall d'Avray, precursor of modern education" in R.S. Patterson et al eds. Profiles of Canadian educators. Toronto: D.C. Heath, 1974. p. 238-339.

1976   Kulak, B. "The making of a President. University of New Brunswick's John Anderson." Atlantic Advocate 66, 8 (1976) 8-10.

Leefe, J. "King's Law School." Atlantic Advocate 66, 7 (1976) 58, 60.

1977   University of New Brunswick, U.N.B. in a changing world: a brief submitted to the Maritime Provinces Higher Education Commission. Fredericton: the University, 1977. 60 p.

Brake, K.A. "An evaluation of the undergraduate professional recreation program at the University of New Brunswick." M.Ed. thesis, Univ. of New Brunswick, 1977.

Finch, M-A. "An analysis of the patterns of communication within the Faculty of Physical Education and Recreation at the University of New Brunswick." M.Ed. thesis, Univ. of New Brunswick, 1977.

1979   University of New Brunswick. The status of women at U.N.B.: task force report to the President. Fredericton: the University, 1979. 81 p.

C. THE UNIVERSITIES OF QUEBEC:
   LES UNIVERSITES DU QUEBEC

1965   Martin, J.-M. "Réformes et perspectives d'évolution de l'enseignement supérieur au Québec." Revue AUPELF 3 (avril 1965) 22-28.

1966   Provost, H. "Le Séminaire de Québec et celui de Paris après la cession." Rev. Univ. Laval 20 (i) 66) 625-635.

1969   Magnuson, R. Education in the Province of Quebec. Washington: U.S. Dept. of Health, Education and Welfare. 1969. 81 p.

1970   Boulianne, R. "The Royal Institution for the Advancement of Learning: the correspondence 1820-1829." Ph.D. thesis, McGill Univ., 1970.

Gauthier, G. "Le conseil des universités du Québec." Revue de l'AUPELF 8 (printemps, 1970) 11-13.

Giguère, G. E. "Les biens de Saint-Sulpice et 'the Attorney General Stuart's opinion respecting the Seminary of Montreal (10 déc. 1828)'" Rev. Hist. (juin 1970).

Marion, S. L'Institution royale, les biens des Jésuites et Honoré Mercier." Cah. des Dix 35 (1970) 96-126.

Pariseau, G. "Monseigneur Ignace Bourget, deuxième évêque de Montréal." Mém.S.R.C. (1970) 177-219.

1971   Audet, L.-P. Histoire de l'enseignement au Québec. Montréal: Holt, Rinehart et Winston, 1971. 2 vol.

Audet, L.-P. "Hydrographes du roi et cours d'hydrographie au Collège de Québec, 1671-1759." Cah. Dix 35 (1971) 104-117.

Crépeau, J.-C. "Le conseil des Universités à la recherche de l'ordre." Educ.Quart. (10 mars 1971) 8-12.

Crépeau, J.-C. "Le milieu parle." Educ. Quart. 1 (14 avril 1971) 14-17.

Lamontagne, J. "Les diplômes universitaires du Québec de 1959 à 1968." Educ.Quart. 1 (12 mai 1971) 21-22.

Savard, M. "La situation des cadres scolaires au Québec." Prospectives 7 (sept. 1971) 221-233.

Whitelaw, J.H. "From CEGEP to university, problems of articulation in Quebec." Canadian University and College. 6 (Mar.-Apr. 1971) 52-55.

1972   Campeau, L. La première mission des Jésuites en Nouvelle-France (1611-1613) et les commencements du Collège de Québec (1626-1670). Montréal: Editions Bellarmin, 1972. 128 p.

Conseil des Universités du Québec. Objectifs généraux de l'enseignement supérieur et grandes orientations des établissements. Québec: Le Conseil, 1972-73. 3 vols.

Conseil des Universités du Québec. Les orientations générales du secteur universitaire de langue anglaise et l'avenir de Bishop's et de Loyola. Québec: Le Conseil, 1972. 35 p.

Dufour, D., et M. Amyot, "Evolution de la scolarisation de la population d'âge scolaire du Québec, 1961-1981." Act. Econ. 45 (oct.-déc. 1972) 487-502.

Gauthier, G. "Evolution récente de l'enseignement supérieur québécois." McGill Jour. Educ. 7 (1972) 135-148.

Lavallée, A. "La Querelle universitaire québécoise 1876-1889." Rev. Hist. 26 (juin 1972) 67-82.

Lefebvre, J.-J. "In memoriam: Marcel Faribault." Rev. Notariat 75 (oct. 1972) 73-90.

Pelletier, M. "Le contrôle des universités québécoises: objectifs, stratégies, escarmouches." Relations 370 (avril 1972) 106-109.

Sylvain, P. "La vie quotidienne de l'étudiant universitaire Québécois au XIXe Siècle." Société Canadienne d'histoire de l'Eglise Catholique, Sessions d'Etude 1972, 41-54.

Whitelaw, J. "The universities of Quebec - guidelines for the 70s." Univ.Aff./Aff.univ. 13 (Nov. 1972) 12-13.

1973 Coté, A. "Le rôle propre des universités québécoises; le rapport du Conseil des universités." Univ.Aff./Aff.univ. 14 (fév. 1973) 4-5.

Hurtubise, R. ed. L'Université québécoise du proche avenir. Montréal: Editions Hurtubise HMH Ltée, 1973. 403 p.

Magnuson, R. "Education and Society in Quebec in the 1970's." Jour. Educ. Thought 7 (Aug. 1973) 94-104.

Tard, L.-M. "Au Québec: une expérience originale et fructueuse: l'enquête du Conseil des universités sur les objectifs et les orientations des institutions d'enseignement supérieur." Revue de l'AUPELF 11 (printemps-automne 1973) 93-87.

1974 Audet, L.-P. "Histoire de la Commission Parent." Mém. S.R.C. 1974, 127-137.

Dion, G. "Le Rapport Parent dix ans après: les relations professionnelles." Mém.S.R.C. 1974, 121-125.

Lavallée, A. Québec contre Montréal: la querelle universitaire, (1876-1891). Montréal: Les Presses de l'Université de Montréal, 1974. 288 p.

Lipkin, J. "The Academic 'Tilt' in Quebec Post-Secondary Education." Can. International Educ. 3 (June 1974) 61-76.

Québec. Ministère de l'Education. L'Education au Québec...en 1973. Québec: L'éditeur officiel du Québec, 1974. 309 p.

Québec. Ministère de l'Education. Les Enseignants du Québec. Québec: Le Ministère, 1974. 121 p.

Québec. Ministère de l'Education. Opération sciences de la santé. Planification sectorielle de l'enseignement supérieur. Québec: L'éditeur officiel du Québec, 1974. 2 vols.

1975 Falardeau, J.-C. Etienne Parent, 1802-1874, biographie, texte et bibliographie. Montréal: La Presse, 1975. 344 p.

Trofimenkoff, S. M. Action Française: French Canadian nationalism in the twenties. Toronto: U. of T. Press. 157 p.

1976   Campeau, L.   "Note critique à propos de l'école des arts et métiers de Saint-Joachim." Rev. Hist. 29 (mars 1976) 567-570.

Gill, R.M. "Universities and Development in Quebec." Ph.D. thesis, Duke University, 1976.

Mallea, J.R.   Matériaux pour l'histoire des institutions universitaires de philosophie au Québec. Quéwec: Les Presses de l'Université Laval, 1976. 2 vols.

Pilkington, G. "Higher education in Quebec: a product of evolution and revolution." Can. and International Educ. 5 (Dec. 1976) 39-70.

1977   Galarneau, G. "L'enseignement des sciences au Québec et Jérôme Demers (1765-1835)." Rev. Univ. Ottawa 47 (1977) 84-94.

Richard, J.-Y. "La participation en milieu universitaire: un rêve habitable." Prospectives 13 (fév. 1977) 37-45.

"Une 'université régionale de la santé' pour l'est du Québec a été proposée." Univ. aff./Aff. univ. 18 (July 1977) 12.

1978   Avis au Ministre de l'éducation sur 26 projets de nouveaux programmes d'enseignement dans les universités du Québec. Québec: Conseil des universités, 1978. 1 vol. (pag. multiple.)

Lajeunesse, M. "Espoirs et illusions d'une réforme scolaire au Québec du XIXe siècle." Culture 31 (juin 1978) 149-159.

1979   Daniel, J.S. and W.A.S. Smith, "Opening open universities: the Canadian experience." Can. Jour. Higher Educ. 9 (1) 63-63.

1980   Bellevance, M.   Le fédéralisme canadien et les subventions aux universités québecoise. Rev. can. d'ens. sup. 10, 2 (1980) 1-20.

Dandurand, P. et M.   Fournier.   Développement de l'enseignement supérieur, classes sociales et luttes nationales an Québec." Sociologies et Sociétés 12, 1 (1980) 101-131.

BISHOP'S UNIVERSITY

1971   Roe, H.   "Reminiscences of the earliest Lennoxville days." Jour. Can. Church Hist. Soc. 13 (Sept. 1971) 38-43.

1972   Conseil des Universités du Québec. Les orientations générales du secteur universitaire de langue anglaise et l'avenir de Bishop's et de Loyola. Québec, Le Conseil, 1972. 35 p.

COLLEGES CLASSIQUES

1970   Gagnon, S. Le clergé, les notables et l'enseignement privé au Québec:
le cas du Collège de Sainte-Anne 1840-1870. Histoire Soc. 5 (avril
1970) 40-65.

1971   Grand'maison, G. "Les élèves du Séminaire de Rimouski, 1862-1900."
M.A. thesis, Univ. d'Ottawa 1971.

Lessard, C. "Le Collège-Séminaire de Nicolet (1803-1863)." Rev. Hist.
25 (juin 1971) 63-88.

Plante, L. "L'enseignement classique chez les Soeurs de la Congréga-
tion de Notre-Dame." Ph.D. thesis, Université Laval, 1971.

1972   Bélanger, R. Le Séminaire de Chicoutimi et la Côte-Nord, 1883-1903.

Gagnon, A. "Collège N.D. de l'Assomption de Nicolet: 1937 à nos
jours." Thèse de maîtrise, Univ. Laval, 1972.

1973   Drolet, J.C. "Séminaire de Chicoutimi: vie financière 1978-1912."
Saguenayensia, 15 (mars-avril 1973), 38-51.

1974   Lamontagne, J. "Les professeurs de collège pendant la réforme
scolaire des annéees soixante au Québec. Analyse psychosociologique
d'un changement social." Ph.D. thesis, Univ. de Montréal, 1974.

Berberi Tran-Khanh, S. "Le Petit Séminaire de St-Georges de Beauce
1946-1968." Ph.D. thesis, Univ. Laval, 1974.

1975   Jean, M. "Histoire du Collège Marie-Anne 1932-1967." Thèse de maîtrise, Univ. de Montréal, 1975.

Stanley, G.F.G. "Les collèges classiques de langue française en
Acadie." Les Cahiers 6 (sept. 1975) 117-37.

1976   Fleurent, M. "L'Education morale au Petit Séminaire de Québec 1668-
1875." Thèse de D.ès L. Univ. Laval 1976.

Giroux, A. Histoire du Collège Basile-Moreau, 1933-1968. Montréal:
Soeurs de Sainte-Croix. 268 p.

1977   Villiard-Bériault D.
Saint-Laurent, un collège se raconte, 120 ans de collège, 10 ans de
cégep, Montréal, Fides, 1977. 157 p.

1978   Galarneau, C. Les collèges classiques au Canada Français (1620-1970).
Montréal: Fides. 287 p.

CONCORDIA UNIVERSITY

1971   Forsythe D. Let the niggers burn! the Sir George Williams University affair and its Caribbean aftermath. Montreal: Our Generation Press, 1971. 209 p.

      Shook, L.K. "Loyola College" in Catholic post-secondary education in English-speaking Canada. Toronto: U. of T. Press, 1971. p. 257-268.

1972   Conseil des Universités du Québec. Les orientations générales du secteur universitaire de langue anglaise et l'avenir de Bishop's et de Loyola. Québec: Le Conseil, 1972. 35 p.

1974   Cinman, I. Loyola, Sir George form Concordia University. CAUT Bull. ACPU XX111, 2 (Oct. 1974) 3.

      Rioux, B. "L'Université Loyola: de la tolérance à la servilité". Maintenant 133 (fév. 1974) 8-9.

1975   Clarke, D. B. "Decades of decision: Sir George Williams University 1952-53 to 1972-73." Unpublished typescript available on interlibrary loan from the Library, Concordia University. 233 p.

      "Concordia reorganizes academic structure and establishes 'theme' colleges." Univ. Aff./Aff. univ. 18 (Dec. 1977) 14.

      Jones G. and J. McCormick. The illustrated companion history of Sir George Williams University. Montreal: Concordia Unversity, 1977. 185 p.

UNIVERSITE LAVAL

1949   Bureau, R. "Le Musée de minéralogie et de géologie de l'Université Laval". Nat. Can. 76, 205-22.

1962   Hamelin, L.-E. "Petite histoire de la géographie dans le Québec et à l'Université Laval." Cah.Géog. 13 (1962/63) 137-153.

1966   Lavallée, J.G. "Monseigneur Antoine Racine, premier évêque de Sherbrooke (1874-1893)." Société canadienne d'histoire de l'Eglise Catholique, Sessions d'étude, 1966, 31-39.

1967   Leclerc, R. "Le centre de documentation de la bibliothèque de l'Université Laval (Québec)." Revue de l'AUPELF 5 (automne 1967) 27-32.

1968   Sargent, R.J. "The Thought of Monseigneur Louis-Adolphe Pacquet as a spokesman for French-Canadian ultramontanism." Doctoral dissertation, Union Theological Seminary, New York, 1968.

1969   Myers, H.B.   "Profile of a Patriot: Msgr. Arthur Maheux."   Queen's
       Quart. 76 (1969) 11-16.

1970   Litalier, R. Le Prêtre québécois à la fin du XIXe siècle: style de
       vie et spiritualité d'après Mgr. L.-Z. Moreau. Montréal: Fides.
       1970. 219 p. (Surtout Ch.I)

1971   Les Grandes orientations de l'Université Laval: mémoire présenté au
       conseil des universités par le conseil de l'Université Laval.
       Québec: Univ. Laval 1971. 88 p.

       Sylvain, P. "Les Difficiles débuts de l'Université Laval." Cah. Dix
       36 (1971) 193-210.

       Vachon, L.-A. "Université Laval, Québec." Revue de l'AUPELF, 9 (juin
       1971) 46-48.

1972   Baillargeon, H. Le Séminaire de Québec sous l'épiscopat de Mgr de
       Laval. Québec, Les Presses de L'Université Laval, 1972. 308 p.

       Blanchard, L.-P. "L'élection du recteur à l'Université Laval." Univ.
       Aff./Aff.univ. 13 (June-July 1972) 6-7.

       Dumouchel, E.   "L'ancienne et la nouvelle chartes de l'Université
       Laval." Revue de l'AUPELF 10 (juin 1972) 15-19.

1973   Trudel, M.   "Les débuts de l'Institut d'histoire à l'Université
       Laval." Rev. Hist. 27 (1973) 397-403.

1975   Lambert, J.H. "Le haut enseignement de la religion: Mgr. Bourget and
       the founding of Laval University." Rev. Univ. Ottawa 45 (juil.-sept.
       1975) 278-294.

1976   Parise, R. Georges-Henri Lévesque, père de la renaissance québecoise
       Montréal: A. Stanke. 172 p.

1977   Galarneau, C. "L'enseignement des sciences an Québec de Jérôme Demers
       (1765-1835)." Rev. Univ. Ottawa 47 (jan. - avril 1977) 84-94.

       Giles, G.J. "University reform in Quebec: the strike at Laval 1976.
       New Haven, Conn.: Institution for Social and Policy Studies, Yale
       University, 1977.   23 p.   (Yale Higher Education Research Group.
       Working Paper YHERG -17).

1978   Coté, A. "Laval University: one year after the strike." CAUT/ACPU
       Bull. 25 (Feb. 1978) 15.

       Laberge, P.-A. L'Université Laval, 1952-1977:   vers l'autonomie.
       Québec: Les Presses de l'Université Laval, 1975. 95 p.

1979   Bonneau, L.-P.   "L'Université Laval - son rôle au Canada" in Higher
       Education in Canada: historical perspectives.   Ed. by A. Gregor and
       K. Wilson.   Monographs in Education II.   Winnipeg: Univ. of Manitoba,
       1979. p. 53-66.

       Université Laval Commission d'étude sur l'avenir de l'Université
       Laval.   Pour la renaissance de l'Université Laval: rapport de la
       Commission ...   Québec: Université Laval, 1979.   347 p.

MCGILL UNIVERSITY

1970   Boulianne, R. "The Royal Institution for the Advancement of Learning:
       the correspondence 1820-1829." Ph.D. thesis, McGill Univ., 1970.

1971   Dumas, P.   "William Osler et la Bibliotheca Osleriane."   Union Méd.

       Ronish, D.   "The Montreal Ladies' Educational Association 1871-1885."
       McGill Jour. Educ.   6 (Summer 1971) 78-83.

       Tunis, B.R. et E.H. Bensly, "A la recherche de William Leslie Logie,
       premier diplômé de l'Université McGill."   Union Méd. 100 (mars 1971)
       536-538.

1972   Collins, P. "The hundred years of engineering at McGill." Engineering
       Jour. 55 (Sept. 1972) 13-21.

1974   "Keen support for educational development: at McGill."   Univ. aff./
       Aff.univ.   15 (Apr. 1974) 9.

       McMurray, D. Four principals of McGill: a memoir 1929-1963. Montreal:
       Graduates' Society of McGill Univ., 1974.   73 p.

1976   Skelton-Passmore, E.   Research and the Allan Memorial Institute.
       Montreal: the Institute, 1976. 55 p.

1977   Cornell, J.   "Sir William Dawson and the theory of evolution."   M.A.
       thesis, McGill Univ., 1977.

       Penfield, W.   No man alone: a neurosurgeon's life.   Boston: Little,
       Brown, 1977.   416 p.

1978   Frost, S.B.   "A Transatlantic wooing."   Dalhousie Rev. 58, 3 (autumn
       1978) 458-70.

       Frost, S.B.   "Trouble with women."   McGilliana 6 (Sept. 1978) 2, 607.

1979   Frost, S.B. The history of McGill in relation to the social, economic
       and cultural aspects of Montreal and Quebec: study commissioned by
       Commission d'étude sur les universités.   Montréal: McGill Univ. 1979.
       57 p.

Markell, H.K.   The Faculty of Religious Studies McGill University, 1948-1978.   Montreal: Faculty of Religious Studies, McGill Univ. 1979.   67 p.

1980   Frost, S.B.   McGill University: for the advancement of learning. Vol 1: 1801-1895.   Montreal: McGill-Queen's Univ. Press, 1980. 334 p.

1981   Frost, S.B.   "Education at McGill."   McGilliana 10 (March 1981), 2-9.

UNIVERSITE DE MONTREAL

1941   Action universitaire 9 (sept. 1942).   Numero spécial pour l'inauguration de l'Université.

1965   Domaradzki, T.   "Monseigneur Olivier Maurault."   Etudes Slaves   13 (1968) 78-81.

1968   Malchelosse, G.   "Mgr. Olivier Maurault."   Cah. Dix 33 (1968) 9-12.

"Université de Montréal" Revue de l'AUPELF 6 (hiver 1968) 122-127.

1969   Université de Montréal.   Commission Conjointe du Conseil et de l'Assemblée Universitaire.

L'Université: son rôle et ses composantes, la relation entre ses composantes. Montréal: Presses de l'Université de Montréal, 1969. 333 p.

1970   Benoist, Jean.   "Centre de recherches caraibes de l'Université de Montréal."   Revue de l'AUPELF. 8 (automne, 1970) 105-108.

Pariseau, G.   "Monseigneur Ignace Bourget, deuxième évêque de Montréal."   Mém. S.R.C. 1970, 177-219.

1971   Crépeau, J.-C.   "A l'Université de Montréal: planification oui... mais."   Educ. Quart.   1 (10 mars 1971) 13-17.

Lacoste, P.   "Université de Montréal."   Revue de l'AUPELF.   9 (juin 1971) 49-50.

1973   Roy, G.   "Roger P. Langlois, directeur, Ecole Polytechnique de Montréal."   Commerce 75 (fév. 1973) 26-33.

1979   Hétu, J.   Album souvenir 1878-1978: centenaire de la Faculté du Droit de l'université de Montréal: corrections et ajouts" Thémis 14 (1979-80) 147-150.

Jacques, L. "Esdras Minville un homme de son temps, un homme de notre temps."   Act. Nat.   45 (oct. 1979) 140-146.

1973   Touchette, C. "Evolution des objectifs et des programmes en education des adultes à l'Université de Montréal 1876-1930." Ph.D. thesis, Univ. of Toronto, 1973.

1974   Dumas-Rousseau, M. "L'Université de Montréal de 1852 à 1865: tentatives de fondation." Thèse de D.E.S., Univ. Laval, 1974.

1976   Angers, F.A. "Minville et les hautes études commerciales." Act.Nat. (mai-juin 1976) 643-676.

       Pouliot, L. Monseigneur Bourget et son temps. Tome V, Montréal: Bellarmin, 1977. 319 p.

1978   Leduc, C." Les orientations des femmes à l'Université de Montréal en 1949-50 et en 1974-75." Can. and International Educ. 7 (June 1978) 51-58.

1980   Assimopoulous, N. et C.H. Bélanger. "Politiques et pratiques d'interdiscipliarité Rev. can. d'ens. sup. 10, 2 (1980) 39-52.

       Carbonneau R. "Les 20 ans de l'Ecole de criminologie" Forum (Université de Montréal) 15, 9 (1980) 5.

       Laurendeau, J.-G. "L'université de Montréal et la coopération europeénne." Forum (Université de Montréal) 14, 18 (1980) 4-5.

UNIVERSITE DU QUEBEC

1971   Riverin, A. "Université du Québec." Revue de l'AUPELF 9 (juin 1971) 50-51.

       Villedieu, Y. "L'université du Québec: avec ou sans les universités l'enseignement supérieur sera planifié." Educ. Quart. 1 (24 mars 1971) 12-13.

       Villedieu, Y. "L'université du Québec à Montréal: pour sortir de 'l'invraisemblable confusion....'" Educ. Quart. 1 (24 mars 1971) 12-13.

1973   Robert, P. et M. Sidier, "La structure modulaire au service de l'innovation pédagogique: l'expérience de l'Université du Québec." Revue de l'AUPELF 11 (printemps-automne 1973) 75-89.

1974   Daniel, J.S. "Quebec's télé-université." Univ. aff./Aff. Univ. 15 (Sept. 1974) 6.

1977   Gagnon, C. "Une université régionale ouverte sur le monde." Educ. Quart. 7 (8: 1977) 14-15.

1978   Côté, F. "Comment à Chicoutimi, on s'est donné un financement privée de la recherche." <u>Univ. Aff./Aff. univ.</u> 19(Feb. 1978) 32.

"Téléenseignement - maintenant le dialogue est assuré." <u>Univ. aff./Aff. univ.</u> 19 (Jan. 1978) 7.

Université du Québec à Montréal. <u>Mémoire présenté par l'UQAM à la Commission d'étude sur les universités.</u> Montréal, 1978. 82 p.

Université du Québec à Rimouski. <u>Mémoire de l'UQAR à la Commission d'étude sur les universités.</u> Rimouski, 1978. 119 p.

1979   Université du Québec. <u>Reseau souvenir: une revue de presse des dix ans de l'Université du Québec.</u> Québec: Service de l'information, Univ. du Québec, 1979. 56 p.

UNIVERSITE DE SHERBROOKE

1969   "Université Sherbrooke." <u>Revue de l'AUPELF</u> 7 (printemps 1969) 70-81.

1971   Pardoen, A. "Université de Sherbrooke: échanger un peu de liberté contre un peu de sécurité." <u>Educ. Quart.</u> 1 (14 avril 1971) 7-9.

1972   Joncas, J. "L'enseignement coopératif à l'Université de Sherbrooke." <u>Act. Péd.</u> 24 (juin 1972) 5-19.

1977   Université de Sherbrooke. <u>Le devenir de l'Université de Sherbrooke: les caracteristiques générales de l'Université, ses priorités et ses axes de développement.</u> Sherbrooke: L'Université, 1977. 25 f.

1979   Imbeault, M.-A. "Sherbrooke - une université au cachet bien spécial." <u>Univ. Aff./Aff. univ.</u> 20, 3 (1979) 14-15.

D.   THE UNIVERSITIES OF ONTARIO
     LES UNIVERSITES D'ONTARIO

1968   Stager, D. "Monetary returns to post-secondary education in Ontario." Ph.D. thesis, Princeton Univ., 1968.

1970   Hanly, C. et al. <u>Who pays? university financing in Ontario.</u> Toronto: Lewis & Samuel, 1970. 168 p.

Lapp, P.A., J. W. Hodgins and C.B. MacKay. <u>Ring of Iron: a study of engineering education in Ontario.</u> Toronto: Committee of Presidents of Universities of Ontario, 1970. 155 p.

Ontario Confederation of University Faculty Associations, Educational Policy Committee. "Report." OCUFA Newsletter 3 (spring 1970) 1-9.

Stamp, R.M. "The campaign for technical education in Ontario, 1876-1914." Ph.D. thesis, Univ. of Western Ontario, 1970.

1971 Benson, E. "The house that Davis built, or university education in Ontario in the sixties." CAUT/ACPU Bull. 19 (Spring 1971) 3-12.

Heick, W.H. "Historical perspective: an interview with Arthur R.M. Lower." Queen's Quart. 75 (Winter 1971) 518-535.

1971 McGregor, A. "Egerton Ryerson, Albert Carman and the founding of Albert College, Belleville." Ont. History 63 (Dec. 1971) 105-16.

Porter, J. et al. Towards 2000: the future of post-secondary education in Ontario. Toronto: McClelland & Stewart, 1971. 176 p.

1972 Commission on Post-Secondary Education in Ontario. Draft Report. Toronto: Queen's Printer, 1972. 112 p.

Commission on Post-Secondary Education in Ontario. Post-Secondary education in North Bay and Sault Ste. Marie. Toronto: Queen's Printer, 1972. 43 p.

Commission on Post-Secondary Education in Ontario. Post-secondary education in Northwestern Ontario. Toronto: Queen's Printer, 1972. 40 p.

"Consideration of post-secondary education by the Policy and Priorities Board of Cabinet." OCUFA Newsletter 5 (Apr. 1972) 1-3.

Cook G.C. and D. Stager. An examination of the draft report of the Commission on Post-Secondary Education in Ontario. Toronto: Institute for the Quantitative Analysis of Social and Economic Policy, University of Toronto, 1972. 14 p.

D'Costa, R. Post-secondary educational opportunities for the Ontario francophone population. Toronto: Queen's Printer, 1972. 109 p.

Fleming, W.G. Education: Ontario's preoccupation. Toronto: U. of T. Press, 1972. 330 p.

1972 Gidney, R.D. "Centralization and education: the origins of an Ontario tradition." Jour. Can. Studies 7 (Nov. 1972) 33-48.

Long, J.C. "An historical study of the establishment of college systems in Ontario and Alberta in the 1960's." M.Ed. thesis, Univ. of Calgary, 1972.

Nicholson, N.L. "The religious factors in the location of Ontario universities." Ontario Geography 7 (1972) 39-49.

Ontario Confederation of University Faculty Associations. "Brief to the Commission on Post-Secondary Education in Ontario." CAUT/ACPU Bull. 20 (Spring 1972) 3-11.

Parr, J.G. "The lowly, the media and higher education." Forum 3 (Nov. 1972) 5-12.

Purdy, J.D. "John Strachan's educational policies, 1815-1841." Ont. Hist. 64 (Mar. 1972) 45-64.

Sidnell, M.J. "Towards bureaupolitocracy." Jour. Can. Thought 7 (May 1972) 3-18.

Smith, A.H. The production of scientific knowledge in Ontario universities. Toronto: Queen's Printer, 1972. 174 p. Study prepared for the Commission on Post-Secondary Education in Ontario.

Stanley, G.F.G. "The big Bishop Alexander Macdonell of Kingston." Historic Kingston 20 (1972) 90-105.

Wright, D.T. "Recent developments in higher education in Ontario", in Universities facing the future, edited by W.R. Niblett & R.F. Butts. San Francisco: Jossey-Bass, 1972, p. 297-309.

1973 Adelman, H. Rebuilding the university, the holiversity. Toronto: New Press, 1973, 152 p.

Allard, J.-L. "Les Franco-Ontariens et l'éducation postsecondaire." Rev. Univ. Ottawa 43 (oct.-déc. 1973) 518-531.

Black, E. "A perspective on the "crises" in post-secondary education." CAUT/ACPU Bull. 21 (Mar. 1973) 16-20.

"The final COPSE report." OCUFA Newsletter 7 (Sept. 1973) 18-20.

Commission on Post-Secondry Education in Ontario. The learning society. Toronto: Ministry of Government Sources, 1973. 263 p.

Laliberté, M. "Rapport d'une commission d'enquête sur l'éducation post-secondaire en Ontario." Rev. Scolaire (mai 1973) 14-15.

Ontario Confederation of University Faculty Associations. "Brief to the Committee on University Affairs." OCUFA Newsletter 6 (Feb. 1973) 4-8.

Ontario Confederation of University Faculty Associations. "Brief to the Committee on University Affairs." OCUFA Newsletter. 7 (Dec. 1973) 3-6.

Sheffield, E.F. "The Learning Society: an overstatement." Queen's Quart. 80 (Autumn 1973) 434-449.

Sheffield, E.F. ed. Agencies for Higher Education in Ontario. Toronto: Ontario Institute for Studies in Education, 1974. 82 p.

Winegard, W.C.
"The last of a kind? another view of relations between the University of Ontario and the Government." OCUFA Newsletter 7 (January 1974) 7.

1975 Charron, K. Education of the health professors in the context of the health care system: the Ontario experience. Paris. OECD, 1975.

Oliver, P.
"Government, industry and science in Ontario: the case of the Ontario Research Foundation", in Public and private persons: the Ontario political culture, 1914-1974. Toronto: Clarke Irwin, 1975. p.156-178.

Payton, L.C. The status of women in Ontario universities: a report to the Council of Ontario Universities. Toronto: C.O.U. 1975. 21 p.

1977 Cinman, I. "Ontario faces 'economic and cultural suicide' if university system not changed." CAUT Bul. ACPU 26 (Sept. 1977) 7.

Kirkness, J. "The Ontario Universities Program for Instructional Development." CAUT Bul. ACPU 25 (6) 10, 1977.

Woodcock, L. "Destiny Canada - where people communicated, listened and learned." Univ. aff./Aff. univ. 18 (Sept. 1977) 2-3.

1978 Cameron, D.M. The northern dilemma: public policy and post-secondary education in Northern Ontario. Toronto: Ontario Economic Council, 1978. 198 p.

Fiorino, A. Historical Overview ... (of education in Ontario). Toronto: Commission on Declining School Enrolments in Ontario, 1978. 60 p.

Frederick, N.O. "The autonomy of universities and colleges: a tentative theory of power distribution based on a comparative case study of government relations with universities and colleges in Ontario." Ph.D. thesis, Univ. of Toronto. 1978.

Royce, M.V. "Methodism and the education of women in nineteenth century Ontario." Atlantis 3 (Spring 1978) 130-143.

1979   Mehmet, O.   "The Ontario university system as wealth-creator: who benefits? who pays?"   Can. Jour. Higher Educ. 9 (3) 41-51.

1980   Council of Ontario Universities, Committee on Operating Grants. Changing public priorities: universities and the future.   Toronto: COU, 1980.   69 p.

       Ontario Ministry of College and Universities.   Polytechnic education in Ontario.   Toronto: M.C.U. 1980.   92 p.

BROCK UNIVERSITY

1961   Need for a University in the Niagara District: a series of articles compiled and published by the Niagara District Joint Committee on Higher Education.   Niagara Falls: the Committee, 1961. 103 p.

1965   Gibson, J.A.   Brock University 1963-1965:   a retrospective report. St. Catharines: the University, 1965.   19 p.

1971   Fleming, W.G.   "Brock University" in Post-Secondary and Adult Education.   Toronto: U. of T. Press, 1971.   p. 86-91.

1972   Brock University.   Student housing: an explanatory study of the Brock University residence.   Prepared by Brock University Planning Department and Trevor Dento.   St. Catharines: the University, 1972. 2 vols.

CARLETON

1971   Fleming, W.G.
       "Carleton University",   in Post-Secondary and Adult Education, Toronto: U. of T. Press, 1971, p.92-101.

1972   Farr, D.M.L.
       "The Dunton Years 1958-1972."   The Carleton Alumneye 1, 1 (1972) 6-9.

1976   George, D.C.
       A report on continuing education and related matters at Carleton University.   Ottawa: Carleton Univ., 1976.

1978   Carleton University.   Report of President's Committee on Carleton University to 1982.   Ottawa: Carleton Univ. 1978.

       Humphreys, E. and J. Porter
       Part-time studies and university accessibility.   Ottawa: Carleton Univ., Dept. of Sociology, 1978.

UNIVERSITY OF GUELPH

1971   Ontario Agricultural College. <u>Programmes and organization of the Ontario Agricultural College for the seventies.</u> Guelph: University of Guelph, 1971. 72 p.

1972   University of Guelph, Committee on Academic Priorities. <u>Aims and objectives of the University: final report.</u> Guelph: the University, 1972. 18 p.

1973   University of Guelph, Three Semester Study Steering Committee. <u>The three semester system at Guelph ... summary and interpretation of research results.</u> Guelph: Univ. of Guelph, 1973. 31 p.

1974   Ross, A.M. <u>The College on the Hill: a history of the Ontario Agricultural College 1874 to 1974.</u> Toronto: Copp Clark, 1974. 180 p.

      "OAC centennial 1874-1974." <u>Guelph Daily Mercury,</u> special issue July 5, 1974.

      "Special Centennial Issue." <u>Guelph Alumnus</u> 7 (Jan.-Feb. 1974).

1975   Barker, C.A.V. "The Ontario Veterinary College: Temperance Street era." <u>Can. Vet. Jour.</u> 16 (Nov. 1975) 319-328.

      University of Guelph. President's Task Force on the Status of Women at the University of Guelph. <u>Report.</u> Guelph, Ont., 1975. 58 p.

      Barker, C.A.V. "John G. Rutherford and the controversial standards of education at the Ontario Veterinary College 1864 to 1920." <u>Can. Vet. Jour.</u> 18 (Dec. 1977) 327-340

1979   Shute, J.C.M. <u>The Ghana-Guelph Project: A story of international cooperation: final project report.</u> Guelph: Univ. of Guelph, 1979. 61 p.

LAKEHEAD UNIVERSITY

1971   Fleming, W.G. "Lakehead University," in <u>Post-Secondary and Adult Education.</u> Toronto: U. of T. Press, 1971. p. 109-114.

      Bohm, W.D. "Swan-song and follow-up." <u>Forum</u> 2 (Nov. 1971) 19-22.

LAURENTIAN UNIVERSITY

1970   Cragg, A.W. "The crisis at Laurentian." <u>OCUFA Newsletter.</u> 4 (Nov. 1970) 12-13.

1971 Fleming, W.G. "Laurentian University," in Post-Secondary and Adult Education." Toronto: U. of T. Press, 1971. p. 114-121.

MCMASTER UNIVERSITY

1970 Campbell, E.J.M. "The McMaster Medical School at Hamilton." Lancet No. 7675 (Oct. 1970) 764-767.

1971 Fleming, W.G. "McMaster University", in Post-Secondary Education in Ontario. Toronto: U. of T. Press, 1971. p. 121-129.

1973 Macdonald L. and M.S. Lenglet. "The status of women at McMaster University", in Women in Canada edited by M. Stephenson. Toronto: New Press, 1973. p.227-244.

McMaster University. Office of Institutional Research. The economic impact of McMaster University on the City of Hamilton and surrounding localities. Hamilton: McMaster Univ. 1973. 18 p.

1976 Johnston, C.M. McMaster University: Vol.1: the Toronto years. Toronto: U. of T. Press, 1976. 295 p.

1978 Russell, C.A. "Thomas Todhunter Shields, Canadian fundamentalist." Ont. Hist. 70 (Dec. 1978) 263-280.

1981 Johnston, C.M. McMaster University 2/ the early years in Hamilton, 1930-1957. Toronto: U. of T. Press, 1981. 330 p.

UNIVERSITY OF OTTAWA/UNIVERSITÉ D'OTTAWA

1971 Fleming, W.G. "The University of Ottawa", in Post-Secondary Education and Adult Education. Toronto: U. of T. Press, 1971. p. 29-34.

Shook, L.K. "University of Ottawa" and "St. Patrick's College", in Catholic post-secondary education in English-speaking Canada. Toronto: U. of T. Press, 1971. p. 242-256.

1973 University of Ottawa Commission on the Revision of Teaching and Research Structures. The University of Ottawa, what is it? Ottawa: Univ. of Ottawa, 1973. 8 vols.

1977 Laframboise, J.-C. "Les Oblats et l'Université d'Ottawa: du "Collège à l'Université 1918-1950." Société canadienne d'histoire de l'église catholique. Sessions d'étude 44 (1977) 81-101.

1978 Paskus, A. The Faculty of Psychology at the University of Ottawa. Ottawa: U. of Ottawa Press, 1978. 256 p.

QUEEN'S UNIVERSITY

1953 Edmison, J.A. St. Andrew's Church and Queen's University. Kingston: Queen's Univ. 10 p.

1965 Dorland, A. "Queen's in the Edwardian era" in Former Days and Quaker Ways. Picton: Picton Gazette Publishing Co., 1965, p.157-177.

Queen's University. Joint Committee on University Government. University Government at Queen's: second report of the Committee on structure of the Senate. Kingston: Queen's Univ., 1969. 28 p.

1970 Gundy, H.P. "Thomas Liddell: Queen's First Principal." Historic Kingston 19 (1970) 17-27.

1971 Strachan, R. "A Canadian experiment." (McGill-Queen's University Press). Scholarly Publishing 2 (1971) 173-77.

1972 Angus, M. "The old stones of Queen's, 1842-1900." Historic Kingston 20 (1972) 5-13.

Lower, A.R.M. "Queen's yesterday and today." Historic Kingston 20 (1972) 77-89.

Neatby, H. "The Honourable William Morris 1786-1858." Historic Kingston 20 (1972) 65-76.

1973 Neatby, H. "Queen's College and the Scottish fact." Queen's Quart. 80 (Spring 1973) 1-12.

1974 Gibson, F.W. "President Franklin Roosevelt's visit to Queen's University, 18 August 1938." Historic Kingston 22 (1974) 9-36.

Haselgrove, A.R. "Robert Sutherland: Queen's first black student." Historic Kingston 22 (1974) 64-69.

Queen's University, Kingston. Principal's Committee on the Status of Women at Queen's University. Report. Kingston: Queen's Univ. 1974. 32 p.

1976 Shortt, S.E.D. "James Cappon: the ideal in nature" and "Adam Shortt: the emergence of the social scientist" in The search for an ideal: six Canadian intellectuals in an age of transition 1850-1930. Toronto: U. of T. Press, 1976, 59-75 and 95-116.

1978 Bindon, K.M. Queen's men, Canada's men: the military history of Queen's University, Kingston. Kingston: Queen's Univ., 1978. 180 p.

Neatby, H. Queen's University: I, 1841-1917: and not to yield. Montreal: McGill-Queen's U.P., 1978. 346 p.

1979 Smith. A. The thought of George Monro Grant," Can. Lit. 83 (Winter 1979) 90-116.

1980 Green, L. Sandford Fleming Toronto: Fitzherry and Whiteside, 1980.

Rawlyk, G. and K. Quinn. The Redeemed of the Lord say so: a history of Queen's Theological College 1912-1972. Kingston: Queen's Theological College, 1980. 270 p.

Strong-Boag, V. ed. A woman with a purpose: the diaries of Elizabeth Smith 1872-1884. Toronto. U. of T. Press, 1980.

ROYAL MILITARY COLLEGE

1973 Gravel, J.-Y. "La fondation du Collège Militaire Royal de Saint-Jean." Revue'Histoire 28 (sept. 1973) 257-280.

1976 Hines, G.W. "The Royal Naval College of Canada, 1911-22", in Swords and Covenants. Edited by A. Preston and P. Deams. Totowa, N.J., Rowman & Littlefield, 1976, p.164-89.

1977 Brock, T.L. "Vignettes of a century of cadeting at R.M.C., Kingston." Historic Kingston 25 (1977) 19-25.

1979 Navran, L. and R. Walker. "Longitudinal changes in vocational interests of Canadian military college graduates." Can. Counsellor 13 (Apr. 1979) 136-139.

UNIVERSITY OF TORONTO

1930 Callaghan, M. "The University of Toronto." College Humour (U.S.) (Feb. 1930) 44-45, 109-11.

1950 Defries, R.D. The Connaught Medical Research Laboratories during the second world war, 1939-1945. Toronto: U. of T. Press, 1950.

1969 Henderson, J.L.H. ed. John Strachan documents and opinions: a selection. Toronto: McClelland & Stewart, 1969. 290 p.

1970 Feeley, J. "A library in crisis: the University of Toronto library, 1890-1892." Ont. Hist. 62 (Dec. 1970) 220-234.

Ladd, D.R. "University of Toronto" in Change in educational policy: self studies in selected colleges and universities. New York: McGraw Hill, 1970.

University of Toronto, Presidential Advisory Committee on Extension. Report. Toronto: Univ. of Toronto, 1970. 62 p.

1971 Engel, D. et al. The campus as the campus centre: a manual. Toronto: Students' Administrative Council, Univ. of Toronto, 1971. 88 p.

Gidney, R.D. "The Rev. Robert Murray: Ontario's first superintendent of schools." Ont. Hist. 67 (Dec. 1971) 191-204.

McGregor, A. "Egerton Ryerson, Albert Carman, and the founding of Albert College." Ont. Hist. 63 (Dec. 1971) 205-216.

Shook, L.K. "University of St. Michael's College" and "Pontifical Institute of Medieval Studies", in Catholic post-secondary education in English-speaking Canada. Toronto: U. of T. Press, 1971. p. 129-228.

1972 Ross, M.G. "The dilution of academic power in Canada." Minerva 10 (April 1972) 241-258.

1973 Burn, B.B. "Comparison of four foreign universities: Frieburg, Paris, Toronto, Cambridge" in The university as organization. Edited by J.A. Perkins. New York: McGraw Hill, 1973. p. 79-103.

Conway, J. "Academic change and crisis - Canadian style," in Academic Transformation. Ed. by D. Reisman and V. Stadtman. N.Y.: McGraw-Hill, 1973. p. 343-66.

Ham, J.M., P.A. Lapp and I.W. Thompson. Careers of engineering graduates 1920-1970, University of Toronto. Toronto: The Engineering Alumni Association and the Faculty of Applied Science and Engineering, Univ. of Toronto, 1973. 89 p.

Harris, R.S. and I. Montagnes, eds. Cold Iron and Lady Godiva: engineering education at Toronto 1920-1972. Toronto: U. of T. Press, 1973. 169 p.

1974 Bissell, C.T. Halfway up Parnassus: a personal account of the University of Toronto 1932-1971. Toronto: U. of T. Press, 1974. 197 p.

Craig, G.M. "Two contrasting Upper Canada figures: John Rolph and John Strachan." Trans. R.S.C. 1974. p.237-248.

Osmond, D.R. "The churchmanship of John Strachan." Jour. Can. Church Hist. Soc. 16 (Sept. 1974) 46-59.

1975 Cosbie, W.G. The Toronto General Hospital 1819-1965: a chronicle. Toronto: Macmillan, 1975. 373 p.

Francis, D. "Frank M. Underhill - Canadian intellectual." Ph.D. thesis, York Univ. 1975.

McCorkell, E.J. Memoirs of Rev. E. J. McCorkell, C.S.B. Toronto: Basilian Press, 1975. 150 p.

University of Toronto. Task Force to Study the Status of Non-Academic Women at the University of Toronto. "Report on the status of non-academic women." University of Toronto Bulletin. 27 (March 21, 1975) S1-S3.

Wasteneys, H.C.F. "A History of the University Settlement of Toronto, 1910-1958: an exploration of the social objectives of the University Settlement and of their implementation." D.S.W. thesis, Univ. of Toronto, 1975.

1976   Angrave, J. "John Strachan and Scottish influence on the character of King's College, York, 1827." Jour. Can. Studies 11 (Aug. 1976) 60-68.

1976   Shortt, S.E.D. "Maurice Hutton: classical-Christian humanist" and "James Mavor: the empirical ideal" in The search for an ideal: six Canadian intellectuals in an age of transition 1850-1930. Toronto: U. of T. Press, 1976, 77-93 and 119-135.

1977   Infeld, L. and L. Pyerson, eds. Leopold Infeld: Why I left Canada: reflections on science and politics. Translated by H. Infeld, Montreal: McGill-Queen's U.P., 1977. 224 p.

Allen, E. "Physics at the University of Toronto, 1907-1977." Physics in Canada. 33 (2:1977) 26-31.

Forward, D. A history of botany in the University of Toronto. Toronto: Dept. of Botany, Univ. of Toronto, 1977. 97 p.

Meikle, W.D. "And gladly teach: G.M. Wrong and the Department of History at the University of Toronto." Ph.D. thesis, Michigan State Univ. 1977.

Owen, G.W. "Projects for Trinity College Toronto." Jour.Can.Art Hist. 4 (Spring 1977) 61-72.

Patterson, G.N. Pathway to excellence: UTIAS - the first twenty five years. Toronto: Institute for Aerospace Studies, Univ. of Toronto. 1977. 288 p.

Phillips, C.E. College of Education Toronto: memoirs of OCE. Toronto: Faculty of Education, Univ. of Toronto, 1977. 220 p.

Scollard, R.J., comp. Footprints in the sand of Clover Hills: anniversaries, and notable events in the history of St. Michael's College, 1852-1977. Toronto: St. Michael's College, 1977, 55 p.

1978   Bassam, B.   The Faculty of Library Science, University of Toronto,
and its predecessors 1911-1972. Toronto: Faculty of Library Science,
Univ. of Toronto, 1978. 141 p.

Bladen, V.   Bladen on Bladen: memoirs of a political scientist.
Toronto: Scarborough College, Univ. of Toronto, 1978. 218 p.

Edinborough, A., ed.   The enduring world: a centennial history of
Wycliffe College. Toronto: U. of T. Press, 1978. 136 p.

Simon, G.T., ed.   The first North American electron microscope 1938.
Toronto: Microscopical Society of Canada, 1978. 26 p.

1979   Robinson, G. de B.   The mathematics department in the University of
Toronto 1827-1978. Toronto: Dept. of Maths., Univ. of Toronto, 1979.
114 p.

1980   Greenlee, J.G.   "The song of a people: Sir Robert Falconer on
empire." Jour. Can. Studies 15, 1 (1980) 80-92.

Horn, M.   "Free speech within the law":   the letter of the
sixty-eight Toronto professors, 1931." Ont. Hist. 72 (Mar. 1980)
27-48.

TRENT UNIVERSITY

1970   "Trent University: gem of academic architecture." Anaconda Spearhead
33 (Autumn 1970).

1971   Fleming, W.G.   "Trent University", in Post-secondary and adult education. Toronto: U. of T. Press, 1971. p. 168-71.

1975   "Otonabee College." Can.Arch. 20 (July 1975).

UNIVERSITY OF WATERLOO

1971   Fleming, W.G.   "The University of Waterloo", in Post-secondary and
adult education. Toronto: U. of T. Press, 1971. p. 180-190.

1972   Lambert, R.   "Liberalism at Waterloo State: a case history." This
Magazine is about Schools 6 (Fall 1972) 80-96.

1976   Woodruff, M.E. et al.   "A survey of the progress and direction of
research at the School of Optometry, University of Waterloo." Can.
Jour. Public Health 67 (Oct. 1976) 401-404.

WILFRID LAURIER UNIVERSITY

1971 Fleming, W.G. "Waterloo Lutheran University", in Post-secondary and adult education. Toronto: U. of T. Press, 1971. p. 171-180.

Lyon, B. The first 60 years: a history of Waterloo Lutheran University from the opening of Waterloo Lutheran Seminary in 1911, to the present day. Waterloo: the University, 1971. 68 p.

UNIVERSITY OF WESTERN ONTARIO

1970 Overduin, H. People and ideas: nursing at Western 1920-1970. London: Faculty of Nursing, Univ. of Western Ontario, 1970. 150 p.

1971 Shook, L.K. "Brescia College", in Catholic post-secondary education in English-speaking Canada. Toronto: U. of T. Press, 1971. p. 299-304.

1973 University of Western Ontario President's Advisory Committee on Women's Salaries (Academic). "Report". Western News 11, 13 (Oct. 30, 1973), Supplement.

1975 University of Western Ontario, President's Advisory Committee on the Status of Women at the University. "Report" Western News 11, 7(Sept. 18, 1975), Supplement, 32 p.

1977 Barr, M.L. A century of medicine at Western: a centennial history of the Faculty of Medicine. London: Univ. of Western Ontario, 1977. 672 p.

1978 Gwynne-Timothy, J. Western's first century. London: Univ. of Western Ontario, 1978. p. 854.

Lutman, J.H. Heritage western: a celebration 1878-1978: an illustrated history of the University of Western Ontario in celebration of its first hundred years. London: Univ. of Western Ontario, 1978, 58 p.

Sherrill, R.N. They passed this way: a selection of (honorary degree) citations 1878-1978. London: Univ. of Western Ontario, 1978. 271 p.

UNIVERSITY OF WINDSOR

1971 Fleming, W.G. "The University of Windsor", in Post-secondary and adult education. Toronto: U. of T. Press, 1971. p. 197-202.

Shook, L.K. "Assumption University", in Catholic post-secondary education in English-speaking Canada. Toronto: U. of T. Press, 1971.
p. 275-292.

1974 DeMarco, F.A. Report on extension and continuing education. Windsor:
Univ. of Windsor, 1974. 154p.

YORK UNIVERSITY

1960 Winters, R. "The creation of universities." National Conference of
Canadian Universities, Proceedings. 1960. 29-32.

1971 Fleming, W.G. "York University", in Post-secondary and adult education. Toronto: U. of T. Press, 1971. p. 202-211.

Jansen, C. The York drop-out: an exploratory study. Toronto: York
Univ., Dept. of Sociology, 1971. 68 p.

Tessier, J. "Le Collège universitaire Glendon: une expérience
précaire de bilinguisme." Maintenant 102 (jan. 1971) 18-20.

1972 Anisef, P. and C. Jansen. York Graduate Study. Toronto: Institute
for Behavioral Research, York University, 1972. 7 vols.

1. Background characteristics.
2. The honours and ordinary programme.
3. Atkinson and York graduates.
4. Decisions about university, major, career.
5. The York experience.
6. Present work experiences.
7. Experiences of those presently in graduate school.

1972 Jansen, C. Housing, Transport and Social Participation. Toronto:
Institute for Behavioral Research, York Univ., 1972. 2 vols.

1. The university setting. 67 p.
2. A survey of undergraduates. 200 p.

Lapp, P.A. An assessment of the needs for higher education in Metropolitan Toronto and the role of York University. Toronto: York
Univ., 1972. 108 p.

Olson, T.W. The future of the Faculty of Arts: survey of programmes
and prospects with recommendations: a report to the Dean. Toronto:
York Univ., 1972. 93 p.

1974 Macdonald, H.I. "Installation address (as president)." York Gazette
5 (Oct. 1974) 14, 21-22.

1975 Porticaro, B.F. "The relative statuses of academic men and women at York University." M.A. thesis, York Univ., 1975.

York University, Report of the Senate Task Force on the status of women at York University. Toronto: York Univ., 1975. 261 p.

1977 York University. Report of the President's Commission on goals and objectives. York Univ., 1977. 114 p.

E. THE UNIVERSITIES OF MANITOBA
   LES UNIVERSITES DU MANITOBA

1973 Morgan, J., ed. Report of the Task Force on Post-Secondary Education in Manitoba. Winnipeg: Queen's Printer, 1973. 228 p.

"Organization of provincial system and regional education structure (the) themes of Manitoba Report. Univ.Aff./aff.univ. 14 (April 1973) 8-9.

1974 Bredin, T.F. "The Red River Academy." Beaver 105 (Winter 1974) 10-17.

1976 Choquette, R. "Adelard Langevin et les questions scolaires du Manitoba et du Nord-Ouest 1895-1915." Rev.Univ.Ottawa 46 (1976) 324-344.

1977 Manitoba Federation of Labour and Special Projects Branch, Ministry of Colleges and Universities Affairs. "A report on post-secondary education." Interchange 7 (1) 11-23.

1978 Inter-Universities North. Annual report, 1977-78. Thompson, Man., 1978. 1 vol. (looseleaf).

1979 Duckworth, H. "Higher Education in Manitoba" Higher Education in Canada: historical perspectives Ed. by A. Gregor and K. Wilson Monographs in Education II. Winnipeg: Univ. of Manitoba, 1979. P. 43-52.

BRANDON UNIVERSITY

1978 McLeish, J.A.B. A Canadian for all seasons (the John E. Robbins story). Toronto: Lester & Orpen, 1978. 320 p.

1980 Shore, V. "At Brandon small is beautiful." Univ. aff./Aff. univ. 21, 2 (1980) 2-3.

UNIVERSITY OF MANITOBA

1970 Fridfinnson, A. and M. Sampson. Employment survey of 1967-1969, University of Manitoba B.A. graduates. Winnipeg: Manitoba University Counselling Service, 1970. 71 p.

1971 Lindal, W.J. "Manitoba College, Wesley College and United College." Icelandic Canadian 30 (Autumn 1971) 11-19.

Shook, L.K. "St. Paul's College" in Catholic post-secondary education in English-speaking Canada. Toronto: U. of T. Press, 1971. p. 317-328.

1972 Edwards, J.A. Andrew Baird of Manitoba College. Winnipeg: Univ. of Winnipeg Press, 1972.

University of Manitoba Faculty Association. Governance of the University of Manitoba: a brief presented to the Task Force on Post-secondary Education. Winnipeg: the University, 1972. 50 p.

1974 University of Manitoba, Board of Governors. Response to the Task Force on Post-secondary Education in the province. Winnipeg: Univ. of Manitoba, 1974. 2 vols.

1976 Williamson, N.J. "Lansdowne College: a product of the depression of 1885." Manitoba Pageant 21 (Summer 1976) 15-17.

1977 University of Manitoba Centennial Committee. From rural parkland to urban centre: one hundred years of growth at the University of Manitoba 1877 to 1977. Winnipeg: 1978. 174 p.

University of Manitoba Senate Planning and Priority Committee. Subcommittee on Institutional Goals Inventory. Attitudes towards goals of the University of Manitoba, by P.J. Husby. Winnipeg: 1977. 84 p.

University of Manitoba UM100 1877-1977. Winnipeg: Winnipeg Free Press, 1977. 12 p. Special supplement of Winnipeg Free Press, Oct. 14, 1977.

1979 Gregor, A.D. "The University of Manitoba: the denominational college system" in Higher education in Canada: historical perspectives Ed. by A. Gregor and K. Wilson. Monographs in Education II. Winnipeg: Univ. of Manitoba. 1979. p. 13-28.

Morton, W.L. "The founding of the University of Manitoba: born 25 years too soon?" in Higher education in Canada: historical perspectives. Ed. by A. Gregor and K. Wilson. Monographs in Education II. Winnipeg: Univ. of Manitoba, 1979. p. 7-12.

UNIVERSITY OF WINNIPEG

1976   Bedford, A.G. The University of Winnipeg: a history of the founding
        colleges. Toronto: U. of T. Press for the Univ. of Winnipeg, 1976.
        479 p.

F. THE UNIVERSITIES OF SASKATCHEWAN
    LES UNIVERSITES DE LA SASKATCHEWAN

1972   Small, J. "Saskatchewan: a time of testing." Can. Forum 51 (Oct.-
        Nov. 1972) 73-74.

1973   Province of Saskatchewan, Report of the Royal Commission on Univer-
        sity Organization and Structure. E. Hall, Chairman. Regina, 1973.
        49 p.

1977   de Valk, A. "Independent university or federated college? The debate
        among Roman Catholics during the years 1918-1921." Sask. Hist. 30
        (Winter 1977) 18-32.

        Gorman, J. Père Murray and the Hounds: the story of Saskatchewan's
        Notre Dame College. Sidney, B.C.: Gray's Publishing, 1977. 164 p.

1980   Tausig, C. "Saskatchewan's Universities meet community needs with
        agricultural research." Univ. aff./Aff. univ. 21, 6 (1980) 2-4.

UNIVERSITY OF REGINA

1971   Shook, L.K. "Campion College" in Catholic post-secondary education
        in English-speaking Canada. Toronto: U. of T. Press, 1971. p.325-332.

1974   Riddell, W.A. The first decade: a history of the University of
        Saskatchewan, Regina Campus, 1960-1970. Regina: University of Regina,
        1974. 155 p.

1975   University of Regina. President's Committee on the Status of Women.
        Report. Regina: Univ. of Regina, 1975. 94 leaves.

UNIVERSITY OF SASKATCHEWAN

1966   University of Saskatchewan. Organization and structure: report of a
        committee on the organization and structure of the University of
        Saskatchewan as amended and adopted by the Senate...November 4, 1966.
        Saskatoon: Univ. of Saskatchewan 1966. 35 p.

1970   Currie, B.W.   War research and the university.   Saskatoon: Univ. of Saskatchewan, 1970.   10 leaves.

Thompson, W.P.   The University of Saskatchewan: a personal history. Toronto: U. of T. Press, 1970.   233 p.

1971   MacLeod, T.H.   The role of the University of Saskatchewan within the Community.   Saskatoon: Univ. of Saskatchewan, 1971.   100 p.

Riddell, W.A.   The University in Saskatchewan.   Saskatoon: Univ. of Saskatchewan, 1971.   31 leaves.

Shook. L.K.   "St. Thomas More College" in Catholic post-secondary education in English-speaking Canada.   Toronto: U. of T. Press, 1971. p.341-353.

1972   Spinks, J.W.T.   Decade of change: the University of Saskatchewan 1959-70.   Saskatoon: Univ. of Saskatchewan, 1972.   169 p.

1973   Huel, R.   "Adrien-Gabriel Morice O.M.I. and the University of Saskatchewan."   Rev.Univ.Ottawa 43 (avril-juin 1973) 194-201.

1977   Saskatchewan.   Committee on Service Funding of the College of Medicine, University of Saskatchewan.   Report.   Regina: Dept. of Health and Dept. of Continuing Education, 1977.   73 leaves.

Saskatchewan.   Institute of Apologists.   Brief on the College of Agriculture, University of Saskatchewan presented to the Cabinet, Government of Saskatchewan.   Saskatoon: 1977.   22 leaves.

G. UNIVERSITIES OF ALBERTA
   LES UNIVERSITES DE L'ALBERTA

1971   Baker, H.S. et al.   The Future and Education, Alberta 1970-2005. Edmonton: Alberta Human Resources Research Council, 1971.

1972   Commission on Educational Planning, W. Worth, Chairman.   A future of choices, a choice of futures. Edmonton: Queen's Printer, 1972.   329 p.

Committee of Inquiry into Non-Canadian Influence in Alberta Post-Secondary Education, A.F. Moir, Chairman.   Report.   Edmonton, 1972. 139 p.

Long, J.C.   "An historical study of the establishment of college systems in Ontario and Alberta in the 1980's."   M.Ed. thesis, Univ. of Calgary, 1972.

McIntosh, G.   "Alberta: the reports are in."   Can.Forum (Oct.-Nov. 1972) 75-78.

Sukdeo, F. "An Assessment of student quotas and fees in Alberta Universities." Alta.Jour.Educ.Res., 18 (Sept. 1972) 223-233.

Unger, G. "A Choice of Futures – the public is confused." CAUT.Bull. ACPU 21 (Dec. 1972) 12-15.

Warren, R. "A Choice of Futures: it's up to people." School Progress, 41 (Sept. 1972) 24-27.

1973   Zachariah, M. "Is there a plan in A Choice of Futures?" Jour.Educ. Thought 7 (August 1973) 121-127.

1977   A financial plan for Alberta colleges and universities: recommendations and research results. By Bernard S. Sheehan et al. Calgary: Financial Plan Project for Colleges and Universities, 1977. 625 p. Final volume of a 5 v. report prepared for the Dept. of Advanced Education and Manpower, Alberta.

1978   Alberta Task Force to Review Students' Contribution to the Costs of Post-Secondary Education. Report. Edmonton: 1978. 31 p.

1979   de Valk, A. "Catholic higher education and university affiliation in Alberta 1906-1926." Can. Cath. Hist. Assoc. S.S. 1979, 23-47.

UNIVERSITY OF ALBERTA

1971   Shook, L.K. "St. Joseph's College" in Catholic post-secondary education in English-speaking Canada. Toronto: U. of T. Press, 1971. p. 358-368.

1973   University of Alberta Advisory Committee to the Department of Extension in Learning Resources. The development of a learning resources centre as a base for the expansion of continuing education in Alberta. Edmonton: 1973. 31 leaves.

1974   University of Alberta Association of the Academic Staff of the University of Alberta. Collective bargaining rights for faculty at the University of Alberta. By Bernard Adell. Edmonton: 1974. 161 p.

1975   Nearing, P.A. "Rev. John R. MacDonald, St. Joseph's College and the University of Alberta." Canadian Catholic Historical Association, Study Sessions 42 (1975) 70-89.

1976   Gordon, C.C. "St. Joseph's College, 1926-1976." New Trail: the University of Alberta Magazine. 31 (Spring 1976) 14-16.

1977   Campbell, D.D. Those tumultuous years: the goals of the President of the University of Alberta during the decade of the 1960's. Edmonton: Library, University of Alberta, 1977. 67 p.

ATHABASCA UNIVERSITY

1972   Athabasca University: an experiment in practical planning. Edmonton:
       Athabaska Univ. 1972.

1976   Curtis, E.J. and S.D. Phillips.   The implementations of expressed
       needs and preferences of adults for the design of non-traditional
       adult education programs.   Edmonton: Athabasca University, 1976. 53
       leaves.

1977   Athabasca University.   Athabasca University - the next five years:
       programs, services, processes, structures.   Edmonton: 1977.   100
       leaves.

       Lowe, R. "Growing pains at Athabasca University." CAUT BULL.ACPU 25
       (Apr. 1977).

1979   Daniel, J.S. and W.A.S. Smith.   "Opening open universities: the
       Canadian experience." Can.Jour.Higher Educ. 9 (2) 63-73.

       Meech, A., and J. Daniel.   Television and Athabasca University: a
       patchwork network. Edmonton: Athabasca University, 1979. 12 p.

UNIVERSITY OF CALGARY

1960   Johns, W.H.   "The Creation of new universities." NCCUC Proc. 1960,
       33-37.

1969   Report of the President: review of administrative structures and
       functions. Calgary: Univ. of Calgary, 1969. 32 p.

1976   Mah, D.   Student participation at the University of Calgary: past
       and present.   Calgary: Univ. of Calgary Students' Union, 1976.   58
       leaves.

1977   University of Calgary. Development plan, 1976-1985. Calgary: 1977.
       46 p.

       University of Calgary. President's Task Force to Evaluate the Faculty
       of Social Welfare. Evaluation report. Calgary: 1977. 34 leaves.

1979   University of Calgary. Presidential Task Force to Review the Faculty
       of Science. Report. Calgary: 1979. 52 p.

       University of Calgary.   Response to the report of the Task Force to
       Review Students' Contributions to the Costs of Post-Secondary Educa-
       tion. Edmonton: 1979. 12 leaves.

UNIVERSITY OF LETHBRIDGE

1968   Mardon, E.G.   The founding faculty.   Lethbridge: University of
       Lethbridge, 1968. 108 p.

1972   Smith, W.A.S.   "A Presidency in retrospect."   Univ. Aff./Aff. univ.
       13 (Oct. 1972) 2-3.

1974   Holmes, O.G.   Come hell or high water.   Lethbridge: The Lethbridge
       Herald, 1972, 141 p.

1976   Meyers, G.   A cost study of selected aspects of the Cooperative
       Studies Project Program, the University of Lethbridge.   Calgary:
       Evaluation Research Information Systems, 1976. 62 leaves.

1978   Atkinson, D.   "Work-study programs for liberal arts students work."
       Univ. aff./Aff. univ. 19 (Jan. 1978) 28.

H. UNIVERSITIES OF BRITISH COLUMBIA
   LES UNIVERSITES DE LA COLOMBIE-BRITANNIQUE

1972   Ellis, J.F.   "British Columbia: education - 1972."   Can.Forum 51
       (Oct.-Nov. 1972) 79-81.

1973   Committee on University Governance, John Bremer, Chairman, Working
       Paper on university governance in British Columbia. Victoria: Queen's
       Printer, 1973. 21 p.

1974   "B.C. committee recommends changes in university governance."   Univ.
       Aff./Aff.univ. 15 (Oct.1974) 7-8.

       University Government Committee, W.D. Young, Chairman, Report of
       . . . to the Hon. Eileen Dailly, Minister of Education, Province of
       British Columbia.   Victoria: Queen's Printer, 1974.   39 p.

1976   British Columbia.   Commission on University Programs in Non-
       metropolitan Areas.   Report.   Vancouver, B.C., 1976. 50 p.

1975   Wennevold, H.N.   Projections of post-secondary enrolments for British
       Columbia 1977-1986.   Vancouver: B.C. Post-Secondary Education Enrol-
       ment Forecasting Committee, 1976. 160 p.

       Wennevold, H.N.   Trend analysis of enrolments and participation per-
       centages in British Columbia post-secondary education 1967-1976.
       Vancouver: British Columbia Post-Secondary Education Enrolment Fore-
       casting Committee, 1977.   198 p.

1977 Lowe, R. "NDU closed; B.C. government denies collective bargaining rights to faculty." CAUT Bul. ACPU 26 (Sept. 1977) 6.

UNIVERSITY OF BRITISH COLUMBIA

1936 Williams, M.Y. "Reginald Walter Brock, Dean of the Faculty of Applied Science, University of British Columbia: in memoriam". Typescript, U.B.C. Library, 1935. 24 1.

1966 Committee on Graduate Studies, I. McTaggart-Cowan, chairman. A Review of graduate study at the University of British Columbia. Vancouver: The University, 1966. 100 p.

1969 "Larry looks back (interview with N.A.M. MacKenzie)." U.B.C. Reports 15 (Nov. 29, 1969) 1-3, 7.

1971 Omelusik, N.W. "Ex uno plures - the libraries of the university of British Columbia." Can. Library Jour. 28 (May - June 1971). 186-188.

Shook, L.K. "St. Mark's College", in Catholic post-secondary education in English-speaking Canada. Toronto: U. of T. Press, 1971. p. 373-391.

1973 Day, S. A report on the status of women at the University of British Columbia. Vancouver: Talonbooks, 1973. 100 p.

Gibson, W.C. Westbrook and his university. Vancouver: University of British Columbia Press, 1973. 204 p.

1976 Coleman, B. "McGill British Columbia 1899-1915". McGill Jour. Educ. 11 (Fall 1976) 179-188.

40 years: former UBC extension directors reminisce, 1936-1976. Vancouver: Centre for Continuing Education, Univ. of British Columbia, 1976. 50 p.

Hedgecock, J.K. The bookstore for the eighties. Vancouver: Univ. of British Columbia, 1976. 43 leaves.

1977 Bernard, E. "A University at war: Japanese Canadians at UBC during World War II". B.C. Studies. 35 (Autumn 1977), 36-55.

Robinson, J. Faculty Women's Club: sixty years of friendship and service, 1917-1977. Vancouver: Faculty Women's Club, Univ. of British Columbia, 1977. 134 p.

44

SIMON FRASER UNIVERSITY

1971 Baird, D.A. "Simon Fraser University library". Can. Library Jour. 28 (May–June 1971) 190–192.

1974 Strand, K. Simon Fraser University: a report by the President on its early years. Burnaby, B.C.: Simon Fraser University, 1974. 44 p.

UNIVERSITY OF VICTORIA

1972 University of Victoria. Commission on Academic Development (D.J. MacLaurin, chairman). Report. Victoria: University of Victoria, 1972. 2 vols. (I: Report; II: Appendices).

1975 University of Victoria. Status of women report. Victoria: 1975. 19 p.

1978 University of Victoria. Interior program proposal, 1978–79. Victoria: 1978. 61 leaves.

I. UNIVERSITY OF THE NORTH

1970 Greene, R. "Summary of the commission on the university and the Canadian north." AUCC Proc. 1970, 56–57.

1971 Cleverley, F. "Pioneers bring the university to the northland." Can. Univ. & College 6 (July–Aug. 1971) 30–31.

Judge, D. "Canada's north has its own vision of a university." Can. Univ. & College 6 (July–Aug. 1971) 30–32.

1972 "The University of Canada North," Univ.Aff./Aff.univ. Jan. 1972, 7.

1973 Wilson, D.N. "University of Canada North: promise for an alternative university structure." Can. International Educ. 2 (June 1973) 3–14.

1975 Gray, M. Possibilities for tertiary education in the north. Ottawa: Education Support Branch, Dept. of the Secretary of State, 1975. 44 leaves.

2. Current Trends and Problems/Orientation et problèmes actuels

A. GENERAL/GÉNÉRALITÉS

1969 Balkin, D. "The Hall-Dennis report and the universities." Jour. Council Student Services 4 (Autumn 1969) 9–19.

Deutsch, J. "The role of a changing university in a changing society." Jour. Council Student Services 4 (Autumn 1969) 3-8.

Geoffroy, M. "La contestation," Act. Nat. 58 (fév. 1969) 507-516.

1970 Carrier, H. "L'université dans une société nouvelle." Relations 346 (fév. 1970) 55-57.

Croteau, J. "L'université chrétienne," Act. Nat. 59 (juin 1970) 966-987.

Gaudry, R. "L'université et le développement au Canada." AUCC Proc. (1970) 106-112.

Genest, J. "Où en sommes-nous? La révolution scolaire," Act. Nat. 59 (juin 1970) 929-940.

Hendley, B. "What ails the University", McGill Jour. Ed., 5 (Fall, 1970) 192-204.

Lacoste, P. Le rôle de l'enseignement post-secondaire: buts, questions fondamentales et moyens." Can. Pub. Admin 13 (Fall 1970) 213-276.

Macpherson, C.B. "The university as multiple fool." CAUT Bull ACPU 19 (Autumn 1970) 3-7.

Michaud, D. "Summary of the commission on the university and the environment". AUCC Proc. 1 (1970) 32-34.

Poole, J.M. "The Crisis in the University". McGill Jour. Educ., 5 (Fall 1970) 205-214.

Spady, W.G. "Dropouts from higher education: an interdisciplinary review and synthesis", Interchange, 1 (1970) 64-85.

Tatlow, F. "Summary of the commission on university resources for international cooperation", AUCC Proc. 1 (1970) 40-44.

Thomson, D. and R.F. Swanson. "Scholars, missionaries or counter-imperialists." Jour. Can. Studies 5 (Aug. 1970) 3-11. (On the Americanization of Canadian higher education.)

Winthrop, H. Are the learned professions seceding from American society?" Dalhousie Rev. (Winter 1970-71) 496-509.

1971 Carlos, S. "Les périls de l'éducation", Maintenant 106 (mai 1971) 131.

Carrier, H. "L'université: milieu d'acculturation ou centre de contestation?" Relations 362 (juillet-août 1971) 216-217.

Edwards, R. "Emerging national policies for higher education in Canada" in World Year Book of Education 1971-72. Edited by B. Holmes et al. London: Evans Bros., 1971. p. 317-333.

Gill, A. "More on the universities and the environment." Univ. aff. /Aff. univ. 12 (July 1971) 24-29.

Gill, A. "Que font les universités pour accroître la qualité de la vie?" Univ. Aff./Aff. univ. 12 (jan 1971) 1-2.

Gill, A. "What the universities are doing about the environment." Univ. Aff./Aff. univ. 12 (Jan. 1971) 7-8; 21-23.

Gordon, H.S. Social institutions, change, and progress. Vancouver: University of British Columbia, 1971. 28 p.

Hansen, B.L. and F. Ireland. "Coming changes in higher education." Bus. Quart. 36 (Summer 1971) 31-37.

Hebb, D.O. "The nature of a university education", McGill Jour. Ed. 6 (Spring 1971) 5-17.

Matthews, B.C. "A president looks at registrars." Forum 2 (July 1971) 5-12.

St. John, J.B. "The indispensable institution". Interchange 2 (1971) 71-81.

Stevenson, H.A. "Public and professional disenchantment: the spectre of a new crisis in Canadian education." Lakehead Univ. Rev. 4 (Fall 1971) 83-99.

Verney, D.V. "Canadian experience", in The Task of Universities in a Changing World. Edited by S.D. Kertise. Notre Dame: Univ. of Notre Dame Press, 1971. p. 259-76.

1972   Benson, E. "Canadian universities: problems and solutions." C.A.U.T. Bull ACPU. 20 (Spring 1972) 61-70.

Bonneau, L.-P. "Au va l'AUCC?" Univ. Aff./Aff. univ. 13 (December 1972) 14.

Chénier, H. "Deux perspectives divergentes: la confessionnalité scolaire selon le Rapport Dumont et l'opinion de Mgr Grégoire." Maintenant 116 (mai 1972) 32-34.

Davies, D.I. "Intellectual tradition and academic colonialism." Can. Forum 4 (Oct.-Nov. 1972) 20-26.

Fluxgold, H. "Who killed the goose that laid the golden egg?" Can. Forum 51 (Oct.-Nov. 1972) 32-36.

Harvey, V. "L'université et l'évolution de la société", Maintenant 115 (avril 1972) 26-28.

Harvey, E.B. "University degrees and jobs", Orbit 3 (April, 1972) 7-10.

Hodgins, J.W. "Academic spin-offs and Canadian entrepreneurship." Bus. Quart. 37 (Spring 1972) 64-70.

Ostry, S. ed. Canadian higher education in the seventies. Ottawa: Information Canada, 1972. 307 p.

Ross, M.G. "The university - now and tommorrow: rule by computer?" Univ. Aff./Aff. univ. 13 (March 1972) 2-3.

Shute, J.M. "Canadian university technical assistance programs in Africa," Can. Jour. African Studies 6 (1972) 491-500.

Tremblay, R. "L'idée de l'université et son avenir", Maintenant 114 (mars 1972) 24-33; 115 (avril 1972) 29-32.

Woods, Gordon and Company. Organization of the academic year. Toronto: Queen's Printer, 1972. 210 p.

Wyman, M. "The state of universities." CAUT Bull ACPU. 20 (Winter 1972) 33-38.

1973 Black, E. "A perspective on the "crisis" in post-secondary education". CAUT Bull. ACPU 21 (March 1973) 16-20.

Booth, A.D. "Some thoughts on university education." Lakehead Univ. Review. 6 (winter-fall 1973) 135-45.

Camp, D. "The public image of the university student today." AUCC Proc. 1 (1973) 92-94.

Carrothers, A.W.R. "The role of the university in post-secondary education/Le role de l'université dans l'enseignement postsecondaire." AUCC Proc/Déliberations (1973) 36-52.

"Directives touchant les politiques des universités en matière de brevets." CAUT Bull APCU. 21 (jan. 1973) 25, 7.

Guérin, G. "Structuration du système universitaire." <u>Stoa</u> 3 (1) 29-46.

Harvey, E.B. and J.L. Lennards. <u>Key issues in higher education.</u> Toronto: O.I.S.E., 1973. 128 p.

Harvey, V. "Comment la société en évolution voit-elle évoluer l'université", <u>Maintenant</u> 127 (juin-juillet 1973) 28-34.

Ministry of Colleges and Universities. <u>Seminar on post-secondary learning: resumes of the discussion group sessions.</u> Toronto: Ministry of Colleges and Universities, 1973. 38 p.

Ministry of Colleges and Universities. <u>Seminar on post-secondary learning: transcripts of the presentations and discussions at the plenary sessions.</u> Toronto: Ministry of Colleges and Universities, 1973. 189 p.

Moore, M. "Canadians and their universities". <u>OCUFA Newsletter</u> 6 (April 1973) 3-4.

Semple, W. "Faculty, state and the people". <u>OCUFA Newsletter</u> 6 (April 1973) 6 +

1974   Aitken, H. "Three semester ... good or bad?" <u>Guelph Alumnus</u> 7 (Spring 1974) 12-13.

Belshaw, C.S. <u>Towers besieged: the dilemma of the creative university.</u> Toronto: McClelland & Stewart, 1974. 224 p.

Bourgeault, G. "Une université à l'image de la société", <u>Relations</u> 34, 399 (déc. 1974) 343.

Bowen, H.R. "The manpower vs. the free-choice principle." <u>Univ. Aff./Aff. univ.</u> 13 (Jan. 1974) 2-4.

Campbell, D.D. "Higher education: new avenues to explore." <u>Univ. Aff./Aff. univ.</u> 15 (May 1974) 10.

Cottam, K.J. <u>Canadian universities, American takeover of the mind?</u> Toronto: Gall Publications, 1974. 46 p.

Sibley, W.M. "The transactional frame of accountability", in H.R. Bowen, ed. <u>Evaluating institutions for accountability.</u> San Francisco: Jossey-Bass, 1974. P. 95-118.

Stamp, R.M. "Canadian universities and Canadian identity," <u>Can. International Educ.</u> 3 (June 1974) 17-33.

Thomas, A.M.   A summary and critique of various reports on post-secondary education in Canada, 1969-73.   Toronto: Can. Assoc. for Adult Education, 1974.   51 p.

1975   Gillett, M.   "Sexism in higher education."   Atlantis 1 (Fall, 1975) 68-81.

MacDonald, J.B.   "Relationships between the professions and the universities", in The Professions, universities and the civil service - mutual interaction.   Occasional Paper no. 32.   Report on a Seminar sponsored by the Commonwealth Foundation at the Professional Centre, Jamaica, January 13th - 18th 1975.   London, The Commonwealth Foundation, 1975.   p. 74-84.

Morris, J.F.   "Change in universities in the future: a search for new approaches to growth."   CAUCE Jour.   11 (May 1975) 17-25.

Stager, D.   "The universities."   Can. Public Policy (Summer 1975) 393-401.

Symons, T.H.B.   To know ourselves: the report of the Commission on Canadian Studies.   Ottawa, Ont. Association of Universities and Colleges of Canada, 1975.   2 vol.

"Women and the universities."   AUCC Proc.   (1975) 45-76.

1976   Allen, W.F.   "International aspects of university operations."   AUCC Proc.   1 (1976) 15-21.

Association of Universities and Colleges of Canada.   Committee on the Status of Women in the Universities/Association des universités et collèges du Canada.   Comité sur la situation de la femme dans les universités.   Report on the progress made by AUCC member institutions regarding the status of women/Rapport sur le progrès réalisé par les établissements membres de l'AUCC en ce qui a trait à la situation de la femme.   Ottawa, Ont., 1976.   38 p.

Franklin, M.   "Collaboration between industry and universities could streamline Canadian technology."   Science Forum 9 (October 1976) 12-15.

Isaacs, C.F.W.   Avoiding stagnation in small university departments.   A report prepared for the Ontario Council on Graduate Studies.   Toronto: Council of Ontario Universities, 1976.   52 p.

Leclerc, M.   "L'Université aux prises avec la communication sociale et technique."   Antennes 1 (ler trimestre 1976) 11-16.

Leibu, Y. "La qualité de l'enseignement universitaire: essai d'approche systématique." Rev. Can. d'ens sup. 6, 3 (1976) 1-11.

Wojciechowski, J.A. "Universities and Canadian culture." Rev. Univ. Ottawa 46 (avril-juin 1976) 169-179.

1977 Belshaw, C. "The university in Canadian society." AUCC Proc. (1977) 121-130.

Booth, A. "Higher education in a technological age." AUCC Proc. (1977) 54-69.

Campbell, D.D. "University public service: an agenda for action." Jour. Educ. Thought 11 (Dec. 1977) 237-242.

Cinman, I. "University research and the intelligence community." CAUT Bull. ACPU 25 5 (1977) 13-14, 17.

Girard, M. "Contrôler, évaluer, analyser les institutions d'enseignement." Prospectives 13 (fév. 1977) 11-14.

Giroux, R.F. "The instructional revolution: implications for educational leaders." Jour. ACCC (spring 1977) 1-14.

Patry, R. Survey of programmes of cooperation between Canadian universities and foreign institutions/L'enquête sur les programmes de coopération établis entre les universités canadiennes et les établissements étrangers. Ottawa: Assoc. Univs. & Colleges of Canada, 1977. 146 p.

"Second report of the Committee on the Status of Women." AUCC Proc. (1977) 1-120.

Shore, V. "It is better to jaw than to war." Univ. Aff./Aff. univ. 18 (Dec. 1977) 4-5.

Stevenson, H.A. "Knowledge and the future - perspectives on Canadian prospects." McGill Jour. Educ. 12 (Spring 1977) 3-16.

Sullivan, N. "Today's patrons of the arts are universities and colleges." Univ. Aff./Aff. univ. 8 (July 1977) 2-3.

Vickers, J. and J. Adam. But can you type? Canadian universities and the status of women. Toronto: Clarke Irwin, 1977. 142 p.

von Zur-Muehlen, M. The Canadian universities in a crisis. Ottawa: Statistics Canada, 1977. 138 p.

von Zur-Muehlen, M. The foreign student issues in 1976-1977. Ottawa: Canadian Bureau for International Education, 1977. 143 p.

Woodcock, L. "Merit, selection, excellence take on ugly connotation." Univ. Aff./Aff. univ. 18 (Nov. 1977) 6, 9.

1978 Association des universités et collèges du Canada. Mémoire à la Commission sur l'unité canadienne. Ottawa, 1978. 7 feuilles.

Association of Universities and Colleges of Canada. Brief to the Task Force on Canadian Unity. Ottawa, 1978. 6 p.

Bissell, C.T. "University presidents and politicians." Can. Jour. Higher Educ. 8, 3 (1978) 19-32.

"Canadian universities need international experience." Uni. Aff./Aff. univ. 19 (Jan. 1978) 9.

Côté, F. "Pour l'université moderne, l'espoir est dans la communauté." Univ. aff./Aff. univ. 19 (Feb. 1978) 7,9.

Rankin, M. "Access to information vital to researchers." Univ. aff./Aff. univ. 19 (Jan. 1978) 6-7.

Woodward, C.A. "Diogenes in the Tower of Babel: the generation gap and the role of the university. Jour. Educ. Thought 12 (Dec. 1978) 190-196.

1979 Ayre, D.J., C.E. Pascal and J. Scarfe, eds. Higher education colloqium 78/79 Toronto: Ontario Institute for Studies in Education, 1979. 249 p.

Canadian university experience in international development projects/ Les universités canadiennes et le développement international; a workshop jointly sponsored by the Centre for International Programs, University of Guelph and the International Development Office (AUCC) held at the University of Guelph, 18-19 October, 1979. Guelph: Univ. of Guelph, 1979. 78 p.

Colvin, J. "Colleges and universities: the odd couple." Jour. Assoc. Can. Com. Coll. 3, (Summer 1979) 40-59.

Council of Ontario Universities. Citizenship of students and faculty in Canadian universities: a statistical report. Ottawa, Association of Universities and Colleges of Canada, 1979. 131 p.

International relations of Canadian universities with the developed and industrialized world/Les relations internationales des universités Canadiennes avec les pays evolués et industrialisés; papers presented at a meeting of the Council of University Presidents, Winnipeg, 12 November, 1979. Ottawa: Association of Universities and Colleges of Canada, 1980. 47 p.

Sheffield, E.F. Policy-oriented research on national issues in higher education. Ottawa, Ont., 1979. 46 leaves. [A discussion paper for the Colloquium: Data Needs for Higher Education in the Eighties, March 26, 1979]

Laurent, I. "Transferability: can community colleges and universities meet the challenge?" Jour. Assoc. Can. Com. Coll. 3 (Summer 1979) 24-38.

Mustard, J.F. "The threat to the future of science and Canadian universities." Proc. R.S.C. (1979) 317-327.

Sheffield, E.F., H.J. Noah, H. Hamm-Brucher. "The OECD review and higher education. Can. Jour. Higher Educ. 9 (2) 1-18.

Symons, T.H.B. "Nationalism and higher education", in Issues in Higher Education. Edited by A. Gregor and K. Wilson. Winnipeg: Univ. of Manitoba, 1979. p. 7-17.

1980 Unger, S. "The retention rate: an analysis of enrolment attrition at a Canadian College." Can. Jour. Higher Eudc. 10, 1 (1980) 57-74.

Williams, D.C. Applied science - applied humanities: a strategy for Canadian universities in the 1980s. The Kellogg Lecture, Winnipeg, Nov. 12, 1979. Ottawa: AUCC and W.K. Kellogg Foundation, 1980. 13 p.

B. UNIVERSITY GOVERNMENT/ADMINISTRATION UNIVERSITAIRE

1970 Holmes, J. "Summary of the commission on AUCC guidelines on university government." AUCC Proc. 1 (1970) 51-52.

Swingle, P.G. "Administrative arbiting." CAUT Bull. ACPU. 19 (Autumn 1970) 9-13.

Watt, L.A.K. "The choosing of a university president." OCUFA Newsletter 3, 5 (Spring 1970) 13-14.

1971 Fleming, W.G. "University government", in Post-secondary and adult education. Toronto: U. of T. Press, 1971. p. 212-265.

"National survey on open senate and board meetings." Univ. Aff./Aff. univ. 12 (Ap. 1971) 20-24.

1972 Brown, J. "One tier or two tier government: University of Waterloo's answer." CAUDO. Develop. Journal Développe. 3 (December 1972) 3-4.

Campbell, D.D. "An empirical approach to the inference and classification of university goals: the University of Alberta 1950-6 to 1968/69." Ph.D. thesis, Univ. of Toronto, 1972.

Houwing, J.F. and L.F. Michaud. Changes in the composition of governing bodies of Canadian universities and colleges, 1965-1970. Ottawa: Assoc. of Univs. & Colleges of Canada, 1972. 65 p.

Friedmann, K.A. and B.H. Barker. "Ombudsmen in universities." CAUT Bull. ACPU. 20 (Spring 1972) 43-60.

Ross, M.G. "The dilution of academic power in Canada." Minerva 10 (1972) 241-258. See also C.T. Bissell, 11 (Jan. 1973) 130-133.

Smyth, D.M. "Structures for university government to the beginning of the twentieth century." Ph.D. thesis, Univ. of Toronto, 1972.

1973   Bosetti, R.A. "The process of perception and the administrator." Can. Admin. 12 (May 1973) 35-38.

Committee on University Governance, J. Bremer, chairman. Working paper on university governance in British Columbia. Victoria: Queen's Printer, 1973. 21 p.

Conway, J. "Academic change and crisis - Canadian style", in D. Reisman and V. Stadtman, eds. Academic transformation. New York: McGraw Hill, 1973. p. 343-366.

Flower, G. "Promising design or potential disaster? It depends on where you sit." Education Canada 13 (Sept. 1973) 33-40.

Sheldon, M. "Administering what refuses to be administered." Univ. Aff./Aff. univ. 14 (Sept. 1973) 4.

1974   Hartman, J.B. "Complementary modes of university organization." Jour. Educ. Thought 8 (April 1974) 15-28.

Rocher, G. "La restructuration scolaire de l'université de Montréal." Mém. SRC (1974) 199-204.

University Government Committee, W.D. Young, chairman. Report of the Committee to the Hon. Eileen Dailly, Minister of Education, Province of British Columbia. Victoria: Queen's Printer, 1974. 39 p.

1975   Houwing J.F. and A.M. Kristjanson. Composition of governing bodies of Canadian universities and colleges/Composition des organismes administratifs des universités et collèges du Canada. Ottawa: Assoc. of Univs. & Colleges of Canada, 1975. 51 p.

Smith, R. "Unicameralism at the University of Toronto: a progress report on the Governing Council." Can. Pub. Admin. 18 (Spring 1975) 17-37.

1976   Harvey, H.H.   Inflation: a powerful tool in government science
policy."   CAUT Bull. ACPU.   24 (October 1976) 14-15, 18.

McDougall, W.J., ed.   The role of the voluntary trustee.   London,
University of Western Ontario, 1976.   145 p.

1977   Booth, D.   "Those who chair could use some help."   Univ. aff./Aff.
univ.   18 (Nov. 1977) 24.

Hartman, J.B.   "Change and conflict in the university."   Jour. Educ.
Thought 11 (April 1977) 3-15.

1979   Watson, R.E.L.   "The role of the department head or chairman: discipline, sex and nationality as factors influencing faculty opinion."
Can. Jour. Higher Educ.   9 (3) 19-28.

1980   Fleming, T.   "Beyond survival: policies for academic revitalization."
Can. Jour. Higher Educ.   10, 2 (1980) 103-115.

Konrad, A.G.   "Deans in Canadian higher education."   Can. Jour.
Higher Educa.   10, 2 (1980) 53-72.

C.   UNIVERSITY FINANCE/FINANCE UNIVERSITAIRE

1969   Brown, W.T.   Education finance in Canada.   Ottawa: Can. Teachers
Federation, 1969.   93 p.

1970   Association of Universities and Colleges of Canada.   Federal support
of universities and colleges of Canada: a submission to the Government of Canada and the Council of Ministers of Education concerning
federal financial support of Canadian universities and colleges.
Ottawa: AUCC, September, 1970.   95 p.

Atherton, P.J.   "Financing post-secondary education in Alberta."
Alta. Jour. Educ. Research 16 (Sept. 1970) 137-148.

Hanley, C. et al.   Who pays: university financing in Ontario.
Toronto: Lewis & Samuel, 1970.   168 p.

Huang, R.Y.M. and Hanly, C.M.   "A position paper on the faculty role
in university financing and operation for the OCUFA Conference on
university financing and operation."   OCUFA Newsletter 4 (September,
1970) 14-16.   See also 8-11.

Macpherson, C.B.   "The university as critical capital: a convocation
address."   Queen's Quart.   77 (Autumn 1970) 389-94.

"Mémoire de l'AUCC relatif à l'aide financière fédérale."   Univ. Aff.
/Aff. univ.   11 (Nov. 1970) 20.

Parent, A.-M. "La notion d'utile dans l'éducation." Mém S.R.C. (1970) 103-107.

Primeau, W. "Summary of a commission on higher education in the seventies - financing and other university-government relations." AUCC Proc. 1 (1970) 59-60.

Robinson, G. de B. "University overhead costs: a critical problem in Canada." Science Forum. 3 (Oct. 1970) 20-21.

Salyzyn, V. "Taxation and education." CAUT Bull. ACPU. 19 (Autumn 1970) 21-29.

Stager, D. "Financing post-secondary education in Canada: some policy considerations." Proceedings of the Conference on Community College Finance." Toronto: Can. Assoc. Adult Educ., 1970. p. 6-47.

Tremblay, A. "Accroissement des frais d'éducation et du produit national brut." Prospectives. 6 (juin 1970) 190-193.

Waines, W.J. Federal support of universities and colleges of Canada. Ottawa: Assoc. Univs. & Colleges of Canada, 1970. 95 p.

Watts, R.L. "Further direction in university financing." OCUFA Newsletter 4 (Nov. 1970) 6-7.

Weldon, K.L. Inter-provincial comparisons of cost and quality of higher education in Canada. Toronto: Committee of Presidents of Univs. of Ontario, 1970. 54 p.

1971 Dunton, A.D. "Increased effectiveness and economy in higher education." AUCC Proc. (1971) 95-101.

Glen, J.D. "The challenge of rising educational costs." McGill Jour. Educ. 6 (Fall 1971) 195-203.

Hettich, W. Expenditures, output and productivity in Canadian university education. Ottawa: Information Canada, 1971. 123 p. (Special Study No. 14 prepared for Economic Council of Canada.)

Systems Research Group Inc. Financing post-secondary education. Toronto: Queen's Printer, 1971. 158 p. Study prepared for the Commission on Post-Secondary Education in Ontario.

Wright, D.T. "The financing of post-secondary education: basic issues and distribution of costs." Can. Pub. Admin. 14 (Fall 1971) 595-607.

1972 Babcock, J.K. "Direct mail fund raising." CAUDO Develop. Jour. Développe. 2 (June 1972) 1-3.

Carson, D.A. "The ups and downs of an alumni fund." CAUDO Develop. Jour. Développe. 2 (Feb.-March 1972) 1-2.

Stager, D. "Economics of continuing education", in Canadian higher education in the seventies. Edited by S. Ostry. Ottawa: Information Canada, 1972.

Stager, D. Evolution of federal government involvement in financing post-secondary education in Canada, 1867-1966. Toronto: Council of Ministers of Education, 1972. 247 p.

Stager, D. Federal government grants to Canadian universities. Toronto: Institute for Quantitative Analysis of Social & Economic Policy, Univ. of Toronto, 1972. 19 p.

Stager, D. and G. Cook. Financing post-secondary education: a critique of the draft report of the Commission on Post-Secondary Education. Toronto: Institute for Quantitative Analysis, Univ. of Toronto, 1972. 14 p.

Systems Research Group Inc. Cost and benefit study of post-secondary education in Ontario, school year 1968-69. Toronto: Queen's Printer, 1972. 157 p.

1973 Crowley, R.W. "Towards free post-secondary education?" Jour. Can Studies 8 (August 1973) 43-57.

Daly, T. "The University of Toronto Varsity Fund telethon." CAUDO. Develop. Journal Développe. 3 (May 1973) 2-4.

Drekos, G.E. "L'économique, la politique de l'enseignement universitaire et les frais de scolarité." Act. Econ. 3 (juillet-septembre 1973) 435-440.

Graham, J. and J.R. Cameron. "Equalization in federal support for post-secondary education." Can. Public Admin. 16 (Spring 1973) 139-143.

Hartle, D.G. "The financing of higher education in the 1970's: a viewpoint from Ottawa." Stoa 3, 2 (1973) 113-140.

Horriére, Y. et P. Petit. "Les effets redistributifs de l'enseignement supérieur: une première évaluation." Act. Econ. 2 (juin 1973) 237-258.

Lacroix, R. Une évaluation partielle des pertes ou des gains des provinces résultant de la mobilité des étudiants et diplômés universitaires. Montréal: Université de Montréal, Centre de Recherche en Développement Economique, 1973. 55 p. Also published in Act. Econ. (juil.-sept. 1973) 379-402.

Macdonald, J.B. "Financing of research in universities." _Stoa_ 3, 2 (1973) 157-174.

Oliver, M. "Factors reshaping the financing of higher education in the 1970's. _Stoa_ 3, 2 (1973) 105-111.

Ontario Confederation of University Faculty Associations. "Brief on the Federal role in university finance." _OCUFA Newsletter_. 7 (Sept. 1973) 17.

Parr, J.G. "A little less of the "Who Pays?" ... a little more of the "what for?"" _Stoa_ 3, 2 (1973) 141-149.

Peitchinis, S.G., "Equality and inequality of opportunity: the financing of post-secondary education in Canada." _Australian Jour. Higher Educ_. 5 (Dec. 1973) 64-75.

Proulx, P.-P. "Cost studies in post-secondary education-Canada." _Stoa_ 31 (1973) 5-16.

Proulx, P.-P. "Réflexions sur les facteurs déterminants de l'évolu- tion du financement de l'enseignement supérieur au Canada dans les années 1970 et 1980." _Stoa_ 3, 2 (1973) 151-156.

Stager, D. "Federal government grants to Canadian universities 1951- 66." _Can. Hist. Rev_. 54 (Sept. 1973) 287-297.

1974   Council of Ontario Universities. _The Ontario operating grants for- mula: a statement of principles to the Ontario Council on University Affairs_. Toronto: COU. 1974. 51 p.

Gill, A. "This year's dollar story." _Univ. Aff./Aff. univ_. 15 (May 1974) 8, 9.

1976   Coté, F. "La proposition fédérale et la réaction de l'AUCC." _Univ. Aff./Aff. univ_. 17 (7) 4.

Council of Ontario Universities. _A companion of provincial contribu- tions to Canadian universities_. Toronto: COU, 1976. 16 p.

Masleck, C. "Federal-provincial governments hold talks to determine future of cost-shared programs." _CAUT Bull. ACPU_. 24 (Sept. 1976) 1.

Ontario Council of Universities. _Brief to the Canadian and Ontario governments on the financing of higher education in Canada_. Toronto: COU, 1976. 24 p.

Council of Ontario Universities. _Approach to the eighties: demand/ quality/resources_. Toronto: COU, 1976. 59 p.

Prakash, B. "The demand for and financing of higher education in Canada." Ph.D. thesis, Univ. of Toronto, 1976.

Saskatchewan Universities Commission. Survey of university fiscal systems. Regina: the Commission, 1976. 126 p.

1977 Hettich, W. Foreign student costs: a report on the cost of educating foreign students at Canadian universities. Ottawa: Can. Bureau for International Education, 1977. 28 p.

"Where will the universities stand in the provincial queue as they compete for funds?" Univ. Aff./Aff. univ. 18 (February 1977) 3, 8.

Conférence des Recteurs et des Principaux des Universités du Québec. Principes et pratiques comptables ainsi que forme de présentation des états financiers des universités du Québec. Montréal: La Conférence, 1977. 30 p.

1978 Conférence des Recteurs et des Principaux des Universités du Québec. Analyse de quelques indicateurs du niveau de développement du système d'enseignement supérieur de Québec, de l'effort relatif de la société et du gouvernement et de la productivité des universités québécoises. Montréal: La Conférence, 1978. 88 p.

Council of Ontario Universities. The price of restraint: brief to the Ontario Council on University Affairs. Toronto: COU, 1978. 61 p.

1979 Bottomley, A. and R. Cook. "Calcul des coûts unitaires dans les universités francophones." Can. Jour. Higher Educ. 9 (2) 19-34.

D'iorio, A. Le financement de l'enseignement supérieur au Canada: l'exemple de l'Ontario. Rev. de L' AUPELF 17 (déc. 1979) 221-233.

Ontario Council of Universities. Who pays the price?: brief to the Ontario Council on University Affairs. Toronto: COU, 1979. 62 p.

Thibault, C. "University financing", in Issues in higher education. Edited by A. Gregor and K. Wilson. Winnipeg: Univ. of Manitoba, 1979. p. 19-27. (Monographs in Education I)

D. THE UNIVERSITY AND THE STATE/L'UNIVERSITÉ ET L'ETAT

1961 Stewart, F.K. "Government control of education in Canada." Current History (June 1961) 353-360.

1969 McCarter, J.A. "Why not nationalize the universities?" Science Forum 2 (Feb. 1969) 21-23.

1970   Amy, J. "Summary of the commission on the impact of federal policies on university planning." AUCC Proc. 1 (1970) 58.

"AUCC statement on Rowat-Hurtubise study." Univ. Aff./Aff. univ. 11 (November 1970) 15.

Hanly, C.M.T. "Considering the CUA report." OCUFA Newsletter 3 (January 1970) 13-17.

Judge, D. "Deadline Ottawa, universities seek federal policy on higher education." Can. Univ. & Coll. 5 (Nov. 1970) 13-14.

Macdonald, J.B. "Change and the universities: university-government relations." Can. Public Admin. 13 (Spring 1970) 6-18. See also 19-27.

Schreyer, E. "Excerpts from an address." AUCC Proc. (1970) 115-117.

1971   Benson, E. "The house that Davis built: or university education in the sixties." CAUT Bull. ACPU. 19 (Spring 1971) 3-12.

Crépeau, J.C. "McGill: Garder le pouvoir aux universités." Educ. Quart. 1 (24 mars 1971) 18-21.

Rowat, D.C. "The Commission on the Relations between Universities and Governments: summary report." Can. Public Admin. 14 (Winter 1971) 608-620.

1972   Cole, R.T. "The universities and governments under Canadian federalism." Jour. of Politics [U.S.] 34 (May 1972) 524-553.

Gill, A. "Science in Ottawa." Univ. Aff./Aff. univ. 13 (Sept. 1972) 6-7.

Ontario Confederation of University Faculty Associations. "The state and the universities subject of conference." OCUFA Newsletter 6 (Oct. 1972) 10-11.

"Policies for science and the universities." [Interview with Alistair Gillespie, Minister of Science and Technology] Univ. Aff./Aff. univ. 13 (June-July 1972) 2-4.

Smiley, D.V. "Inter-university and inter-governmental planning — federal provincial relations in matters of university research." AUCC Proc. (1972) 113-120.

1973   Allard, J.-L. "Les Franco-Ontariens et l'éducation post-secondaire." Rev. Univ. Ottawa 43 (1973) 518-531.

Dupré J.S. et al. Federalism and policy development: the case of adult occupational training in Ontario. Toronto: U. of T. Press, 1973. 264 p.

Holland, J.W. "A reappearance of national and provincial educational policy styles." Can. and International Educ. 2 (June 1973) 47-66.

Nicholson, N.L. "The federal government and Canadian universities: a review." Stoa 3, 1 (1973) 17-28.

1974 "Debating a national science policy: provinces call for autonomy." Univ. Aff./Aff. univ. 15 (March 1974) 4.

Faulkner, J.H. "A federal view of the federal role." Univ. Aff./Aff. univ. 15 (May 1974) 5.

Hare, F.K. "Interchange Canada: as one academic sees it." Univ. Aff./Aff. univ. 15 (May 1974) 24.

Hayes, F.R. The chaining of Prometheus: the evolution of a power structure for Canadian science. Toronto: U. of T. Press, 1974. 217 p.

Munroe, D. "Le Conseil supérieur de l'éducation." Mém. S.R.C. (1974) 193-198.

"National involvement requires federal presence/Une participation aux affaires nationales exige une présence fédérale." Univ. Aff./Aff. univ. 15 (April 1974) 2-4.

1976 Coté, F. "La proposition fédérale et la réaction de l'AUCC." Univ. Aff./Aff. univ. 17 (Sept. 1976) 4.

Globerman, S. "Canadian science policy and economic nationalism." Minerva 14 (Summer 1976) 191-208.

Hitschfeld, W. "Reflections on federal research support to universities." Univ. Aff./Aff. univ. 17 (Nov. 1976) 11.

Holdaway, E.A. "Federal initiatives in education in Australia; have they implications for Canada?" Education Canada 16 (Fall 1976) 4-13.

Manitoba Federation of Labour and Special Projects Branch, Ministry of Colleges and Universities Affairs. "A report on post-secondary education." Interchange 7 (1) 11-23.

Morin, L. "Considérations sur les fins de l'enseignement universitaire." Rev. Sci. Educ. 2, 3 (1976) 157-175.

Sullivan, N. and L. Woodcock. "Federal government proposes new financing options." Univ. Aff./Aff. univ. 17 (Sept. 1976) 2-3.

Traub, R.E. et al. "Interface project II and Ontario's review of educational policy." Interchange 7 (4) 24-31.

1977   Cody, H.H. "Towards a perspective on the perpetuation of the Canadian federal system: Federal-Provincial relations in university education since 1945." Ph.D. thesis, McMaster Univ., 1977.

Losey, N. "Why fund a university?" CAUT Bul. ACPU 25 (5) 2, 3, 1977.

Mitchell, L.A. "The future of Canadian education: greater Ottawa participation." CAUT Bul. ACPU 25, 6 (1977) 11.

Sullivan, N. "Post-secondary education - federal role on the wane?" Univ. Aff./Aff. univ. 18 (February 1977) 2-3.

Vipond, D. and R.A. Richert. "Contributions of Canadian psychologists to the war effort." Can. Psych. Rev. 18 (Apr. 1977) 169-174.

1978   Canadian Association of University Business Officers (CAUBO). Submission to the Tariff Board regarding Reference no. 155: exemption from duties for certain institutions and goods, tariff items 69605-1 and 69610-1. Ottawa: Association of Universities and Colleges of Canada, 1978. 67 p.

De Bresson, C. "Is the government responsible for declining R. and D.?" Can. Research 11 (Sept. 1978) 23-27.

Young, W.R. "Academics and social scientists versus the press: the policies of the Bureau of Public Information and the Wartime Information Board, 1939-1945." Hist. Papers 1978, 217-240.

1979   Oliver, M. "Post-secondary commissions." Higher Education in Canada: historical perspectives. Ed. by. A. Gregor and K. Wilson. Monographs in Education II. Winnipeg: Univ. of Manitoba, 1979. p. 29-42.

Gregor, A. "The re-alignment of post-secondary education systems in Canada." Can. Jour. Higher Educ. 9 (2) 35-49.

Young, D.G. "A futures perspective of control of education in Canada." Can. Admin. 18 (April 1979) 5 p.

1980   Fellagi, I. "Cooperations between the universities and Statistics Canada in the field of social statistics." Can. Rev. Soc. and Anth. 17, 1 (1980) 74-77.

Frederick,N. "The autonomy of universities and colleges: a tentative theory of power distribution based on a comparative case study of government relations with universities and colleges in Ontario." Ph.D. Thesis, Univ. of Toronto, 1980.

E. THE UNIVERSITY AND THE ECONOMY/L'UNIVERSITÉ ET L'ECONOMIE

1966   Organization for Economic Cooperation and Development. Training of and demand for high-level scientific and technical personnel in Canada. Paris: OECD, 1966.

1968   Stager, D. "Measuring the output of educational institutions" , in The Canadian labour market. Edited by A. Kruger and N. Meltz. Toronto: Centre for Industrial Relations, Univ. of Toronto, 1968. P. 297-312.

1970   Atkinson, A.J., K.J. Barres and E. Richardson. Canada's highly qualified manpower resources. Ottawa: Dept. of Manpower and Immigration, 1970. 340 p.

Carrier, H. L'université dans un monde à développer." Relations 354 (novembre 1970) 306-309.

Salyzyn, V. "Taxation and education." CAUT Bull. ACPU. 19 (Autumn 1970) 21-29.

1971   Riverin, A. L'université et le développement socio-economique. Montréal: Publications Les Affaires, 1971. 162 p.

1972   Axworthy, L. "The university as innovator in the urban community." Univ. Aff./Aff. univ. 13 (October 1972) 8.

Carrier, H. "L'école et la liberté." Relations 376 (novembre 1972) 306-307.

Crean, J.F. "Taux de rentabilité attendu et la demande d'éducation: quelques résultats empiriques." Relations Ind. 27 (août 1972) 382-402.

Ostry, S. ed. Canadian higher education in the seventies. Ottawa: Information Canada, 1972. 307 p.

Holland, J., et al. Manpower forecasting and educational policy. Toronto: Queen's Printer, 1972. 267 p.

Joris, A. "La scolarité de la main-d'oeuvre au Saguenay-Lac Saint-Jean dans une optique de développemnt économique." Act. Econ. 48 (juil.-sept. 1972) 335-47.

1973 Fleming, R.J. and R. Billington. "The role of the universities in power development." Engineering Jour. 56 (Feb. 1973) 30-34.

Harrière, Y. et P. Petit. "Les effets redistributifs de l'enseignement superieur: une première évaluation." Act. Econ. 39 (juil.-sept. 1973) 379-402.

Wilson, A.H. "Outreach of the Canadian universities into manufacturing industry." Can. R. and D. 6 (March-April 1973) 40-41.

1974 Farine, A. Les diplômés de l'Université de Montréal sur le marché du travail. Montréal: Université de Montréal, Centre de Recherche en Développement Economique, 1974. 223 p.

Stager, D. "Economic issues in Canadian education", in Issues in Canadian economics. Edited by L.H. Officer and L.B. Smith. Toronto: McGraw Hill-Ryerson, 1974. P. 311-320.

1975 Holland, J. and M. Skolnik. Public policy and manpower development. Toronto: Ontario Institute of Studies in Education, 1975. 160 p.

Phidd, R.W. "The Economic Council of Canada: its establishment, structure, and role in the Canadian policy-making system." Can. Pub. Admin. 18 (Fall 1975) 428-473.

1979 Colvin, J.A. "Higher education and manpower needs." Can. Jour. Higher Educ. 9, 2 (1979) 87-94.

F. UNIVERSITY PLANNING/LA PLANIFICATION UNIVERSITAIRE

1970 "Campus construction 1970-72." Can. Univ. & College. 5 (July 1970) 7-26.

"Campus projects win excellence merit awards in design competition." Can. Univ. & College 5 (Oct. 1970) 26-27.

Christensen, E.M. "Location and needs surveys are vital in selection of the university centre site." Can. Univ. & College 5 (July 1970) 27-31.

"Report examines role of Catholic colleges and universities." Univ. Aff./Aff. univ. 11 (May 1970) 25.

"Un engagement au caractère chrétien et l'excellence universitaire." Univ. Aff./Aff. univ. 11 (May 1970) 26.

1971 Desbarats, Guy. "Towards a university model: a structure for permanent evolution." Univ. Aff./Aff. univ. 12 (Oct. 1971) 2-4.

Lefebvre, J.B. "Building for change: the case for systems buildings on campus." Can. Univ. & College 6 (July-August 1971) 17-18.

Légaré, J. "Aspects démographiques de la planification de l'enseignement." Act. Econ. 47 (avril-juin 1971) 74-83.

Pardoen, A. "Pourquoi planifier." Educ. Quart. 1 (10 mars 1971) 6-7.

Pelletier, D. "Planification: l'initiative aux universités." Educ. Quart. 1 (14 avril 1971) 10-13.

Pierre, G. "Systemia and academia: a tale of two universities." Univ. Aff./Aff. univ. 12 (Oct. 1971) 1.

Stahmer, M. "Planning administration space by function - not by prestige." Can. Univ. & College 6 (May-June 1971) 28-29.

Systems Research Group Inc. The connect/campus individual specific file system: an overview. Toronto: Systems Research Group, 1971. 33 p.

Systems Research Group, Inc. Campus planning and budgeting manual: an outline. Toronto: Systems Research group, 1971. 25 p.

Systems Research Group Inc. Introduction to planning with a campus model. Toronto: Systems Research Group, 1971. 33 p.

1972 Commission on post-secondary education in Ontario. Libraries and information storage and retrieval systems. Toronto: Queen's Printer, 1972. 113 p.

Farine, A. "La comptabilité démographique et sociale et son application aux activités éducatives." Act. Econ. 47 (jan-mars 1972) 734-744.

Holland, J. et al. Manpower forecasting and educational policy. Toronto: Queen's Printer, 1972. 482 p.

Richards, D.M. "Predicting the demand for teaching." Alta. Jour. Ed. Res. 18 (June 1972) 133-139.

Tremblay, A. "La planification de l'éducation." Bien-Etre 24 (jan-fév. 1972) 18-23.

Woods, Gordon and Co. Organization of the academic year. Toronto: Queen's Printer, 1972. 230 p.

1973 Adams, W.A. and E.A. Holdaway. "Communication networks in formal organizations." Can. Admin. 13 (November, 1973) 7-11.

Austin, T.A. "The analysis, design, and complementation of a data base and report generation system for the physical resources data of the University of New Brunswick." M.Sc. thesis, Univ. of New Brunswick, 1973.

Ingram, E.J. "Knowledge utilization: an alternative model." Man. Jour. Educ. 9 (November 1973) 15-22.

Jackson, R.W.B. "A new model of the university: not one thing, but many." Science Forum 6 (August 1973) 9-13.

1976 Dupré, S. "Problems of changing growth rates." AUCC Proc. (1976) 45-52.

Evans, J.R. "Problems of changing growth rates." AUCC Proc. (1976) 9-14.

Lapointe, S. "La planification sectorielle: l'opération sciences fondamentales." Can. Jour. Higher Educ. 6 (3) 43-49.

Lauzon, M. "Système informatisé et intégré de la gestion des études à l'Université Laval." Rev. Can. d'ens sup. 6, 1 (1976) 69-88.

Smith, R. "Ontario university system financing and staffing policies: a quantitative model for policy analysis. Can. Jour. Higher Educ. 6, 3 (1976) 51-72.

Zsigmond, Z., et al. Future trends in enrolment and manpower supply in Ontario. Ottawa, Statistics Canada, 1976. 302 p.

1977 Mehmet, O. Le rendement économique des diverses disciplines dans les universités canadiennes du 1961-1972." Relations Ind. 32 (1977) 321-337.

Sheehan, B.S. et al. A financial plan for Alberta Colleges and universities: recommendations and research results. Calgary: Financial Plan Project for Colleges and Universities, Univ. of Calgary, 1977. 625 p.

Thomson, D.C. "The state of planning at McGill." McGill Jour. Educ. 12 (Spring 1977) 47-56.

1978 Creet, M. and B. Trotter "Statistics for policy and planning in Canadian higher education: an Ontario perspective." Can. Jour. Higher Educ. 8, 1 (1978) 47-60.

Fleming, T. "Some considerations of the goal setting and planning processes in public higher education." Can. Jour. Higher Educ. 8, 3 (1978) 33-46.

Jones, L.R. "A model for academic planning." Can. Jour. Higher Educ. 8, 3 (1978) 1-10.

Nobel, H., R.A. Stoll and I.S. Calvert. "A participatory approach to the development of centralized information systems." Can. Jour. Higher Educ. 8, 1 (1978) 1-24.

Worth, W. "Perspectives on policy formulation" Can. Jan. Higher Educ. 8, 2 (1978) 1-8.

1980 Griew, S. "A model for the allocation and utilisation of academic staff resources." Can. Jour. Higher Educ. 10, 2 (1980) 73-84.

G. ACCESS TO HIGHER EDUCATION/ACCÈS À L'ENSEIGNEMENT SUPÉRIEUR

1970 Blishen, B.R. "Social class and opportunity in Canada." Can. Rev. Sociology & Anthrop. 7 (May 1970) 110-127.

Fisher, E.A. "Financial accessibility to higher education in Canada during the 1960's." CAUT Bull. ACPU. 18 (Summer 1970) 92-106.

Manley-Casimir, M. and I.E. Housego. "Equality of educational opportunity: a Canadian perspective." Alta. Jour. Educ. Res. 16 (1970) 79-88.

Pike, R.M. Who doesn't get to university -- and why: a study on accessibility to higher education in Canada. Ottawa: Assoc. of Univs. and Colleges of Canada, 1970. 210 p.

1971 Farina, A. "Fonds d'autofinancement des frais de scolarité." CAUT Bull. ACPU. 19 (Spring 1971) 13-18.

1972 Buttrick, J. "Who goes to university in Ontario." This Magazine 6, 2 (1972) 81-100.

Environs Research Group. Post-secondary educational opportunity for the Ontario Indian population. Toronto: Queen's Printer, 1972. 187 p.

1973 Crowley, R.W. "Towards free post-secondary education?" Jour. Can. Studies 8 (August 1973) 43-57.

Gordon, A. "Accessibility and equal opportunity." AUCC Proc. (1973) 103-109.

Pike, R. "Enrolment and accessibility: retrospect and prospect." Univ. aff./Aff. univ. 14 (Nov. 1973) 2-4.

Porter, M.R., J. Porter and B. Blishen. Does money matter? prospects for higher education. Toronto: Institute for Behavioral Research, York Univ., 1973. 318 p.

1974 Fleming, W.G. Educational opportunity: the pursuit of equality. Scarborough: Prentice Hall of Canada, 1974. p. 133.

1976 Quelques caractéristiques des étudiants du niveau post-secondaire au Canada. Ottawa: Secrétariat d'État, 1976. 91 p.

Some characteristics of post-secondary students in Canada. Ottawa, Department of the Secretary of State, 1976. 91 p.

1977 Daniel, J.S. "The open university concept." Can. Jour. Information Science 2 (1) 129-38.

Daniel, J.S. and W.A.S. Smith. "Opening open universities: the Canadian experience." Can. Jour. Higher Educ. 9 (2) 63-73.

Davis, J.T., Jansen, C., and T.W. Olson. Factors influencing student enrolment, performance and experience at York University. Toronto, Office of Research Administration, York University, 1977. 141 p. in 3 v.

Harvey, E. "Accessibility to postsecondary education - some gains, some losses." Univ. aff./Aff. univ. 18 (Oct. 1977) 10-11.

Woodcock, L. "Planning: you may not like it but it's good for you." Univ. Aff./Aff. univ. 8 (July 1977) 4, 17.

1978 Pike, R.M. "Part-time undergraduate studies in Ontario," Innovations and access to higher education. New York: International Council on Educational Development, 1978. p. 1-146.

Von Zur-Muehlen, M. The educational background of parents of post-secondary students in Canada: a comparison between 1968-69 and 1974-75 and related to the educational level of the population. Ottawa: Statistics Canada, 1978. 74 p.

1979 Pascal, C.E. and S. Kanowitch. Student withdrawals from Canadian universities: a study of studies. Toronto: Higher Education Group, Ontario Institute for Studies in Education, 1979. 35 p.

1980 Darling, A. "The impact of the participation rate - whatever it is - on university enrolment." Can. Jour. Higher Educ. 10, 1 (1980) 37-56.

Goyder, J.C. "Trends in the socioeconomic achievement of the university educated : a status attainment model interpretation." Can. Jour. Higher Educ. 10, 2 (1980) 21-38.

Pike, R.M. "Open access in Canadian higher education during the seventies." Can. Jour. Univ. Cont. Educ. 7 (Summer 1980) 4-7.

3. Curriculum and Teaching/Programmes d'étude et méthodes d'enseignement

A. THE FACULTY OF ARTS AND SCIENCE/FACULTÉ DES ARTS

1970 Bélanger, P. "Une expérience d'enseignement: la formule cours-discussions." Act. Péd. 9-10 (janvier 1970) 83-97.

Michaud, D. "Summary of the commission on teaching in the university." AUCC Proc. (1970) 67-70.

Sheffield, E.F., ed. Curriculum innovation in arts and science: report of a Canadian universities' workshop. Toronto: Higher Education Group, Univ. of Toronto, 1970. 38 p.

1971 Randhawa, B.S. "Meaningful learning and individualized instruction in relation to tote unit for an evaluation paradigm." Man. Jour. Educ. 7 (Nov. 1971) 57-68.

Stockholder, F.E. "The relevance of UBC's Arts I program to designing new curricula." Univ. Aff./Aff. univ. 12 (Dec. 1971) 5.

1972 Anisef, P. and C. Jansen. "The honours and ordinary programme", in York Graduate Study. Vol 2. Toronto: Institute for Behavioural Research, York Univ. 1972. 77 p.

Duval, R. "La pédagogie universitaire, un problème de relations humaines." Act. péd. 25 (août 1972) 11-46.

Harvey, E.B. Education and employment of arts and science graduates: the last decade in Ontario. Toronto: Queen's Printer, 1972. 314 p.

Leclerc, M. et S. Dumas. Cent quatorze professeurs parlent de l'enseignement à l'université: rapport présenté au Service de Pédagogie universitaire, étude exploratoire. Québec: ·Université Laval, 1972. 180 p.

Lemire, V. "Le micro-enseignement: un bilan provisoire." Prospectives 8 (mai 1972) 203-205.

1973 Boyd, G.M. "Educational technology and the re-creation of the university." McGill Jour. Educ. 8 (Fall 1973) 169-75.

Daem, J.-P. "Education is fragmented and isolated within specialties." Univ. Aff./Aff. univ. 14 (Sept 1973) 20.

Dussault-Dumas, H. "Pour un réseau universitaire de didactiques."
Prospectives 9 (avril 1973) 131-133.

Fletcher, A.G. "The engineering role in modern liberal education."
Engineering Jour. 56 (Apr. 1973) 29-32.

Goldschmit, B. and M.L. Goldschmit. "Modular instruction in higher
education: a review." Higher Education 2 (Feb. 1973) 15-32.

Harvey, D. "De-schooling the self." Our Generation 9 (Summer 1973)
34-40.

Hilborn, J. "Education and control." Our Generation 9 (Summer 1973)
18-33.

Mariyama, M. "Future education and a new epistemology." McGill Jour.
Educ. 7 (Spring 1973) 86-94.

Samson, J.-M. "Une source de créativité à l'université: l'évaluation
par activités cumulatives." McGill Jour. Educ. 7 (Spring 1973) 64-72.

Sheffield, E.F. "Approaches (mostly elsewhere) to the improvement of
teaching in higher education." Improving College and University
Teaching. 21 (winter, 1973) 5-9.

Shore, B.M. "Strategies for the implementation of modular instruction
and their implications in university education." Jour. Higher Educ.
[U.S.] 44 (December 1973) 680-697.

Tomkins, G.S. "National consciousness, the curriculum and Canadian
studies." Jour. Ed. Thought 7 (April 1973) 5-24.

Vidal, F. "What has happened to foreign language instruction?" Univ.
Aff./Aff. univ. 14 (December 1973) 7.

Weber, M.E. and O.M. Fuller, "Problem solving in PSI." McGill Jour.
Educ. 8 (fall 1973) 179-87.

1974   Anderson, M. "A new subject: women's studies." McGill Jour. Educ.
9 (Spring 1974) 67-76.

Fuller, O.M. et al. "A course in experimentation." McGill Jour.
Educ. 9 (Spring 1974) 96-109.

Motulsky, B. "La pédagogie universitaire au premier cycle: un sujet
de réflexion pour l'Université du Québec." Educ. Quart. 4 (août
1974) 25-27.

Sterling, T.D. and R.C. Brown. "For the students who don't know why:
a new curriculum." Univ. Aff./Aff. univ. 15 (May 1974) 6-7.

Wilson, H.B. "Cultural literacy laboratory." McGill Jour. Educ. 9 (Spring 1974) 85-95.

1976 Canadian Association of Latin American Studies. Directory of Canadian scholars and universities interested in Latin American studies. Edited by W.C. Soderland. 2nd edition. Ottawa: the Association, 1976. 71 p.

1977 Harris, J. "Literacy and liberal education." Can. Forum 57 (April 1977) 7-12.

Creigh, J.C. "Skipping through the open door: the unprepared student and his problems." English Quart. 10 (Winter 1977/78) 37-44.

Thomson, C. "The emergence of Native American education at the University of Lethbridge." Can. and International Educ. 6 (Dec. 1977) 34-48.

Woods, M.J. "The buck stops here: one remedy for university illiteracy." English Quart. 10 (Winter 1977/78) 7-13.

B. THE HUMANITIES/LES HUMANITÉS

GENERAL/GÉNÉRALITÉS

1968 Priestley, F.E.L. "The future of the humanities in Ontario universities." Humanities Assoc. Bull. 19 (1968) 3-13.

1970 Lebel, M. "L'Enseignement universitaire de la littérature canadienne française au Canada et à l'étranger." Culture 31 (1970) 238-44.

Onimus, J. "Les nouvelles méthodes critiques et l'enseignement de la littérature." Etudes Lit. 3 (août 1970) 203-208.

Pizzorusso, A. "Critique littéraire et enseignement: réflexions d'un professeur." Etudes Lit. 3 (août 1970) 191-202.

Saint-Jacques, D. "Les études de lettres: une supercherie"? Etudes Lit. 3 (août 1970) 221-243.

Somville, L. "Critique littéraire et enseignement." Etudes Lit. 3 (août 1970) 173-190.

1971 Gutteridge, D. "The subject central curriculum: last chance or lost cause?" English Quart. 4 (Winter 1971) 17-27.

Lamonde, Y. "Histoire, sciences humaines et culture au Québec (1955-1970)." Rev. Hist. 25 (juin 1971) 106-113.

1975 Lebel, M. "Les humanités dans l'enseignement supérieur au Canada", in J.R. Perkins, ed., The undoing of Babel: Watson Kirkconnell, the man and his work. Toronto: McClelland & Stewart, 1975. P. 50-63.

Vardy, S.B. "Hungarian studies at American and Canadian universities." Canadian-American Review of Hungarian Studies. 2 (Fall 1975) 91-121.

1976 Chiasson, A. "Le centre d'études acadiennes de l'Université de Moncton et son folklore." Laurentian Univ. Rev. 8 (Feb. 1976) 115-121.

1980 Painchaud-Leblanc, G. Le rôle de l'université dans l'enseignement des langues secondes aux adultes." Can. Jour. Univ. Cont. Ed. 6 (Winter 1980) 20-23.

ART/ARTS PLASTIQUES

1972 Journal of the Universities Art Association of Canada. I, 3 (December 1972)
Includes: "Graduate programs booming." 4.
"New and proposed programs summarized." 5-9.
"Simplified credit transfer needed." 11-12.

1973 Journal of the Universities Art Association of Canada. I, 4 (April 1973)
Includes: "The Relations of art and design." 3-4.
W. Junkind. "Art and design at university." 4-5.
E. Doré. "Relations between art and design." 5-6.
S. Harrison. "A designer's view of art and design." 7-8.
L. Ferrabee. "The National Design Council and design education." 14-17.

1974 Calvé, M. "L'éducation artistique et l'université." M.A. thesis, Concordia Univ., 1974.

1976 Chalmers, F.G. "The master of fine arts and master of visual art: graduate studio degrees in Canada." CAUT/ACPU Bull. 24, 8 (October 1976), 16-18.

Fleming, M. 100 years: evolution of the Ontario College of Art. Toronto: Art Gallery of Ontario, 1976. 160 p.

1980 Gerson, M. "Training arts administrators for a perilous profession." Perf. Arts. Can. 17 (Spring 1980) 36-38.

Singen, K. "A school for all seasons" Perf. Arts Can. 17 (Fall 1980) 50.

LANGUAGE AND LINGUISTICS/
LANGUES ET LINGUISTIQUE

GENERAL/GÉNÉRALITÉS

1970 Halamandaris, P.G. "Linguistics and the language teacher." Man. Jour. Educ. 6 (November 1970) 15-27.

1971 Lemire, G. "L'enseignement - recherche en linguistique au collégial." Prospective 7 (juin 1971) 171-175.

1972 Joos, M. "Reading knowledge testing." Can. Jour. Linguistics 17 (1972) 191-215.

1976 Tetraw, J. Etat actuel et notre sinologie". Act. Nat. (avril 1976) 547-561.

1977 Rebuffo, J.J. "Le dilemme du professeur de langue: théorie ou pratique?" McGill Jour. Educ. 12 (printemps 1977) 159-169.

1979 Yalden, J. "Second language at the universities: a look into the future." Can. Mod. Lang. Rev. 35 (Mar. 1979) 431-441.

CLASSICS/LANGUES ANCIENNES

1972 Barrett, A.A. "The classics in Canada." Classical Outlook [U.S] 50 (December 1972) 37-38.

ENGLISH/ANGLAIS

1970 Jones, L.W. Canadian graduate studies in American literature: a bibliography of theses and dissertations, 1921-1968. Can. Rev. American Studies 1 (Fall 1970) 116-129.

1971 Patterson, L.F. "Report re speech courses taught in Canadian universities and colleges." Can. Speech Jour. 3 (Fall 1971) 52-61.

1972 Kreisel, H. "Graduate programs in English in Canadian universities." English Quart 5 (Spring and Summer 1972) 95-103.

1976 Priestley, F.E.L. and H.I. Kerpneck. Report of The Commission on Undergraduate Studies in English in Canadian Universities. Toronto, Association of Canadian University Teachers of English, 1976. 111 p.

Shortt, S.E.D. "Archibald MacMechan: romantic idealist," and "James Cappon: the ideal in culture," in The search for an ideal: six Canadian intellectuals and their convictions in an age of transition, 1890-1930. Toronto: U. of T. Press, 1976. P. 41-57 and 59-75.

1977 Bennet, B. The teaching and study of Australian literature in the universities." English Quart. 10 (Summer 1977) 45-61.

Nichols, O.M. "Checking out the freshman research paper." English Quart. 10 (Fall 1977) 51-57.

1978 Horning, A. "Getting out from under: a ready and easy way to teach freshman composition." English Quart. 11 (Fall 1978) 35-44.

Morgan, P. "Interface 1978: relations between school and university English." English Q. 11 (Winter 1978-79) 1-8.

Priestley, F.E.L. "The uses of literature." Dalhousie Rev. 58 (Spring 1978) 5-16.

Rodman, L. ESL in freshman English." English Quart. 11 (Summer 1978) 138-146.

Stewart, M.F. "Sentence-combining and syntactic maturity in first year university." Alta. Jour. Educ. Research 24 (December 1978) 262-274.

Wright, V. "The English language programme." English Quart. 11 (Summer 1978) 95-103.

1979 Bramwell, R.D. "On teaching semantics to education students." English Q. 12 (Winter 79-80) 81-94.

Freedman. A. "Writing and the university." English Q. 12 (Spring - Summer 1979) 33-42.

Esch, M. and Gladstein, M.R. "Teaching the research process. English Q. 12 (Spring-Summer 1979) 57-66.

FRENCH/FRANÇAIS

1963 Rigault, A. "Etat et perspectives de l'enseignement du français dans les universités anglo-canadiennes." Revue de l'AUPELF 1 (juillet 1963) 30-35.

1970 Lebel, M. "L'enseignement universitaire de la littérature canadienne-française au Canada et à l'étranger." Culture 31 (septembre 1970) 238-244.

1972   "French departments mostly ignore French-Canadian survey shows."
        Univ. Aff./Aff. univ. 13 (Dec. 1972) 9.

1973   Gagnon, J.-C. "Pour une didactique de la littérature." Prospectives.
        9 (juin 1973) 96-74.

1976   Pelletier, J.   "L'enseignement de la littérature d'aujourd'hui."
        Liberté 18, 1 (1976).

1977   Holmes, G.   "The problem of anglicized French at the university."
        Can. Mod. Lang. Rev. 33 (March 1977) 520-531.

1978   Kaufman, D. and S. Shapson. "Overview of secondary and post-secondary
        French immersion: issues and research." Can. Mod. Lang. Rev.   34
        (February 1978) 604-620.

        Lister, A.   "A third-year university French course using recorded
        news broadcasts." Can. Mod. Lang. Rev. 34 (January 1978) 207-210.

        Martin, I. et al.   "Shared bilingualism - a learning experiment."
        English Quart. 11 (Summer 1978) 125-134.

SLAVIC STUDIES/ETUDES SLAVES

1971   Domaradski, T.F. "Les études slaves et est-européennes à l'Université
        de Montréal." Etudes Slav. 16 (1971) 138-139.

1976   Barratt, G.   "Doctoral dissertations in the Slavic field accepted by
        Canadian universities, 1950-75." Can. Slav. Papers 18 (June 1976)
        187-198.

HISTORY/HISTOIRE

1969   Dyer, M.G.   "Military history and war studies in Canadian universi-
        ties. Military Affairs 3 (1969).

        MacKenzie, N.A.M.   "Frederic H. Soward and the development of inter-
        national studies in Canada."   in H.L. Dyck and H.P. Krosby, eds.,
        Empire and Nations: essays in honour of Frederick H. Soward. Toronto:
        U. of T. Press, 1969. p. 17-21. See also 11-16.

1970   Dubuc, A.   "L'Histoire au carrefour des sciences humaines."   Rev.
        Hist. 34 (déc. 1970) 331-340.

        Bernard, J.-P. "Quelques interrogations sur la formation des profes-
        seurs d'histoire." Cahiers U.Q., 25 (1970) 161-166.

Eid, N.F. "Pour une méthodologie plus exigeante de l'apprentissage en histoire." Cahiers U.Q., 25 (1970) 155-159.

1971 Goutor, J.R. "The historian as moralist: some implications for teaching history." Can. Jour. Hist. & Soc. Sci. 6 (March-April 1971) 25-31.

Trueman, J. "Has history a future?" Can. Jour. Hist. & Soc. Sci. 6 (March-April 1971) 1-8.

1972 Lower, A.R.M. "That humble fellow the historian: some reflections on writing history." Jour. Can. Studies 7 (Feb 1972) 45-50.

McNaught, K. "Frank Underhill: a personal interpretation." Queen's Quart. 79 (Summer 1972) 127-35.

1973 "The anti-American ingredient in Canadian history." Dalhousie Rev. 53 (Spring 1973) 57-77.

Trudel, M. "Les débuts de l'institut d'histoire à l'Université Laval." Rev. Hist. 27 (1973) 397-403.

1974 Heick, W.H. and R. Graham, eds. His own man: essays in honour of Arthur Reginald Marsden Lower. Montréal: McGill-Queen's Univ. Press, 1974. 187 p.

1975 Francis, D.H. "Frank H. Underhill - Canadian intellectual." Ph.D. thesis, York Univ. 1975.

Heick, W.H. ed. History and myth - Arthur Lower and the making of Canadian nationalism. Vancouver: UBC Press, 1975.

Johnson, M. "Le concept de tempo dans l'enseignement de l'histoire." Rev. Hist. 28 (1975) 483-517.

1976 Berger, C.C. The Writing of Canadian History. Toronto: Oxford Univ. Press, 1976. 320 p.

1977 Bailey, A.G. "Retrospective thoughts of an ethnohistorian." Can. Hist. Assoc. Papers. (1977) 14-29.

Hanham, H.J. "Canadian history in the 1970s." Can. Hist. Review 58, 1 (March 1977) 2-22.

Karr, C.G. "A remote hinterland in a centralist conception: the Atlantic Provinces and the development of the Canadian historiographic tradition." Dalhouse Rev. 57 (Spring 1977) 90-106.

Meikle, W.D. "And gladly teach: G.M. Wrong and the Department of History at the University of Toronto." Ph.D. thesis, Michigan State University, 1977.

1979 Patterson, G. "Harold Innis and the writing of history." Can. Lit. 83 (Winter 1979) 118-130.

Woodcock, G. "The servants of Clio." Can. Lit. 83 (Winter 1979) 131-141.

1980 Peake, F.A. "Reflections on Canadian church history." Can. Church Hist. Soc. Jour. 22 (April 1980) 46-50.

Smith, A. "The writing of British Columbia history." B.C. Studies 45 (Spring 1980) 73-102.

MUSIC/MUSIQUE

1947 Walter, A. "Music in Canadian higher education." in W. Kirkconnell and A.S.P. Woodhouse The Humanities in Canada. Ottawa: Humanities Research Council, 1947. P. 217-220.

1968 Florestan, X. "Situation actuelle de l'enseignement musical au Québec." Musicien éducateur du Québec 1, 4 (1968) 3-10.

1969 Brown, A.M. A study of music curriculum with degree and diploma programs in Canadian institutions of higher learning, 1968-1969. Calgary: Canadian Association of University Schools of Music, 1969. 34 p.

1971 Chartier, Y. "Rapport de la Conférence 1971 du Conseil Canadien de la Musique." Cah. Can. de Musique (automme-hiver 1971) 37-45.

Le Dain, A. "Les professeurs du Centre d'Art d'Oxford donnent leur avis." Jour Jeunesses Musicales 16, 3 (1971) 6-7.

Little, G. "La formation de l'artiste pour 2001." Cah. Can. de Musique (printemps 1971) 67-70.

St. Marcelle, C. "La formation des spécialistes en musique." Musicien educateur du Québec. 3, 4 (1971) 3-6.

1974 Beoudet-Léonard, L. "Perspectives d'écoute - incidences pédagogiques" Cah. Can. de Musique (printemps 1974) 87-94.

1975 Skipper, J. "Musical tastes of Canadian and American college students." Can. Jour. Sociology 1 (Spring 1975) 49-59.

1977   Murray, P. "Ernest MacMillan - music educator." <u>Can. Music Educator</u> 19 (Autumn 1977) 3-12.

Pederson, P. "A note on current teaching and research in the psychology of music in Canada." <u>Can. Psych. Rev.</u> 18 (July 1977) 264-267.

Strangeland, R.A. "Music in the academic setting: opportunities and responsibilities." <u>Can. Music Educator</u> 19 (Autumn 1977) 29-33.

1979   Green, P. "Doctoral programs in music: reform or rhetoric." <u>Can. Music Educator</u> (Winter 1979) 34-39.

Jorgensen, E.R. "Some observations on the methodology of research in music education." <u>Can. Music Educator.</u> 20, 3 (1979) 45-50.

PHILOSOPHY/PHILOSOPHIE

1935   Roy, M. "Pour l'histoire du Thomisme au Canada." <u>Can. français</u> 23 (1935) 161-171.

1951   Forest, C.-M. "Vingt-cinq ans de philosophie à l'Université de Montréal." <u>Actualités philosphiques</u> (1951) 9-30.

1968   Cauchy, V. "Philosophy in French-Canada: its past and its future." <u>Dalhousie Rev.</u> 48 (1968) 384-401.

1970   Lamonde, Y. "L'enseignement de la philosophie au Collège de Montréal 1790-1876." <u>Culture</u> 26 (1970) 109-123, 213-229, 312-326.

1972   Lamonde, Y. "Historiographie de la philosophie au Québec (1853-1970)" <u>Collections Philosophie les Cahiers du Québec.</u> Montréal: Editions AMH. 241 p.

1974   Braybrooke, D. "The philosophical scene in Canada." <u>Can. Forum</u> 53 (January 1974) 29-33.

Collin, C. and Z. Isana. <u>L'ensignement de la philosophie, essai de didactique expérimentale.</u> Montréal: Fides, 1974. 104 p.

1976   Brindamour, M. "Enseigner la philosophie." <u>Educ. Québec</u> 7, 1 (1976) 8-13.

Mallea, J.R. <u>Matériaux pour l'histoire des institutions universitaires de philosophie.</u> Québec: Les Presses de l'Université Laval, 1976. 2 vols. 551 p. and 198 p.

1977   Lamonde, Y. "Histoire de la philosophie au Québec, 1665-1920." Thèse de D. ès L., Univ. Laval 1977.

1979   McKillop, A.   "John Watson and the idealist legacy."   Can. Lit.   83
       (Winter 1979) 72-88.

       Owens, J.   The philosophical traditions of St. Michael's College
       Toronto.   Toronto: College Archives St. Michael's College, Univ. of
       Toronto.   40 p.

1980   Page, F.H.   "William Lyall in his setting."   Dalhousie Rev.   60
       (Spring 1980) 49-66.

RELIGION

1959   Conway, J.S.   "The universities and religious studies."   Can. Jour.
       Theology 5 (1959) 269-272.

1969   Anderson, C.P. and T.A. Nosanchuk, eds. 1969 Guide to religious stud-
       ies in Canada.   Vancouver: Can. Society for the Study of Religion,
       1969.   178 p.

1975   Montoniny, J.P. et S. Crysdale. La Religion au Canada: bibliographie
       annotée des travaux en sciences humaines des religions, 1915-1970.
       Québec Presses de l'Université Laval, 1975.   192 p.

1978   Classen, H.G.   "Religious studies in Canada."   Queen's Quart.   85
       (Autumn 1978) 389-402.

       C. SOCIAL SCIENCES/SCIENCES SOCIALES

GENERAL/GÉNÉRALITÉS

1972   Clarkson, S.   "Lament for a non-subject: reflections on teaching
       Canadian-American relations."   International Jour.   27 (Spring 1972)
       265-275.

       Social Science Research Council of Canada.   The social sciences and
       science policy/Les sciences sociales et la politique scientifique.
       Ottawa: Information Canada, 1972.   21 p.

1973   Chambers, D.W. and J. Southim.   "Collaborative studies in science and
       human affairs."   Univ. Aff./Aff. univ.   14 (March 1973) 2-3.

       Fournier, M.   "L'Institutionnalisation des sciences sociales au
       Québec"   Sociologie et Sociétés   5 (mai 1973) 27-58.

       Lambert, R.D. and J. Curtis.   "Nationality and professional activity
       correlates among social scientists: data bearing on conventional
       wisdoms."   Can. Rev. Soc. Anthrop.   10 (February 1973) 62-80.

Warnock, J.W. "International relations as a Canadian academic discipline." Jour. Can. Studies 8 (February 1973) 46-57.

1974 Guinsburg, T.N. and G.L. Reuber. Perspectives on the social sciences in Canada. Toronto: U. of T. Press, 1974. 196 p.

1975 Barthes, M. "Un stage à l'Assemblée nationale." Educ. Québec 6, 3 (1975) 20-23.

Social Science Research Council of Canada. Problems of social science research at smaller Canadian universities. Edited by H. Overgaard. Ottawa: the Council, 1975. 73 p.

ANTHROPOLOGY/ANTHROPOLOGIE

1962 Dubreuil, G. "Les sciences anthropologiques à l'Université de Montréal." Revue de l'AUPELF 1 (oct. 1962) 12-17.

1973 Cole, D. "The origins of Canadian anthropology." Jour. Can. Studies 8 (February 1973) 33-45.

1979 McFeat, T. "Anthropology changing." Proc. R.S.C. (1979) 215-228.

ECONOMICS AND POLITICAL SCIENCE/ECONOMIE ET SCIENCES POLITIQUES

1970 Verney, D.V. "The education of a political scientist." Can. Jour. Pol. Sci. 3 (Sept. 1970) 345-;358.

1973 Hull, W.H.N. "The 1971 survey of the profession." Can. Jour. Pol. Sci. 6 (March 1973) 89-120.

1974 Loriot, G. et T.Q. Bas. "L'enseignement de la science politique dans les collèges du Québec." Prospectives 10 (juin 1974) 187-196.

Smiley, D. "Must Canadian political science be a miniature replica?" Jour. Can. Studies 9 (February 1974) 31-42.

1975 Bélanger,G. et J.L. Mique. "Réflexion sur l'enseignement et la recherche en économique de la santé." Act. Econ. (1975) 446-452.

1976 Drache, D. "Rediscovering Canadian political economy." Jour. Can. Studies 11 (August 1976) 3-18.

Mallory, J.R. "The political economy tradition in Canada." Jour. Can. Studies 11 (August 1976) 18-20.

O'Neil, D.J. and Wagner, J.R. "Teaching Canadian politics at American universities: some recommendations." Am. Rev. Can. Studies. 6 (Spring 1976) 126-50.

Shortt, S.E.D. "Adam Shortt: the emergence of the social scientist" and "James Mavor: the empirical ideal", in The search for an ideal: six Canadian intellectuals and their convictions in an age of transition 1890-1930. Toronto: U. of T. Press, 1976. p. 95-116 and p. 119-135.

1977   Christian, W. "Harold Innis' idea file." Queen's Quart. 84 (Winter 1977) 535-544.

Journal of Canadian Studies 12 (Winter 1977) devoted entirely to articles assessing the work and influence of Harold Innis (1894-1952).

Parker, I. "Harold Innis, Karl Marx and Canadian political economy." Queen's Quart. 84 (Winter 1977) 545-563.

1979   Eccles, W.J. "A belated review of Harold Adams Innis, The Fur Trade in Canada." Can. Hist. Rev. 60 (December 1979) 419-441.

Higgins, D.J.H. "Municipal politics and government: development of the field in Canadian political science." Can. Public Admin. 22, 3 (1979) 380-401.

Macpherson, C.B. "By Innis out of Marx: the revival of Canadian political economy." Can. Jour. of Political and Social Theory/Revue canadienne de théorie politique et sociate 3, 2 (1979) 134-138.

Phillips, P. "The Hinterland perspective: the political economy of Vernon C. Fowke." Can. Jour. Political Social Theory 2, (Spring-Summer 1978) 73-96.

Whitaker, R. "Confused alarms of struggle and flight: English-Canadian political science in the 1970's." Can. Hist. Rev. 60 (March 1979) 1-18.

GEOGRAPHY/GÉOGRAPHIE

1971   Laverdière, C. "Jacques Rousseau (1906-1970) n'est plus." Rev. Géog. Montréal 25 ,1 (1971) 3-4.

1976   St. Yves, M. "Matériel didactique et méthodes en géographie." Cah. Géog. 20 (1976) 505-519.

1977   Helleiner, F.M. and C.J. Sparrow. "Careers for geographers: the case of Ontario 1953 to 1972." Can. Geographer. 21 (Summer 1977) 182-189.

PSYCHOLOGY/PSYCHOLOGIE

1970   Myers, C.R.   "Journal citations and scientific eminence in contempo-
       rary psychology." American Psychologist 25 (November 1970) 1041-1048.

       Myers, C.R.   "Whatever happened to Canadian psychology?" Can. Psych.
       11 (April 1970) 128-32.

1971   Nelson, T.M. and W. Poley.   "Publication habits of psychologists in
       Canadian universities." Can. Psych. 12 (Jan. 1971) 68-76.

       Wright, M.J.   "The psychological organizations of Canada." Can.
       Psych. 12 (July 1971) 420-431.

1973   Berry, R.   "The changing role of the clinical psychologist: psychol-
       ogists and the system." Ont. Psych. 5, 1 (1973) 27-31.

       Gottlieb, B.H.   "Professional training of the generic community psy-
       chologist: four core competencies." Ont. Psych. (Dec. 1973) 52-55.

       Mahrer, A.R.   "Defining characteristics of a humanistic program of
       community change and specimen: the facilitation of self-confidence
       in the neonate." Ont. Psych. 5 (December 1973) 45-50.

       Ricks, J.   "The OPA Convention: study in professional self-image."
       Ont. Psych. 5, 1 (1973) 14-17.

       Weinstein, M.S.   "The community psychologist as a specialist in
       research and development." Ont. Psych. 5 (December 1973) 7-9.

1974   Berry, J.W. "Canadian psychology: some social and applied emphases."
       Can. Psych. 15 (April 1974) 132-139.

       Morf, M.E.   "Report from Utopia: a note on professional training."
       Can. Psych. 15 (April 1974) 157-164.

       Roche, D.S.   "Psychologists in education: a renewed search for role
       definition." Ont. Psych. 6 (April 1974) 4-7.

       Sullivan, S.M.   "Psychology and teaching." Can. Jour. Behav. Science
       6 (January 1974) 1-29.

       Torney, D.J.   "A note on legislation affecting Canadian psychology:
       the Ontario model." Can. Psych. 15 (April 1974) 178-185.

1977   Bowd, A.D.   "Relevance of professional journals for Canadian educa-
       tional psychologists and counsellor educators." Can. Counsellor 11
       (July 1977) 192-195.

Burwell, E.J. "Issues in the education and training of women in Canadian psychology." Can. Psych. Rev. 18 (Jan. 1977) 34-45.

1978 Bowd, A. "Professional characteristics of Canadian educational psychologists." Alta. Jour. Educ. Res. 24 (Dec. 1978) 223-229.

Paskus, A. The Faculty of Psychology of the University of Ottawa. Ottawa: U. of Ottawa Press, 1978. 256 p.

1979 Furedy, J. "Berlyne as a disinterested critic: a colleague's account of some academic interactions." Can. Psychol. Rev. 20 (April 1979) 95-98.

Haccoun, D.M. and J. Breslau. The evaluation of university experience: an examination of motives and satisfactions." Can. Jour. Behav. Science 11 (July 1979) 205-213.

Lambert, R. and M. West. "North America's first graduate training program in the psychology of sensory deficits." Can. Psych. Rev. 20 (Oct. 1979) 184-188.

Osborne, J. "The status of the psychology of consciousness within Canadian academic psychology." Can. Psychol. Rev. 20 (April 1979) 92-94.

Schaeffer, D. and M. Sulyma. "Citation rates and the quality of Canadian psychology departments." Can. Psychol. Rev. 29 1 (Jan. 1979) 22-37.

SOCIOLOGY/SOCIOLOGIE

1970 Loubser, J., ed. The future of sociology in Canada/L'avenir de la sociologie au Canada. Montréal: Can. Sociology and Anthropology Association, 1970. 64 p.

Morgan, J.G. "Contextual factors in the rise of academic sociology in the U.S.A." Can. Rev. Soc. Anthrop. 7 (August 1970) 159-171.

1971 Herold, E.S. "Student attitudes toward the use of televised lectures in introductory sociology at the University of Manitoba." Man. Jour. Educ. 6 (June 1971) 39-47.

1972 Gurstein, M. "Towards the nationalization of Canadian sociology." Jour. Can. Studies 7 (August 1972) 50-58.

1973 Clark, S.D. "The American take-over of Canadian sociology: myth or reality." Dalhousie Rev. 53 (Summer 1973) 205-218.

Hedley, R.A. and T.R. Warburton. "The role of national courses in the teaching and development of sociology: the Canadian case." Sociological Review [U.K.] 21 (May 1973) 299-319.

1975 Clark, S.D. "Sociology in Canada: an historical over-view." Can. Jour. Sociology 1 (Summer 1975) 225-234.

"Département de sociologie Université de Montréal: maîtrise et doctorat 1955-1975." Sociologie et Sociétés 7 (novembre 1975) 143-152.

Felt, F. "Nationalism and the possibility of a relevant Anglo-Canadian sociology." Can. Jour. Sociology. 1 (Fall 1975) 377-385.

Mackie, M. "Sociology, academia, and the community: maligned within, invisible without?" Can. Jour. Sociology. 1 (Summer 1975) 203-221.

Smith, D.E. "What it might mean to do a Canadian sociology: the everyday world as problematic." Can. Jour. Sociology 1 (Fall 1975) 363-376.

Stolzman, J. and H. Gamberg. "The national question and Canadian sociology." Can. Jour. Sociology 1 (Spring 1975) 91-106.

Watson, G.L. "The poverty of sociology in a changing Canadian society." Can. Jour. Sociology (Fall 1975) 345-362.

1977 Decore, A.M. "Sociology of education in Canada: a review essay." Jour. Educ. Thought 11 (Dec. 1977) 243-252.

1978 Ralston, H. "The uses of a bachelor's degree in sociology: careers of recent graduates of a Maritime university." Can. Jour. Higher Educ. 8, 3 (1978) 47-66.

Tepperman, L. "Sociology in English speaking Canada." Can. Hist. Rev. 59 (Dec. 1978) 435-446.

1979 Brym, R.J. "Introduction: new directions in anglo-canadian historical sociology." Can. Jour. of Sociology 4, 3 (1979) vii-xi.

Clark, S.D. "The changing image of sociology in English-speaking Canada." Can. Jour. of Sociology 4, 4 (1979) 393-403.

Hiller, H.H. "The Canadian sociology movement. Can. Jour. Sociology 4, 2 (1979) 125-150.

1980 Clement, W. "Searching for equality: the sociology of John Porter." Can. Jour. Pol. and Soc. Theory 4 (Spring-Summer 1980) 97-114.

Sociologie et Sociétés 12, 2 (oct. 1980). cahier spécial consacré à des reflexions sur la sociologie. Whole issue devoted to reflections on sociology.

D. MATHEMATICS AND THE SCIENCES/LES MATHÉMATIQUES ET LES SCIENCES

GENERAL/GÉNÉRALITÉS

1969 Doerne, G.B. "Scientists and the making of science policies in Canada." Ph.D. thesis, Queen's Univ., 1969.

1970 Doerne, G.B. "Science policy making: the transformation of power in the Canadian scientific community." Jour. Can. Studies 5 (November 1970) 23-25.

     Rogers, D. "Hostility to science in the university: a science student view." Science Forum. 3 (Aug. 1970) 3-6.

1971 Slivitzky, Michel. "Le Centre québécois des sciences de l'eau." Univ. Aff./Aff. univ. 12 (nov. 1971) 19.

1972 Lamontagne, M. et al. A science policy for Canada Vol. 2. Ottawa: Information Canada, 1972. 608 p.

1973 Cadenhead, G. and G. Bindon. "Science, technology and society – an inter-disciplinary concern." Univ. Aff./Aff. univ. 14 (Mar. 1973) 4-5.

1976 Babbitt, J.D. "Science policy as ideology: the collectivization and socialization of research." Can. Research 9, 4 (July-August 1976) 22-25, 28-29.

1977 Galarneau, C. "L'enseignement des sciences au Québec et Jérome Demers, 1765-1835." Rev. Univ. Ottawa 47 (janvier-février 1977) 84-94.

     Jarrell, R.A. "The rise and decline of science in Quebec." social History/Histoire Sociale (May 1977) 77-91.

     Jarrell, R.A. "Why do many Canadians know nothing of Canadian science?" Science Forum 10, 2 (April 1977) 23-26.

1979 Kucharczyk, J. "Manpower – the emerging crisis for Canadian science and technology." Physics in Canada 35 (Nov. 1979) 163-167.

     Page, J.E. A Canadian context for science education. Ottawa: Science Council of Canada, 1979. 52 p.

1980 Roemer, E.   "Technological studies and the curriculum in higher education." Curriculum Inquiry 10 (Fall 1980) 293-302.

ASTRONOMY/ASTRONOMIE

1972 Kennedy, J.E.   "Our heritage in Canadian astronomy." Royal Astron. Soc. Jour. 66 (April 1972) 83-98.

1975 Jarrell, R.A.   "Origins of Canadian government astronomy." R. Astron. Soc. Jour. 69 (April 1975) 77-85.

1978 Bishop, R.L.   "Joseph Everett and the King's College observatory [Windsor, Nova Scotia]." Royal Astron. Soc. Jour. 72 (June 1978) 138-148.

1979 Fernie, J., ed.   "People and places: collected reminiscenses of John Frederick Heard." R. Astron. Soc. Jour. 73 (April 1979) 53-73; (June 1979) 109-132; (August 1979) 177-197.

1980 Calnen, W.   "Astronomy at King's College, Windsor, Nova Scotia." R. Astron. Soc. Jour. 74 (April 1980) 57-63.

      Donovan, K.   "Canada's first astronomical observatory, 1750." Can. Geog. Jour. 100, 6 (1980) 36-43.

1981 Stebbins, R.   "Looking downwards: sociological images of the vocation and avocation of astronomy." R. Astron. Soc. Jour. 75 (February 1981) 2-14.

BIOLOGY/BIOLOGIE

1977 Forward, D.   A history of botany in the University of Toronto. Toronto: Department of Botany, University of Toronto, 1977. 97 p.

1979 Gridgeman, N.T.   Biological sciences at the National Research Council of Canada: the early years to 1952. Waterloo: Wilfred Laurier Univ. Press, 1979. 105 p.

CHEMISTRY/CHIMIE

1976 Young, E.G.   The development of biochemistry in Canada. U. of T. Press, 1976. 129 p.

1979 Atkinson, G.   "Chemistry laboratory courses - a comparison of some Ontario and United Kingdom findings." Can. Jour. Higher Educ. 9, 3 (1979) 67-71.

GEOLOGY/GÉOLOGIE

1968 Stearn, C.W. "Geological education in Canada", in E.R.W. Neale, ed. The Earth Sciences in Canada. Toronto: U. of T. Press, 1968. P. 52-74.

MATHEMATICS/MATHÉMATIQUES

1976 Beltzner, K.P. et al. Mathematical Sciences in Canada. Ottawa: Science Council of Canada, 1976. 339 p.

Souline, V. "Les tristes conséquences de l'enseignement des mathématiques au secondaire." Prospectives 12 (février 1976) 50-53.

Woodcock, L. "Mathematics departments follow old patterns, fail to meet today's needs - Science Council study says." Univ. Aff./Aff. univ. 17 (October 1976) 2.

1979 Robinson, G. de B. The mathematics department in the University of Toronto 1827-1978. Toronto: Dept. of Mathematics, Univ. of Toronto, 1979. 114 p.

PHYSICS/PHYSIQUE

1972 Stoichiff, B.P. "G.H. [Gerhard Herzberg]." Physics in Canada 28 (April 1972) 11-28.

Welsh, H.L. "Gerhard Herzberg - Nobel Laureate, 1971." R. Astron. Soc. Jour. 66 (Aug. 1972) 183-188.

1974 Martin, C. "Les relations entre les attitudes envers la physique et la performance dans cette discipline chez les étudiants des cours de physique de première année à l'Université de Moncton." M.A. thesis, Université de Moncton, 1974.

1976 Rogers, D.W. et al. "The plight of the young physicist in Canada." Physics in Canada 32 (April 1976) 16-18.

1977 Allin, E.J. "Physics at the University of Toronto 1907 to 1977." Physics in Canada 33, 2 (1977), 26-31.

Jarrell, R.A. "The birth of Canadian astrophysics: J.S. Plunkett at the Dominion Observatory." R. Astron. Soc. Jour. 71 (June 1977) 221-233.

Sayer, M. "Engineering physics". Physics in Canada 33, 7 (1977) 99-103.

1979 Jarrell, R., The Reception of Einstein's theory of relativity in Canada." R. Astrom. Soc. Jour 73 (Dec. 1979) 358-369.

1981 Gingras, Y. La physique à MᶜGill entre 1920 et 1940: la réception de la méchanique quantique par une commonauté scientifique périphérique. Journal for the History of Canadian Science, Technology and Medicine 1 1 (January 1981) 15-40.

E. PROFESSIONAL EDUCATION/ENSEIGNEMENT PROFESSIONNEL

GENERAL/GÉNÉRALITÉS

1970 McLeish, J.A.B. "Continuing professional education in Canada." Convergence 3, 4 (1970) 76-83.

1971 Applied Research Associates. Professional education: a policy option. Toronto: Queen's Printer, 1971. 159 p. (Study prepared for Commission on Post-Secondary Education in Ontario.)

1972 Applied Research Associates. Certification and post-secondary education. Toronto: Queen's Printer, 1972. 103 p. (Study prepared for the Commission on Post-Secondary Education in Ontario.)

Comay, Y. "The migration of professionals: an empirical analysis." Can. Jour. Econ. 5 (August 1972) 419-429.

1973 Coisman, N. "Enseignement professionel: enseignement dominé?" Prospectives 9 (décembre 1973) 274-283.

McLeish, J.A.B. The advancement of professional education in Canada: the report of the professional education project, Kellogg Foundation. Toronto: Ontario Institute for Studies in Education, 1973. 59 p.

1974 Leibu, Yhal. "Aspects educatif et sociaux de la formation professionnelle de niveau collégiat." Prospectives 10 (juin 1974) 178-186.

1977 Stager, D. and N. Meltz. "Manpower planning in the professions." Can. Jour. Higher Ed. 7 (1977) 73-83.

Sullivan, N. "Speakers agree on need for change in professional education." Univ. Aff./Aff. univ. 18, 1 (January 1977) 8-9.

1979 Trebilcock, M. et al. Professional regulation: a staff study of accountancy, architecture, engineering and law in Ontario. Toronto: Ministry of the Attorney General, 1979. 421 p.

AGRICULTURE

1971 Lachance, R.O. et Y. Chartier. "La vocation et les objectifs de la faculté d'agriculture (Université Laval)." _Agr._ 28 (1971) 3-11.

Rioux, A. "La tragédie de l'enseignement agricole." _Act. Nat._ 60 (janvier 1971) 373-380.

Rioux, A. "Le fiasco de l'enseignement agricole." _Act. Nat._ 60 (février 1971) 457-464.

1972 Forest, B. "L'avenir agricole: rôle et formation de l'agronome." _Agr._ 29 (1972) 10, 12, 14-16.

1974 Ross, A.M. _The college on the hill: a history of the Ontario Agricultural College, 1874-1974._ Toronto: Copp Clark, 1974. 180 p.

1975 Marett, C.M. "The Ontario Agricultural College (1874-1974): some developments in scientific agriculture." M.A. thesis, Univ. of Guelph, 1975.

1976 Dutchak, P. _College with a purpose: a history of the Kemptville College of Agricultural Technology, 1910-1973._ Belleville, Ont.: Mika Publishing Co., 1976. 170 p.

1977 Bouchard, A. "The rôle des institutions d'enseignement dans la formation continue." _Agr._ 34 (1977) 10-12.

1978 Lemay, M.A. "La formation continue." _Agr._ 35 (1978) 3-6.

1979 Genest, J. et al. "La formation de l'agronomie." _Agr._ 36 (Mars. 1980) 3-16.

Jones, D.C. "We cannot allow it to be run by those who do not understand education - agricultural schooling in the twenties." _BC Studies_ 39 (autumn 1978) 30-60.

Lettre, J.-P. "La formation professionnelle de la relève agricole au Quebec" _Agr._ 36 (juin 1979) 3-7, 36 (Sept. 1979) 13-17.

ARCHITECTURE, TOWN PLANNING/ARCHITECTURE, URBANISME

1970 Koerte, A. "Architectural education: part I, the global village." _Can. Arch._ 15 (Sept. 1970) 51-54; "Part II, trends in Europe." 11 (Nov. 1970) 39-42. See also N. Pressman, 12 (Dec. 1970) 61-63.

Manning, P. "Architectural education & the wider view." _Can. Arch._ 15 (June 1970) 40-42.

1976   Council of Ontario Universities. <u>Commoditie, firmenes, and delight:</u> <u>a study of architectural education in Ontario.</u> Toronto: C.O.U., 1976.

Carver, H. <u>Compassionate landscape: places and people in a man's</u> <u>life.</u> Toronto: U. of T. Press, 1976. 251 p.

BUSINESS ADMINISTRATION AND PUBLIC AFFAIRS/ COMMERCE, FINANCE ET ADMINISTRATION

1970   Débanné, J.G. "L'orientation de la faculté des sciences de la gestion à l'Université d'Ottawa." <u>Ottawa Bulletin des Anciens/Alumni News</u> 20 (1970) 4-7.

Lincourt, M. "Les étudiants Québecois en aménagement manquent-ils d'agressivité?" <u>Arch. Concept</u> 25 (1970) 11-14.

Malanchuk, B. "I Came Back." <u>Bus. Q.</u>, 35 (Winter 1970) 19-24.

Wheelan, T.L. "The market's view of the M.B.A." <u>Bus. Q.</u> 35 (Winter 1970) 38-42.

1971   "Rapports des travaux des ateliers au Colloque: Poly, foyer d'animation de l'économie industrielle." <u>Ing.</u> 57 (mar 1971) 34-49.

Zur-Muellen, M. von. <u>Business education and faculty at Canadian uni-</u> <u>versities.</u> Ottawa: Economic Council of Canada, 1971. 269 p.

1972   Edds, J.A. "Who says management is a profession?" <u>Bus. Q.</u> 37 (Winter 1972) 47-51.

Hurtubise, R.A. "L'enseignement de l'informatique et l'analyse de systèmes à l'ENAP." <u>Commerce</u> 74 (avril 1972) 30-32.

Larivière, J., et C. Perron. "Quel marché attend les diplômés en administration." <u>Commerce</u> 74 (janvier 1972) 9-14; (février 1972) 20-23; (mars 1972) 40-44; (avril 1972) 50-55.

Ostiguy, F. et P. Auger. "Le technicien en administration." <u>Commerce</u> 74 (mai 1972) 28-32.

1973   Perkins, C.M. "Queen's MBA - or - a strategy for management education leadership." <u>Queen's Univ. Alumni Review.</u> 47 (1973) 5-13.

Porter, G. and R. Cuff, eds. <u>Enterprise and national development:</u> <u>essays in Canadian business and economic history.</u> Toronto: Hakkert, 1973. 138 p.

Wilson, A.H. "Outreach of the Canadian universities into manufacturing industry." Can. Research 6 (March-April 1973) 40-41, 46-47.

Wilson, H.T. "Rationality and decision in administrative science." Can. Jour. Pol. Sci. 6 (June 1973) 271-94.

1975 Vachon, R. "Le rôle de l'université dans le milieu local québecois." Commerce (May 1975) 24-30.

1976 Angers, F.A. "Minville et les Hautes études commerciales." Act. Nat. (mai-juin 1976) 643-676.

Pross, H.P. and S. Wilson. "Graduate education in Canadian public administration: antecedents, present trends and portents." Can. Public Admin. 19 (Winter 1976) 515-541.

1977 Zur-Muehlen, M. von. University business education in Canada during the sixties and seventies. Ottawa: Statistics Canada, 1977. 59 p.

1978 Auger, R. et al. "La formation des dirigeants - l'expérience du Saguenay - Lac St Jean." Rev. Desjardins 44, 1 (1978) 38-42.

Schneck, R. "The americanization of Canadian faculties of business." Jour. Can. Studies 13 (Summer 1978) 109-118.

Zur Muehlen, M. von. Current issues in university management education. Ottawa: Statistics Canada, 1978. 36 p.

Zur-Muehlen, M. von. A review of university management education in Canada. Ottawa: Statistics Canada, 1978. 68 p.

1978 Hurka, S. Business faculty in Canadian universities: importance and satisfaction related to job characteristics." Can. Jour. Higher Educ. 8, 3 (1978) 67-76.

1979 Guerin, G. "Formation-emploi des diplômes en relations undustrielles: une étude de cas: Université de Montréal." Relations Ind. 34 (1979) 740-767.

1980 Consultative Group on Research and Graduate Education in Business, Management and Administrative Studies. University management education and research: a developing crisis. Ottawa: Information Division of SSHRCC, 1980. 81 p.

Hurka, S. "Business administration students in five Canadian universities: a study of values." Can. Jour. Higher Educ. 10, 1 (1980) 83-94.

DENTISTRY/ART DENTAIRE

1952 Geoffrion, P. "Evolution de l'enseignement à la faculté de chirurgie dentaire de l'Université de Montréal." Jour. Can. Dent. Assoc. 18 (1952) 379-381.

Godin, C. "Histoire des sociétés dentaires de la province de Québec." Jour. Can. Dent. Assoc. 18 (1952) 395-397.

Hamel, P. "Evolution de la dentisterie dans Québec et la région de 1902 à nos jours." Jour. Can. Dent. Assoc. 18 (1952) 372-378.

1965 Hall, O. Utilization of dentists in Canada. Ottawa: Queen's Printer 1965. 59 p.

1969 Ontario Council of Health. "Dentistry and its allied disciplines", in Education of the health disciplines. Annex D. Toronto: Ontario Department of Health, 1969. P. 27-42.

1970 House, R.K. Dentistry in Ontario. (A study for the Committee on the Healing Arts.) Toronto: Queen's Printer, 1970. 274 p.

Ontario. Report of the Committee on the Healing Arts. Toronto: Queen's Printer, 1970. 3 vols.

1971 Gullet, D.W. A history of dentistry in Canada. Toronto: U. of T. Press, 1971. 308 p.

1975 Dale, J.C. "Centennial of dental education in Canada." Can. Dent. Assoc. Jour. 41 (June 1975) 340-343.

1976 Harrop, T.J. and R.S. MacKenzie. "The future of dental education in Canada." Can. Dent. Assoc. Jour. 42 (February 1976) 69-76.

Melcher, A.H. "Postgraduate training and graduate education in dentistry." Can. Dent. Assoc. Jour. 42 (December 1976) 591-595.

Roteroek, Jeanette. "Su Geiku and the Dentists." New Trail 37. 1 (Fall 1976) 5-8.

ENGINEERING/GÉNIE

1970 Coupal, B. "Le génie chimique à l'Université de Sherbrooke." Ing. 56 (janvier 1970) 15.

"Création d'un institut de génie nucléaire à l'Ecole Polytechnique." Ing. 56 (avril 1970) 18.

Juteau, L. "Centre d'ingénierie nordique à l'Ecole Polytechnique." Ing. 56 (mai 1970) 8-9.

Lapp, P.A., J.W. Hodgins and C.B. MacKay. Ring of iron: a study of engineering education in Ontario. Toronto: Committee of Presidents of Universities of Ontario. 155 p.

McMullen, W.F. and M.L. Skolnik. An analysis of projections of the demand for engineers in Canada and Ontario and an inquiry into substitution between engineers and technologists. Toronto: Committee of Presidents of Ontario, 1970. 64 p.

1971   Gendron, L. "Le service de l'extension de l'enseignement de l'Ecole polytechnique." Ing. 57 (août 1971) 3-6.

Langlois, R.P. "Allocution de M. Roger P. Langlois, ing., Directeur de l'Ecole polytechnique, présentée au cours du banquet de clôture du Colloque." Ing. 57 (mai 1971) 23-26.

Laurence, J. "Les domaines d'emploi des diplômés de Polytechnique." Ing. 57 (décembre 1971) 20-23.

"Polytechnique s'interroge." Le Devoir [Montréal] 18 Feb. 1971. Supplément de 6 pages sur l'Ecole Polytechnique.

1972   Chant, R.E. "Continuing education for engineers." Eng. Jour. 55 (Jan./Feb. 1972) 15-19.

Deschênes, P.A. et P.C. Aïtcin. "Une expérience pédagogique originale à la faculté des sciences appliquées de l'Université de Sherbrooke." Ing. 58 (fév. 1972) 8-9.

Normandin, M. et P. Perron. "Le centre de recherche industrielle du Québec." Ing. 58 (mai 1972) 3-6.

1973   Blais, B.A. "La réorganisation de la recherche à l'Ecole Polytechnique." Ing. 59 (1973) 21-25.

"Les départements de l'Ecole Polytechnique." Ing. 59 (janvier 1973) 27-73.

Ham, J.M., P.A. Lapp and I.W. Thompson. Careers of engineering graduates 1920-1970, University of Toronto. Toronto: The Engineering Alumni Association and The Faculty of Applied Science and Engineering, University of Toronto, 1973. 89 p.

Harris, R.S. and I. Montagnes, eds. Cold iron and Lady Godiva: engineering education at Toronto, 1920-1972. Toronto: U. of T. Press, 1973. 150 p.

Khan, S.B. and V.R. D'Oyley. "Prerequisite abilities for success in engineering: a discussion from Canadian data." Eng. Educ. [U.S.] 64 (Oct. 1973) 43-45.

Lanctôt, B. "L'enseignement de l'informatique aux ingénieurs." Ing. 59 (mai 1973) 11-15.

Langlois, R.P. "L'Ecole Polytechnique." Commerce 75 (février 1973) 36-38.

L'équipe des services de l'enseignement: le polytechnicien de 1973." Ing. 59 (janvier 1973) 17-19.

Lortie, L. "Il était une fois." Ing. 59 (janvier 1973) 13-15.

Windish, E.J. "Fonctions et formation de l'ingénieur de demain." Ing. 59 (avril 1973) 17-22.

1975 Wilson, A.H. "The market for engineers." Eng. Jour. 58 (July/Aug. 1975) 77-82.

1976 Shemilt, L.W. Research report on engineering education in the Maritimes. Fredericton: Maritime Provinces Higher Education Commission 1976. 362 p.

1979 Gervais, Y. Enseignement supérieur et interaction avec le milieu professionnel: l'experience du Département de génie electrique de l'Ecole Polytechnique de Montréal Ing. 65 (Oct. 1979) 31-34.

O'Keefe, J. "Wedepohl's budget fight at the U. of M: does engineering belong in a liberal arts university? Can. Research 12 (June 1979) 20-22.

Turgeon, A.B. "La démarche systematique et la formation professionnelle de l'ingénieur." Ing. 65 (Avril 1979) 17-22.

1980 Fazio, P. "Programme de recherche universitaire en génie du bâtiment." Ing. 66 (Oct. 1980) 19-23.

1977 Sayer, M. "Engineering physics." Physics in Canada 33, 7 (1977) 99-103.

FORESTRY/GÉNIE FORESTIER

1961 Harrison, J.B., and D.W. MacLean. "Survey of forest and forest products research, organization and activities." Resources for Tomorrow 2 (1961) 703-715.

1962 Ker, J.W. "Canadian experience with the five-year undergraduate forestry curriculum." For. Chron. 38 (1962) 63-69.

1969 Garratt, G.A. "The status of forest technician training in Canada." For. Chron. 45 (1969) 5-13.

1970 Vézina, P.E. "Le développement de l'enseignement forestier supérieur à l'Université Laval." For. et Cons. 36 (septembre 1970) 30-31.

1971 Garratt, G.A. Forestry education in Canada. Macdonald College: Canadian Institute of Forestry, 1971. 408 p.

1974 Mathiew, P. "Les futurs ingénieurs forestiers manquerout-ils d'air ... et de compétence." For. et Cons. 40, 9 (1974) 8-10.

1976 Gilbert, J.-C. "Les projets étudiants ne sont plus." For. et Cons. 42, 4 (1976) 29, 32-33.

HOUSEHOLD SCIENCE/SCIENCES DOMESTIQUES

1953 Macdonald Institute, A fiftieth anniversary sketch of the development of the Macdonald Institute, Ontario Agricultural College. Guelph: Ontario Agricultural College, 1953. 30 p.

1960 University of Manitoba, School of Home Economics. Home economics 1910-1960. Winnipeg: Univ. of Manitoba, 1960. 48 p.

1972 Fewster, J. "New dimensions in international home economics programs." Can. Home Econ. Jour. 22 (July 1972) 3-10.

Woods, M.J. "An analysis of home economics programs in Ontario universities based on the development of four theoretical patterns." M.A. thesis, Univ. of Toronto, 1972.

Young, W. "Professional development - this is what was said." Can. Home Econ. Jour. 22 (Oct. 1972) 3-17.

1973 Hulse, J.H. "The household scientist in international development." Can. Home Econ. Jour. 23 (April 1973) 3-16.

Simpson, E.C. "Home economics - a vital force in the life of the individual." Can. Home Econ. Jour. 23 (July 1973) 3-10.

Simpson, E.C. "Home Economics - A Vital Force in the Life of the Individual." Can. Home Econ. Jour. XXIII, 3 (July 1973) 3-10.

1977 Engberg, L.E. "Improving our international competence in home economics." Can. Home Econ. Jour. 27 (Oct. 1977) 20-26.

Wardlaw, J.M. "Perspectives on home economics and family life programs in Canada." Can. Home Econ. Jour. 27, (July 1977) 55-60.

JOURNALISM/JOURNALISME

1971 Chauveau, M. "Le programme de journalisme à l'Université Laval." Educ. Quart. 1 (mai 1971) 16-17.

1979 Buckler, G. "The little college that could: journalism at King's." Atlantic Advocate 69 (Feb. 1979) 36-39.

LAW/DROIT

1970 Guy, M. "Facultés de droit et chambres professionnelles." Rev. Notariat 73 (août-septembre 1970) 3-7.

1971 Lederman, W.R. "Canadian legal education in the second half of the twentieth centruy." Univ. Tor. Law Jour. 21 (1971) 141-161.

1972 Andrew Roman and Associates. Legal education in Ontario 1970. Toronto: Queen's Printer, 1972. 159 p.

"Apprendre à apprendre le droit." Cahiers Québec 13 (1972) 266-269.

Bertrand, M.A. "La querelle autour du centre international de criminologie comparée." Maintenant 116 (mai 1972) 18-21.

Charles, B. "La criminologie éclairant le monde." Maintenant 118 (sept. 1972) 21-22.

Cheviette, J. "De l'enseignement clinique du droit aux "cléricatures imaginaires." Thémis 7 (1972) 315-324.

Chouinard, A. "Vers un meilleur apprentissage du droit à la faculté de droit de l'université Laval." Thémis 7 (1972) 325-368.

Lebel, H. "Formation juridique et formation professionnelle; quelques réflexions." Thémis 7 (1972) 305-313.

Moison, J. "Barreau et universités." Thémis 7 (1972) 287-288.

Normandeau, A. "La criminologie québécoise, parlons-en." Maintenant 118 (sept. 1972) 12-14.

Rothman, A. et H. Marx. "Les attentes et les perceptions des étudiants en première année de droit." Thémis 7 (1972) 289-303.

Roy, L. "Le Bureau des Services juridiques: l'action sociale d'étudiants en droit." Educ. et Soc. 3 (avril 1972) 6-7.

Silverman, H.W. "The practitioner as a law teacher." Chitty's Law Jour. 20 (April 1972) 113-122.

1973 Carter, R. "Legal studies for native people." Can. Bar Assoc. Jour. 4 (December 1973) 6-8.

Colas, E. "Le Barreau, les facultés de droit et le stage." Rev. Barr. 33 (janv. 1973) 2-16.

1974 Grant, A. "Clinical training within community legal services: a phenomenon in search of an organizational structure." Chitty's Law Jour. 22 (1974) 15-21.

Lajoie, A. et al. "Eléments de réflexion pour une réforme des études de droit, note de recherche." Rev. Barr. 34 (1974) 97-103.

Macdonald, R. St. J. "An historical introduction to the teaching of international law in Canada." Canadian Yearbook of International Law 1974, 67-110.

Parker, G. "The masochism of the legal historian." Univ. Tor. Law Jour. 24 (1974) 279-317.

Willis, J. "Canadian administrative law in retrospect." Univ. Tor. Law Jour. 24 (1974) 225-246.

Weuster, T. "Cafeteria-style legal education?" Chitty's Law Jour. 22 (1974) 255-260.

1975 Macdonald, R. et al. "The new lawyer in a transnational world." Univ. Tor. Law Jour. 25 (1975) 343-357.

Savage, H. "The Dalhousie legal aid service." Dal. Law Jour. 2 (Sept. 1975) 505-520.

1976 Bories, S. "L'information juridique comme instrument de formation et de culture du juriste." Thémis 11 (1976) 357-391.

Brenner, P.J. and J.A. Lahey. "Development and shortcomings of first year legal aid skills courses: progress at Osgoode Hall." Osgoode Law Jour. 14 (1976) 161-215.

1976 Gibson, R.D. "Legal education -- past and future." Manitoba Law Jour. 6 (1976/1977) 21-38.

Grant, A. "New trends in Canadian legal education." Chitty's Law Jour. 24 (1976) 172-176.

Lortie, L. "The early teaching of law in French Canada." Dalhousie Law Jour. 2 (Sept. 1976) 521-532.

Soberman, D. A. Legal Education in the Maritime Provinces. Fredericton: Maritime Provinces Higher Education Commission, 1976. 94 p.

1977 Arthur, H.W. "Paradoxes of Canadian legal education." Dalhousie Law Jour. 3 (Jan. 1977) 639-662.

Barnes, J. "The department of law, Carleton University, Ottawa." Dalhousie Law Jour. 3 (Jan. 1977) 814-827.

Fraser, F.M. "The law faculty at the University of Victoria." Dalhousie Law Jour. 3 (Jan. 1977) 828-836.

Green, L.C. "McGill's Institute of Air and Space Law at twenty-five." Chitty's Law Jour. 25 (1977) 244-245.

Harvey, C., ed. The Law Society of Manitoba 1877-1977. Winnipeg: Peguis Publishers, 1977. 288 p.

Janisch, H.A. "Law schools and continuing legal education: the Dalhousie experience." Can. Bar Rev. 55 (Mar. 1977) 57-74.

LeFebvre, J. "Banque de cours: formation permanente." Rev. Barr. 37 (1977) 120-123, 266-270, 403-408, 547-553, 697-703.

London, J.R. "The admissions and education committee: a perspective on legal education and admission to practice in the Province of Manitoba, past, present and future." Manitoba Law Jour. 8 (1977/1978) 553-595.

Soberman, D.A. "The Symons report and legal education." Univ. Aff./Aff. univ. 18, 1 (January 1977) 13.

1978 Cooke, B. and J. Taylor. "Developing personal awareness and examining values: inter-connected dimensions of supervision in clinical legal education." U.B.C. Law Rev. 12 (1978) 276-294.

1979 Morel, A. La reception du droit criminel anglais au Québec (1760-1892) Thémis 13 (1978) 449-541.

Beetz, J. "Le professeur de droit et le juge." Rev. Notariat 81 (juin 1979) 506-513.

Fraser, F.M. "Recent developments in legal education: the Victoria experience." UBC Law Rev. 13 (1979) 221-239.

MacDonald, R.A. "Law schools and public legal education: the community law programme at Windsor." Dal. Law Jour. 5 (May 1979) 779-790.

Willis, J. A history of the Dalhousie Law School. Toronto: U. of T. Press, 1979. 302 p.

1980 Bickenbach, J.B. "The English influence in legal education in Ontario." The Advocate 15 (1980-81) 12-19.

Cossette, A. L'acte authentique et l'avenir du notariat." Rev. Notariat 83 (déc. 1980) 178-203.

Emmanueli, C.C. Le droit comparé selon une perspective canadienne. Rev. Barr. 40 (fév. 1980) 75-110.

Frankman, L.E. "Canadian law schools: in search of excellence." Dal. Law Jour. 6 (Nov. 1980) 303-312.

Létourneau, G. "La formation des redacteurs de lois." Rev. Barr. 40 (fév. 1980) 42-57.

Macfarlane, P. "The legal profession in Canada: a research perspective and prospectus." Chitty's Law Jour. 28 (Feb. 1980) 50-59.

Morris, N. "Law schools and other reformatories." Dal. Law Jour. 6 (Nov. 1980) 213-228.

LIBRARY SCIENCE/BIBLIOTHÉCONOMIE

1969 Marshall, J. "Major issues in library education: Toronto's approach to its new program." Sask. Lib. 23 (1) 3-15.

1971 Greene, R. "Library co-operation and the rationalization of curricula." Can. Library Jour. 28 (May-June 1971) 206-208.

Oureshi, M.J. "Academic status, salaries and fringe benefits in community college libraries of Canada." Can. Library Jour. 28 (Jan.-Feb. 1971) 41-45.

1972 Denis, L.G. and L.J. Houser. "A study of the need for Ph.D.'s in library science in large Canadian libraries." Can. Library Jour. 29 (January-February 1972) 19-27.

1973 Beacock, E.S. "A view of continuing education of librarians by an employer." CACUL newsletter. 4 (March 1973) 419-25.

Cheda, S. "The free-lance alternative in librarianship: an interview with Susan Klement." Can. Library Jour. 30 (Sept.-Oct. 1973) 401-6.

Cockshutt, M.E. "Education for librarianship: the view of the library school." CACUL newsletter. 4 (March 1973) 426-35.

Lando, F. "Why six librarians chose other careers." Can. Library Jour. 30 (Mar.-Apr. 1973) 100-105.

McDonough, I. "Education for public librarians." Ont. Library Rev. 57 (September 1973) 149-51.

1974 Halpenny, F.G. "Excellence in library education: the Canadian universities and their library schools." Can. Library Jour. 31 (April 1974) 126-133.

Henderson, S.D. "Accreditation of library school programmes in Canada: a review of the literature." Can. Library Jour. 31 (April 1974) 134-136.

Land, R.B. "Accreditation procedures." Can. Library Jour. 31 (April 1974) 84-89.

1976 Schrader, A.M. "Library science education in Canada." Inst. Prof. Librarians Ont. Q. 17 (April 1976) 199-264.

Wallace, C. "The four-fifths minority: continuing education for library personnel." Can. Library Jour. 33 (April 1976) 75-79.

1977 "Counterpoint. Archival education"; ACA Annual Meeting: "A conspiracy against the Canadian identity." Archivaria 5 (Winter 1977/78) 184-194.

"Library schools present statistical reports for 1975/76." Feliciter 23 (Oct. 1977) 4-6.

North, J. "Librarianship: profession." Can. Library Jour. 34 (August 1977) 253-257.

Welch, E. "Archival education" Archivaria. 4 (Summer 1977) 49-59.

1978 Houser, L.J. The search for a scientific profession: library science education in the U.S. and Canada. Metuchen, N.J.: Scarecrow Press, 1978. 180 p.

1979 Bassam, B. "Education of librarians is put in historical perspective." Can. Library Jour. 36 (June 1979) 77-86.

Denis, L.-G. "Full-time faculty survey describes educators." Can. Library Jour. 36 (June 1979) 107-121.

Foster, M. "Philosophy of librarianship." Can. Library Jour. 36 (June 1979) 131-137.

Sessions, V.G. "Continuing education courses are few and disparate." Can. Library Jour. 36 (June 1979) 101-105.

Tague, J. "Information science in graduate library programs." Can. Library Jour. 36 (June 1979) 89-99.

1980 Bertrand-Gastaldy, S. and D. Reicher. "Information science in a library school context." Can. Jour. Information Science 5 (May 1980) 171-182.

Bewley, L. "Library schools react to continuing education demands." Can. Library Jour. 37 (Dec. 1980) 403-407.

MEDICINE/MÉDECINE

General/Généralités

1963 Hanson, E.J. The public finance aspects of the health sciences in Canada. Ottawa: Queen's Printer, 1963. 206 p.

MacLeod, J.W. "The curriculum in Canadian medical education." Can. Med. Assoc. Jour. 88 (1963) 705-712.

1966 Kohn, R. Emerging patterns of health care. Ottawa: Queen's Printer, 1966. 145 p.

McKerracher, D.G. Trends in psychiatric care. Ottawa: Queen's Printer, 1966. 256 p.

Mills, D.L. Study of chiropractors, osteopaths and naturopaths in Canada. Ottawa: Queen's Printer, 1966. 254 p.

Richman, A. Psychiatric care in Canada: extent and results. Ottawa: Queen's Printer, 1966. 458 p.

1968 Medical Research Council. Canadian medical research, survey and outlook: a report to the Medical Science Council of Canada. Ottawa: Queen's Printer, 1968. 416 p.

1970 Hall, O. The paramedical occupations in Ontario: a study for the Committee on the Healing Arts. Toronto: Queen's Printer, 1970. 140 p.

Hanly, C. et al. Mental health in Ontario: a study for the Committee on the Healing Arts. Toronto: Queen's Printer, 1970. 436 p.

Ontario Committee on the Healing Arts. Report. Toronto: Queen's Printer, 1970. 3 vols.

1971   Desjardens, E.   "Prospective sur l'enseignement de la médecine."
        Union Méd.   100 (février 1971) 230-231.

1972   Adams, D.W. and R.G. Roy.   "McMaster field unit: an experiment in
        mental health consultation.   Can. Jour. Public Health 63 (November-
        December 1972) 499-503.

        Genest, J.   "Perspectives de la recherche médicale et clinique pour
        les prochaines décennies."   Union Méd.   101 (oct. 1972) 2051-54.

        Lemieux, G.   "La socialisation et l'avenir de la médecine académique
        au Québec.   Quelques réflexions à l'occasion du deuxième numéro
        annuel sur la recherche clinique."   Union Méd.   101 (avril 1972) 645-
        47.

1973   Desmartis, A.   "Le regroupement des sciences de la santé à Laval."
        Univ. Aff./Aff. univ.   14 (November 1973) 15.

        Hacon, W.S.   "Health manpower development in Canada."   Can. Jour.
        Public Health (January-February 1973) 5-12.

        Hogan, T.W.   "Program evaluation in the health field: nature and
        problems."   Ont. Psych.   5 (August 1973) 4-13.

        Palkiewicz, J.   "La formation des maîtres.   Au Québec: comme les
        médecins."   Prospectives 9 (fév. 1973) 8-10.

        Queen's University, Kingston.   Canadian workshop conference on the
        economics of medical education 1973.   Ottawa: Association of Canadian
        Medical Colleges, 1973.   141 p.

1974   Beaudoin, J.   "Les responsabilités pédagogiques d'une faculté de
        médecine.   Vie Médicale 3 (1974) 450-455.

        Brown, M.C.   "Medicare and the medical monopoly."   Can. Forum 54
        (April 1974) 5-9.

        Castonguay, C.   L'orientation des politiques de la santé au Québec et
        l'enseignement médical.   Vie Médicale 3 (1974) 455-464.

        Firstbrook, J.   "The accreditation of Canadian medical schools."   Can.
        Library Jour.   31 (April 1974) 90-91.

        Phillipson, D.   "Medical research policy for Canada.   Part I: the
        evolution and convolution of policy, politics and $."   Can. Med.
        Assoc. Jour.   110 (June 1974) 1388-1394.

        Saucier, G.   "L'université et le formation des professionnels de la
        santé au Québec."   Vie Médicale 3 (1974) 464-467.

1975   Roos, N.P. and D.G. Fish. "Career and training patterns of students entering Canadian medical schools in 1965." <u>Can. Med. Assoc. Jour.</u> 112 (January 1975) 65-67, 70.

Spitzer, W.O. "Career choices of physicians 15 years after entering medical school." <u>Can. Med. Assoc. Jour.</u> 112 (February 1975) 468-474.

1976   Biehn, J.T. "Characteristics of an effective medical teacher." <u>Can. Family Physician</u> 22 (October 1976) 135-136.

Des Marchais, J. et P. Jean. "La pédagogie médicale à l'intérieur d'une faculté de médecine." <u>Union Méd.</u> 105 (1976) 1354-1358.

Miles, S.E. et al. "The medical student therapist: treatment outcome." <u>Can. Psych. Assoc. Jour.</u> 21 (November 1976) 467-472.

1977   Hould, F.J. "La formation du médecin conscient des coûts de la santé." <u>Vie Médicale</u> 6 (1977) 946-954.

1978   Bernatchez, J.-P. et al. "La méthode du jeu de rôle dans l'enseignement de la relation médecin - malade: évaluation rétrospective d'un projet pilote." <u>Union Méd.</u> 107 (1978) 413-417.

Cormier, G. et C. Bélanger. "Apprendre à enseigner la médecine." <u>Union Méd.</u> 107 (1978) 310-317.

Taylor, M.B. <u>Health insurance and Canadian public policy.</u> Montréal: McGill-Queen's Univ. Press, 1978. 473 p.

1979   Baskett, T.F. "A university department's involvement with medical care in the Canadian North." <u>Can. Med. Assoc. Jour.</u> 120 (February 1979) 298-300.

Historical Development/Développement historique

1954   Mitchell, R. <u>Medicine in Manitoba: the story of the beginnings.</u> Winnipeg: Stovel-Advocade Press, 1954. 141 p.

1967   Curtis, J.F. "The first medical school in Upper Canada." <u>Ont. Med. Rev.</u> 34 (1967) 449-452.

Kett, J. "American and Canadian medical institutions, 1800-1870." <u>Jour. Hist. Med. & Allied Sciences</u> [U.S.] (October 1967) 343-356.

1970   Miller, G. "The teaching of medical history in the U.S. and Canada: historical resources in medical school libraries." <u>Bull. Hist. Med.</u> [U.S.] (May-June 1970) 251-278, 482-483.

1972 Amyot, R. "Remémoration d'événements dans le monde médical entre les 75e et 100e anniversaires de l'Union Médicale du Canada." Union Méd. 101 (nov. 1972) 2368-2375.

Desjardins, E. "Un précurseur de la recherche médicale au 19e siècle: le docteur Joseph-Alexandre Crevier." Union Méd. 101 (avril 1972) 708-711.

1973 Angus, M. Kingston General Hospital: a social and intellectual history. Montréal: McGill-Queen's University Press, 1973.

Best, C.H. "Reminiscences of the insulin era." Newsletter Can. Diabetic Assoc. 20 (1973) 4-17, 23.

1974 Desjardins, E. "La vieille école de médecine Victoria." Union Méd. 103 (1974) 117-125.

Godfrey, C.M. "The evolution of medical education in Ontario." M.A. thesis, Univ. of Toronto, 1974.

Hacker, C. The indomitable lady doctors. Toronto: Clarke Irwin, 1974. 259 p.

Stewart, W.B. Medicine in New Brunswick. Moncton: New Brunswick Medical Society, 1974. 413 p.

1975 Cosbie, W.G. The Toronto General Hospital 1819-1965: a chronicle. Toronto, Macmillan, 1975. 373 p.

Desjardins, E. "Histoire de la profession médicale au Québec." Union Méd. 103 (1974) 732-743, 918-30, 1112-1119, 1279-1292, 1450-1458, 1891-1895, 2040-2049; 104 (1975) 138-151, 448-470, 626-634, 810-819, 981-990, 1137-1142, 1426-1428, 1563-1567, 1876-1882.

1976 Ray, J. Emily Stowe. Toronto: Fitzhenry & Whiteside, 1976. 62 p.

1977 Barr, M.L. A century of medicine at Western: a centennial history of the faculty of Medicine, University of Western Ontario. London: Univ. of Western Ontario, 1977. 672 p.

Barr, M.L. "James Bertram Collip (1892-1965): a Canadian pioneer in endoctrinology." Hannah Institute for the History of Medicine. 1 (1, 1977) 6-15.

Galter, R.B. "Scientific contributions to orthopaedic surgery by the staff of the Hospital for Sick Children, Toronto, 1875-1975." Hannah Institute for the History of Medicine. 1 (1, 1977) 40-56.

1978 Harris, R.I. et al. William Edward Gallie: surgeon, seeker, teacher, friend. Toronto: The Gallie Club. (Dept. of Surgery, University of Toronto) 1978. 62 p.

1979 Bourassa, M.G. L'evolution de la recherche à l'Institute de cardiologie de Montréal." Union Méd. 108 (oct. 1979) 1128-1138.

1980 Audet-Lapoint, P. et al. "Les cent ans de l'Hôpital Notre-Dame de Montréal. Union Méd. 109 (jan. 1980) 13-18.

Bernier, J. "François Blanchet et le mouvement réformiste en médecine au début du XIXe siède." Rev. Hist. 34, 2 (1980) 223-244.

Roland, G. "Dr. Earl Scarlett: melding tradition and beauty in historical writing." Can. Med. Assoc. Jour. 122 (April 1980) 822-826.

Shortt, S. "The new social history of medicine: some implications for research." Archivaria 10 (Summer 1980) 5-22.

Strong-Boag, V., ed. A woman with a purpose: the diaries of Elizabeth Smith 1872-1884. Toronto: U. of T. Press, 1980.

Kutcher, S.P. "Toronto's metaphysicians: the social gospel and medical professionalization in Victorian Toronto." Jorn. Hist. Can. Sci. Tech. Med. 1 (Jan. 1981) 41-51.

The M.D. Programme/Doctorat en Médecine

1970 Kinch, R.A.H. et al. "The teaching of behaviour, growth and development in the preclinical years of medicine." Laval Méd. 41 (avril 1970) 495-499.

1971 Bury, J.A. et al. "Enseignement médical: le malade, le milieu hospitalier et l'étudiant: Réflexions sur la première semaine de stage de la session clinique des étudiants de troisième année des études médicales." Laval Méd. 42 (avril 1971) 373-375.

Hould, F. "Nouveau système d'application de l'enseignement clinique à la Faculté de médecine de l'Université Laval." Laval Méd. 42 (avril 1971) 376-379.

1972 Rothman, A.I. "Longitudinal study of medical students: long-term versus short-term objectives." Jour. Med. Educ. 40 (Nov. 1972) 901-902.

1976 "Formation médicale." Union Méd. 105 (1976) 1668-1708.

1979   Heffernan, M.W.   "Faculty development : some thoughts about the process and context" Can. Family Physician 25 (May 1979) 631-634.

1980   Black, D.P.   "Medical education in a rural health centre" Can. Family Physician 26 (Aug. 1980) 1074-1077.

Forster, J.M.   "A safe doctor - or a good doctor?" Can. Family Physician 26 (July 1980) 980-982.

Gagnon, A.   "La course aux études médicales." Union Méd. 109 (nov. 1980) 1158-1168.

Hould, F.J.   "La sélection des étudiants en médecine: tendance au Québec et plaidayer pour l'arbitraire." Union Méd. 109 (août 1980) 1188-1191.

Sawchuck, V.N.   "The role of family and emergency medicine in undergraduate medical education." Can. Family Physicians 26 (Oct. 1980) 1413-1420.

Shah, C.P., Janicek, M., Munan, L.   Spasoff, R.   "Objectives of teaching community health to medical undergraduates." Can. Jour. Public Health 71-6 (Nov-Dec. 1980) 371-380.

Continuing Education/Education permanante

1972   Woodsworth, A. and V.R. Neufeld.   "A survey of physician self-education patterns in Toronto.   Part I: Use of Libraries." Can. Library Jour. 29 (Jan.-Feb. 1972) 38-44; "Part II: Use of journals and personal filing systems." (March-April 1972) 104-109.

1976   Ivernois, J.F. et al.   "L'enseignement par ordinateur est-il aussi efficace pour les médecins praticiens que pour les étudiants en médecine?" Union Méd. 105 (1976) 1359-1371.

1977   "Education médicale continue: Colloque." La Vie Médicale au Canada. 6 (1977) 505-879.

1980   Spitzer, W. et al.   "The relevance to family physicians of core content review: evaluation of a program of continuing education." Can. Med. Assoc. Jour. 122 (Feb. 1980) 429-432.

Specialization/Spécialités

1971   Jean, C. et R. Garneau.   "Réunions scientifiques du département de pathologie sous la direction du professeur Carlton Auger." Laval Méd. 42 (mai 1971) 428-430.

Meisels, A. et B. Van Open-Toth. "Le service de cytodiagnostic du département de pathologie de l'Université Laval: les dix premières années: 1960-1970." Laval Méd. 42 (mai 1971) 519-522.

1972 Rhodes, A.J. et al. "Postgraduate education in Medical microbiology: a report of eleven years' experience at the School of Hygeine, University of Toronto, Sessions 1958-59 to 1968-69." Can. Jour. Public Health 63 (Mar./April 1972) 152-156.

1973 Byrne, N. and R. Cohen. "Observational study of clinical clerkship activities." Jour. Med. Educ. 48 (October 1973) 919-927.

1974 Mueller, C. and F. Amers. "Postgraduate clinical education - the Canadian experience." Can. Med. Assoc. Jour. 111 (October 1974) 813-817.

1976 Lawson-Smith, C. et al. "McGill Cancer Research Institute: a profile." Can. Research 9 (Nov./Dec. 1976) 9-11, 15-20.

1977 Leichner, P. "Present psychiatric postgraduate trends in Canada: a survey of the opinions of fourth-year residents." Can. Psych. Assoc. Jour. 22 (April 1977) 123-136.

1978 Farkas-Himsley, H. and A.J. Rhodes. "Postgraduate education in medical microbiology: a survey of seventeen years of the course leading to the diploma in bacteriology." Can. Jour. Public Health 69 (May-June 1978) 253-256.

Skelton, D. "A department of geriatric medicine in a Canadian teaching hospital." Modern Med. Can. 33 (November 1978) 1620-1622, 1783-1788.

1979 Vinger, I. "Graduate training in family medicine: two years or three?" Can. Family Physician 25 (Sept. 1979) 1107-1108.

1980 Hannay, D.R. "Post graduate training in family medicine at McMaster University and in West Scotland." Can. Family Physician 26 (Mar. 1980) 448-455.

NURSING

1918 MacMurchy, H. "University training for the nursing profession." Can. Nurse 14 (1918) 1284-1288.

1967 Robson, R.A.H. Sociological factors affecting recruitment into the nursing profession. Ottawa: Queen's Printer, 1967, 244 p.

1969 Ontario Council of Health. "Nursing education", in Education of the health disciplines. Annex D. Toronto: Ont. Dept. of Health, 1969. P. 43-53.

1970 Murray, V.V. Nursing in Ontario: a study for the Committee on the Healing Arts. Toronto: Queen's Printer, 1970. 284 p.

1971 Checkley, K. "The influence of a human relations laboratory on the effectiveness of third-year psychiatric nurses." Ph.D. thesis, Univ. of Alberta, 1971.

Given, J. "A study of anticipatory socialization on prospective nursing students." M.A. thesis, Univ. of Toronto, 1971.

"National conference on research in nursing practice." Can. Nurse 67 (April 1971) 34-40.

Syposz, D.M. "Trends for diploma programs in nursing in Ontario as reflected by the nursing literature and the opinions of selected nurse educators". Ph.D. thesis, Univ. of Toronto, 1971.

1973 Overduin, J. People and idea: nursing at Western 1920-1970. London: Faculty of Nursing, Univ. of Western Ontario, 1973. 150 p.

1974 Callbeck, C. A history of the Prince Edward Island Hospital School of Nursing, 1891-1971. Charlottetown: PEI Hospital Nurses Alumnae Assoc., 1974. 72 p.

Dyson, R., et al. "Training for psychiatric nursing." Can. Mental Health 22 (December 1974) 15-17.

1975 Flaherty, M.J. "Continuing education should be voluntary." Can. Nurse 71 (July 1975) 19-21.

1976 Alderson, H.J. Twenty-five years a-growing: the history of the School of Nursing. Hamilton: McMaster Univ., 1976. 333 p.

Field, B.C. "Orientation and inservice programs for teachers in Canadian two year schools of nursing and sources of satisfaction and dissatisfaction as perceived by these teachers." M.Ed. thesis, Univ. of New Brunswick, 1976.

Smith, D.L. "Skills and competence required of nurses working in occupational health and their need for education." Can. Jour. Public Health 67 (Supplement 2, Sept./Oct. 1976) 68-71.

1977 La Sor, B. and M.R. Elliott. Issues in Canadian Nursing. Scarborough: Prentice Hall of Canada, 1977. 240 p.

Zilm, G. "The trend in nursing education and what it means for health care delivery." Can. Med. Assoc. Jour. 116 (23 April 1977) 936-946.

1978 Lefort, S. "The nurse practitioner - what happened?" Can. Nurse (April 1978) 14-23.

1979 Hurd, J.M. "Nursing and the degree mystique." Can. Nurse (April 1979) 36-39.

1980 Lambert, C. "L'enseignement infirmier dans les cégeps." Infirmière. Can. 22 (avril 1980) 33-36.

Lapointe, G. L'Université Laurentienne et son cadre unique." Infirmière law. 22 (fév. 1980) 26-29.

OPTOMETRY/OPTOMETRIE

1976 Woodruff, M.E. et al. "A survey of the progress and direction of research at the School of Optometry, University of Waterloo." Can. Jour. Public Health 67 (Sept./Oct. 1976) 401-404.

1978 Andrew, D.E. "Optometry: then and now." Can. Jour. Public Health 69 (November-December 1978) 85-89.

Pellowe, R.D. "Clinical training and community service in the School of Optometry, University of Waterloo." Can. Jour. Public Health 69 (November-December 1978) 81-84.

Samek, M. "Quality in continuing education?" Can. Jour. Public Health 69 (November-December 1978) 90-95.

PHARMACY/PHARMACIE

1967 Ross, T.M. Pharmacist manpower in Canada Ottawa: Queen's Printer, 1967. 136 p.

1970 Gagnon, J. "Le Collège décerne ses premiers certificats d'éducation continue." Pharm. 44 (avril 1970) 10.

1971 Pharmacy in a new age: report of the Commission on Pharmaceutical Services. Toronto: Can. Pharmaceutical Assoc., 1971. 463 p.

1973 Knolman, L. "L'A.P.C. crée une Conférence Canadienne d'éducation permanante en pharmacie". Pharm (juillet 1973) 32-35.

1974 Carpentier, J.-M. et P.-P. Leblanc. L'Ecole de pharmacie a cinquante ans." Au fil des événements [Univ. de Montréal] 10 (novembre 1974) 8-9.

L'Ecole de pharmacie de Laval fête son cinquantième anniversaire."
Pharm (novembre 1974) 3-6.

Stieb, E.W.   "Pharmaceutical education in Ontario: 1. prelude and
beginnings (the Shuttleworth era)"   Pharm. Hist. [U.S.] 16, 2 (1974)
64-71.

1975   McIver, N.   "Women in pharmacy."   Can. Pharm. Jour.   108 (February
1975) 12-18.

1977   "The CCCEP role in continuing pharmaceutical education."   Can. Pharm.
Jour.   110 (November 1977) 8-19.

"Continuing education in the provinces."   Can. Pharm. Jour.   110
(November 1977) 20-24.

"The history of the Canadian Conference on Continuing Education in
Pharmacy."   Can. Pharm. Jour.   110 (November 1977) 4-7.

Pitt, F. "La formation de techniciens en pharmacie s'avère indispensable."   Pharm.   (October 1977) 16-22.

Robert, P.   "L'étudiant et les diverses conceptions de la pharmacie."
Pharm (juin 1977) 22, 24, 28-29.

"Mandatory continuing education adopted by Manitoba pharmacists."
Can. Pharm. Jour.   110 (August 1977) 26-29.

1980   Lundgren, G.O. et al.   "What's new for pharmacy education - panel
discussion."   Can. Pharm. Jour. 113 (Oct. 1980) 346-349.

Stewart, G.   "Training and education for pharmacists in the Canadian
Armed Forces."   Can. Pharm. Jour.   (Nov. 1980) 363-366.

PHYSICAL & HEALTH EDUCATION/EDUCATION PHYSIQUE

1916   Cartwright, E.M.   "Physical education and the Strathcona Trust."   The
School 4 (1916) 306-310.

1947   Mercier, A.   "Education physique dans les universités canadiennes
françaises."   M.A. thesis.   Univ. de Montréal, 1947.

1953   Eckert, H.   "The development of physical education and organized
recreation in Alberta."   M.Ed. thesis, Univ. of Alberta, 1953.

1963   Neil, G.I.   "History of physical education in the protestant schools
of Quebec."   M.A. thesis, McGill Univ., 1963.

Gill, S. "A history of physical education in New Brunswick schools." M.Sc. thesis, Univ. of Maine, 1963.

1965 Howell, M.L. "Physical education research in Canada", in Physical education in Canada. Ed. by M.L. Howell. Scarborough, Ont: Prentice Hall, 1965. p 249-75.

Passmore, J.H. "Teacher education", in Physical education in Canada. Ed. by M.L. Howell. Scarborough: Prentice Hall, 1965. p. 50-63.

1966 Potts, R. "The development of physical education in Nova Scotia schools." M.Ed. Thesis, Acadia Univ., 1966.

1967 Ashton, N. "The evolution of a discipline." Can. H.P.E.R. Jour. 33, 6 (1967) 5-10.

Day, J. "Robert Tait McKenzie: physical education's man of the century." Can. H.P.E.R. Jour. 33, 4 (1967).

"The Department of Physical Education of the University of New Brunswick." Can. H.P.E.R. Jour. 33, 4 (1967) 34, 36.

1971 Caldwell, S.F. "Humanistic physical education: tomorrow's challenge." Can. H.P.E.R. Jour. (July-August 1971) 7-8.

Consentino, F. and M.L. Howell. A history of physical education in Canada. Toronto: General Publishing Co., 1971. 154 p.

Enos, E.F. "A philosophical approach to contemporary physical education and athletics." Can. H.P.E.R. Jour. 37 (July-Aug. 1971) 34-37 and (Sept.-Oct. 1971) 16-17.

Leyshon, G.A. "Motor learning and the physical educator." Can. P.H.E.R. Jour. 38 (Sept.-Oct. 1971) 30-34; (Nov.-Dec. 1971) 7-16.

L'Heureux, W.J., "Mass, man and me." Can. H.P.E.R. Jour. 38 (Sept.-Oct. 1971) 3-8.

Schlegel, R.P. and J.C. Nash. "Professional preparation of the health specialist." Can. H.P.E.R. Jour. 37 (July-Aug. 1971) 12-15.

Schneidman, N. "Academic training and athletic performance." Can. H.P.E.R. Jour. 37 (July-Aug. 1971) 30-33.

Smith, M. "New approaches in teaching physical skills." Can. H.P.E.R. Jour. 38 (September-October 1971) 18-26.

1972 Brunelle, J., et al. "Le micro-enseignement: un outil de formation des enseignants en éducation physique." Mouvement 7 (sept. 1972) 143-151.

Hupé, A. "Spécificité de l'enseignement de l'éducation physique: mythe ou réalité?" Mouvement (déc. 1972) 201-202.

Petrie, B.M. "Education for leisure: a gap between ideology and practice." Can. H.P.E.R. Jour. 38 (Jan.-Feb. 1972) 3-12.

1973 West, J.T. "Physical fitness, sport and the federal government 1909-1954." Can. Jour. History Sport Recreation 4 (December 1973), 26-42.

1974 Metcalfe, A. "Some background influences on nineteenth century Canadian sport and physical education." Can. Jour. History Sport Recreation 6 (May 1974) 62-73.

1976 Chelladurai, P. "A composite model for degree programs in institutions of physical education." Can. H.P.E.R. Jour. 42 (5) 30-5.

Moriarty, D. "Integrate or disintegrate." Can. H.P.E.R. Jour. 42, 5 (1976) 23-29.

1978 Oldridge, N.B. "Adapted physical education practicum in the hospital setting - the McMaster experience." Can. H.P.E.R. Jour. 44 (July-August 1978) 15-17, 36-39.

Pooley, J.C. Comparative physical education and sport programmes in Canadian universities: an analysis." Can. and International Educ. 7 (December 1978) 5-16.

1979 Soucie, D. et A. Brodeur. "Le profil de carrière des diplômés en éducation physique à l'Université d'Ottawa (1948-1975)." Can. H.P.E.R. Jour. 45 (mar./apr. 1979) 6-14.

1980 Slack, T. "The employment status of physical education and recreation graduates and the perceived value of their undergraduate training." Can. H.P.E.R. Jour. 46 (Jul.-Aug. 1980) 272-29 and 38-39.

Soucie, D. and T. Bedecki. "Trends in physical education/sport/athletic administration in Canadian universities and colleges." Can. H.P.E.R. Jour. 47 (Nov.-Dec. 1980) 30-36.

1981 Davidson, S.A. Twentieth century torchbearers in Canadian physical education." Can. H.P.E.R. Jour 47 (Jan.-Feb. 1981) 3-5.

PHYSICAL AND OCCUPATIONAL THERAPY/
THERAPEUTIQUE PHYSIQUE ET PROESSIONNELLE

1972 Trider, M. "The future of occupational therapy." Can. Jour. Occ. Therapy 39 (September 1972) 3-8.

1977   Currier, D. "Research in programs of initial physical therapy educa-
       tion." Physiotherapy Can. 29 (October 1977) 211-213.

       Gartland, G.J. "Synopsis of a study of admissions criteria for phys-
       ical therapy programs." Physiotherapy Can. 29 (March 1977) 6-10.

       Olney, S. "Prediction of clinical competence of students of physical
       therapy." Physiotherapy Can. 29 (December 1977) 254-257.

       Pickles, B. "Correlations between matriculation entry requirements
       and performance in the diploma program in physical therapy at the
       University of Alberta." Physiotherapy Can. 29 (December 1977) 249-
       253.

       Walker, J.M. and J.A. Gordon. "Canadian physiotherapy education: a
       changing pattern." Physiotherapy Canada 29 (Mar. 1977) 12-14.

1979   Bridle, M. "Standards - who needs them? Setting standards for the
       education of occupational therapists." Can. Jour. Occup. Therapy
       (Dec. 1979) 206-210.

       Maxwell, J. and M. Maxwell. "Graduate education: the case of occupa-
       tional therapy. Can. Jour. Occup. Therapy (Dec. 1979) 189-196.

       Raymonde H. and F. Ferland. "Evaluation par objectifs de la forma-
       tion clinique en ergothérapie à l'Université de Montréal." Can. Jour.
       Occup. Therapy (June 1979) 109-112.

1980   Bridle, M. and J. Burton. "The clinical learning centre revisited."
       Can. Jour. Occup. Therapy (Dec. 1980) 203-205.

       Hachey, R. "A modularized self-instructional course in psychiatric
       occupational therapy." Can. Jour. Occup. Therapy (June 1979) 95-102.

PUBLIC HEALTH/HYGIÈNE PUBLIQUE

1940   Defries, R.D., ed. The development of public health in Canada.
       Toronto: Canadian Public Health Assoc., 1940.

1973   Anderson, D.O. "Certification in public health - training for obso-
       lescence." Can. Jour. Public Health 63 (September-October 1973)
       405-412.

SOCIAL WORK/SCIENCES SOCIALES

1970   "Aspects du service social en milieu scolaire: à propos d'éducation."
       Serv. Soc. 19 (juillet-décembre 1970) 2-5.

Landauer, M. Social work in Ontario: a study for the Committee on the Healing Arts. Toronto: Queen's Printer, 1970. 89 p. and appendices.

"Le 25ième anniversaire de l'Ecole de service social de l'Université Laval." Serv. Soc. 19 (janvier-juin 1970) 2-5.

Meloche, D. "La formation en service social: récit d'une expérience de stage en milieu scolaire." Serv. Soc. 19 (juillet-décembre 1970) 16-29.

Zay, N. "Le nouveau programme de maîtrise de l'Ecole de service social de l'Université Laval." Serv. Soc. 19 (juillet-décembre 1970) 120-45.

Zay, N. "Rétrospective et perspective d'avenir de l'Ecole de service social de l'Université Laval." Serv. Soc. 19 (janvier-juin 1970) 167-74.

1972 AUCC. Proceedings of the Conference on Social Services Manpower. February 21-23, 1971. Ottawa: AUCC, 1972. 94 p.

Belzite, L. et al. "Teaching and learning conference groups in a bachelor's program." Soc. Worker 40 (February 1972) 43-49.

Clark, F. and A. Comanor. "Implications of the socio-behavioral framework for social work education." Soc. Worker 40 (Fall 1972) 296-303.

De Jongh, J.F. "Regard rétrospectif sur l'enseignement du service social." Serv. Soc. 21 (janvier-août 1972) 22-44.

Desai, A.S. "L'élaboration du programme d'études en service social." Serv. Soc. (janvier-août 1972) 105-34.)

Doolan, M. and W.A. Herington. "An educational model for teaching practice with individuals, families and small groups." Soc. Worker 40 (Fall 1972) 245-255.

Goldberg, E.M. "L'utilité de la recherche dans la formation au service social." Serv. Soc. (janvier-août 1972) 156-170.

Hill, M.A. "Introduction to field practice: the UBC practicum." Soc. Worker 40 (Summer 1972) 186-197.

Latimer, E.A. "An analysis of the social action behaviour of the Canadian Association of Social Workers from its organizational beginning to the modern period." D.S.W. dissertation, Univ. of Toronto, 1972.

1973   Comanor, A. et N. Zay.   "Deux indicateurs de la situation de la
        gérontologie au Canada: la gérontologie dans la formation en service
        social et la recherche sur le bien-être en gérontologie." Serv. Soc.
        22, 2-3 (1973) 5-37.

        Kelly, M.V. "Educating social workers for research." Soc. Worker
        41, 3 (1973) 252-258.

        Kendell, K.A. "Etude comparative de la formation au service social
        en différents pays." Serv. Soc. 24, 2 (1973) 91-114.

        Melichercik, J. "Social work education and social work practice."
        Soc. Worker 41 (Spring 1973) 22-27.

        Schlesinger, B. "Social work education and family planning." Soc.
        Worker 41 (Summer 1973) 93-99.

1974   Mathiew, M. "The accreditation of Canadian schools of social work."
        Can. Library Jour. 31 (April 1974) 94-98.

1975   Goldstein, H. "The B.S.W. as the first professional degree: some
        opinions and questions." Can. Jour. Soc. Work Educ. 2, 1 (1975)
        49-55.

        Katz, A. "Problem oriented education: an alternative social work
        curriculum." Can. Jour. Soc. Work Educ. 1, 2 (1975) 48-56.

        Rose, A. "Teaching social welfare policy and services in the social
        work curriculum of Canadian schools." Can. Jour. Soc. Work Educ. 1,
        3 (1975) 4-12.

        Segal, B. "Dilemmas in the social work education - social work man-
        power equation." Can. Jour. Soc. Work Educ. 1, 2 (1975) 4-12.

        Turnbull, A. "Teaching family-centred practice in a BSW programme:
        a field experience." Soc. Worker 43, 3 (1978) 153-155.

1976   Barnes, J. "An overview of the one-year MSW programme in Canada."
        Soc. Worker 44, 2-3 (1976) 34-42.

        Dupras, A. "L'enseignement de la sexualité de l'handicapé dans les
        écoles canadiennes de service social." Soc. Worker 44 (Winter 1976)
        100-107.

1977   Drover, G. and E. Shragge. "General systems theory and social work
        education: a critique." Can. Jour. Soc. Work Educ. 3, 2 (1977) 28-39.

        Findlay, P.C. "Social work education and the problem of critical
        theory." Can. Jour. Soc. Work Educ. 3, 2 (1977) 40-52.

Hutton, M. Continuum or network: curriculum alternatives for education for the social services." Can. Jour. Soc. Work Educ. 3, 1 (1977) 16-22.

1978 Santilli, M.P. "Training social work students." Soc. Worker 46 (Winter 1978) 101-105.

1979 Hutton, M. Accessibility: an examination of what is involved in making social work education more accessible. Winnipeg. the author, 1979. 72 p.

Olyna, S.D. "Integration a divergence? Field instruction and the social work curriculum." Soc. Worker 47 (Summer-Fall 1979) 57-61.

TEACHER TRAINING AND EDUCATION/FORMATION DES ENSEIGNANTS ET ENSEIGNEMENT

1952 Hutton, H.K. "French Canadian normal schools: an historical, interpretive and evaluative study." Ph.D. thesis. Pennsylvania State Univ. 1952.

1957 Bertrand, R. L'Ecole Normale Laval: un siècle d'histoire (1857-1957). Québec: Société Historique de Québec, Université Laval, 1957. 52 p.

1968 Macdonald, J. "Teacher education: a functional approach." Teacher Educ. 1 (Spring 1968) 1-10.

Robinson, F.G. "Teacher education: a parody of behavioural change." Teacher Educ. 1 (Spring 1968) 17-23.

Skinner, A.F. "Teacher training and the foundational studies." Teacher Educ. 1 (Spring 1968) 26-38.

1969 Ellis, J.F. "Crisis in teacher training: storm warning." Queen's Q. 83 (1969) 285-290.

Hedley, R.L. and C.C. Wood. "Teaching teacher behaviour." Teacher Educ. 2 (Spring 1969) 48-55.

Shorey, L.L. "Teacher participation in continuing education activities." Ph.D. thesis. Univ. of Toronto, 1969.

1970 Dibisk, D.J. "Private returns to teacher education in Alberta." Ph.D. thesis, Univ. of Alberta, 1970.

Hodysh, H.W. An analysis of history of education as an academic discipline." Jour. Teacher Educ. (Summer 1970).

Ferrari, G. "An evaluation of the M.Ed. degree program in counselling at the U. of A." M.Ed. thesis, Univ. of Alberta, 1970.

Kong, S.L. "Educational psychology for teachers." Teacher Educ. 3 (Spring 1970) 62-67.

Richard, F. "Perception de soi des futurs enseignantes." Ph.D. thesis, Université de Montréal, 1970.

Wallace, K.W.A. "The private monetary return to vocational education: teacher training in Alberta." Ph.D. thesis, Univ. of Alberta, 1970.

1971 Bhattacharya, N.C. "Philosophy, education and teacher education." Teacher Educa. 4 (Spring 1971) 26-34.

Channon, G. "Trends in teacher preparation curricula in Canada." McGill Jour. Educ. 6 (fall 1971) 144-159.

Cheong, G.S.C. "Predicting practice teaching performance from experimentalism and dogmatism ratings." Man. Jour. Educ. 7 (Nov. 1971) 31-35.

Elliott, H. "Predicting success in teaching." Alta. Jour. Educ. Res. 17 (June 1971) 69-76.

Hamilton, H.A. "Teacher education the day after tomorrow." Lakehead Univ. Rev., 4 (Fall 1971) 100-108.

Lynch, J. "From theory to practice in teacher training." Teacher Educ. 4 (Spring 1971) 56-65.

McLeish, J.A.B. "Teacher education for the seventies." Teacher Educ. 4 (Spring 1971) 76-84.

Munroe, D. "Teacher education at McGill." McGill Jour. Educ. 6 (Spring 1971) 29-40.

Pierce, H.L. "Department of Educational Foundations, Faculty of Education, University of Alberta, 1961-1971: the first decade." Edmonton: Faculty of Education, Univ. of Alberta, 1971. 35 p.

Picot, D. "La formation pédagogique: théorie ou pratique?" Act. péd. 18 (juin 1971) 48-55.

Smitheran, V., et al. Teacher education: perseverance or professionalism. Charlettetown: Univ. of Prince Edward Island, 1971. 133 p.

Stamp, R.M. "History of education courses in preparation of Canadian teachers." McGill Jour. Educ. 6 (Fall 1971) 160-169.

Van Dromme, J. "La prédiction de la réussite dans l'enseignement."

1972 Clarke, S.C.T. and H.T. Coutts. "The future of teacher education." Can. Admin. 11 (May 1972) 29-33.

Crewhurst, D. "Indian and métis teacher training." School Progress 41 (May 1972) 26-27.

Hillis, E.S. "Those who can't teach ... " Can. Forum 51 (Oct./Nov.) 44-47.

Jomphe, G. "Etude des besoins des étudiants-maîtres de l'Université du Québec. Description, continuum perceptuel, satisfaction." Ph.D. thesis, Université d'Ottawa, 1972.

Program Committee, Council of The College of Education, University of Toronto (T.H.G. Luther, Chairman). Focus (report on future programs of teacher education, University of Toronto, September, 1971) and Refocus (responses to Focus, 1971-72). Toronto: University of Toronto, 1972. 133 p.

Tompkins, G. "Curriculum planning: a medium for in-service education." Jour. Educ. (N.S.) 22 (October 1972-73) 3-9.

1973 Després, G.-J. "Mise au point d'un programme de quatre ans de formation des maîtres des arts industriels et d'un programme sous-gradué menant au baccalauréat en éducation de l'enseignement professionnel industriel pour la Faculté des sciences de l'éducation de l'université de Moncton." M.A. thesis, Université de Monction, 1973.

Ellis, D. "Opinions des instituteurs sur leur formation pédagogique." Orbit 4 (February 1973) 12-13.

Feger, R. "Le perfectionnement des maîtres en exercice dans la famille formation des maîtres à l'Université du Québec à Montréal." M.A. thesis, Université de Montréal, 1973.

Harker, W.J. "The professional preparation of reading teachers and specialists in Canadian universities and colleges." Man. Jour. Educ. 8 (June 1973) 44-50.

McLeish, J.B. "Some correlates of political and religious beliefs in student-teachers." Alta. Jour. Educ. Res. 19 (June 1973) 159-183.

McLeish, J.B. "Teacher education: environments and outcome." Alta. Jour. Educ. Res. 19 (March 1973) 66-81.

Palkiewicz, J. "La formation des maîtres au Québec: comme les médecins." Prospectives 9, 1 (1973) 8-11.

Piquette, R. "Les programmes de formation des maîtres dans les écoles normales françaises (1857-1970)". Thèse de doctorat, Univ. de Montréal, 1973.

Poupard, D. "Etude exploratoire des valeurs d'éducation, de la satisfaction des expériences vécues chez deux groupes d'étudiants en formation des maîtres." Thèse de doctorat, Université de Montréal, 1973.

Rogue, S.J. "The organization, control and administration of the teacher training system of the Province of Ontario, 1900-1920." Ph.D. thesis, Univ. of Ottawa, 1973.

1974   Aylwin, U. "Les universités et la formation des maîtres." Prospectives 10 (avril 1974) 93-102.

Couture, R.-Z. "La motivation du choix de l'enseignement comme carrière chez les étudiants du Bas-du-Fleuve et de la Gaspésie." M.A. thesis, Université d'Ottawa, 1974, xx-66 p.

Daoust, G. et P. Bélanger. "Les pratiques universitaires de perfectionnement des maîtres et les rapports université-milieu." Prospectives 10 (avril 1974) 81-85.

David, G. "Problèmes de formation et de perfectionnement des maîtres des niveaux élémentaire et secondaire." Prospectives 10 (avril 1974) 107-113.

Desbiens, J.P. "Le tableau noir." Prospectives 10, 2 (1974) 87-93.

Fortier, C. "Pour le perfectionnement des enseignants de niveau collégial: la formation pédagogique continue." Prospectives 10 (avril 1974) 115-19.

Gagnon, M. "Disparue depuis Gutenberg, la formation pédagogique de l'universitaire réapparaît." Prospectives 10 (avril 1974) 133-40.

Hendley, B. "Five mistaken approaches to education." McGill Jour. Educ. 9 (Spring 1974) 25-33.

Hodysh, H.W. and P.J. Miller. "Integration and the professional year." Teacher Educ. 7 (Spring 1974) 25-31.

Lebel, D. "Comment organiser la formation pédagogique continue." Prospectives, 10, 2 (1974) 121-125.

Martin, R.A. Future directions for teacher education: a delphi survey involving educators of teachers and recent graduates of a program in teacher education. Toronto: Faculty of Education, U. of T., 1974. 46 p.

McKay, R.M. "The teacher assistant program at Hamilton Teachers' College." Teacher Educ. 7 (Spring 1974) 68-80.

Myers, D. and F. Reid. Educating teachers: critiques and proposals. Toronto: Ontario Institute for Studies in Education, 1974. 156 p.

Pedersen, G.K. "The case for reform in teacher education." Teacher Educ. 7 (Spring 1974) 3-15.

Picot, J.E. A brief history of teacher training in New Brunswick 1848-1973. Fredericton, Department of Education, 1974. 146 p.

Picot, J.E. Les écoles normales du Nouveau Brunswick, 1848-1973. Fredericton, Department of Education, 1974. 157 p.

"Qui est responsable de la formation et du perfectionnement des maîtres au Québec?" Prospectives 10 (avril 1974) 76-79.

"Les recommandations d'un colloque provincial sur la formation des maîtres de l'élémentaire." Prospectives 10 (avril 1974) 103-06.

Sanders, J.T. "Toward a rationale for practice teaching." Teacher Educ. 7 (Spring 1974) 17-24.

Robichaud, E. "Pour former les maîtres." Educ. et Soc. 5, 7 (1974) 7-9.

Roquet, C. "Quelques notes sur la formation des maîtres d'après le Rapport Parent (1964-1974-1984)." Mém. S.R.C. (1974) 187-192.

Volpe, R. "Theoretical relevance in teacher education." Teacher Educ. 7 (Spring 1974) 33-42.

Wilson, J.D. "The teacher in early Ontario", in F. Armstrong et al. Aspects of nineteenth century Ontario. Toronto: U. of T. Press, 1974. p. 218-236.

1975   Applegate, M. "Ontario faculties of education: their role in continuing education." History and Social Science Teacher 10, 3 (1975) 17-23.

Csapo, M. "Towards accountability in teacher training in special education." Jour. Educ. (Spring 1975) 73-77.

Farine, A. Les diplômés en sciences de l'éducation: étude sur la concordance entre l'emploi et la formation universitaire. Montréal: Faculté des sciences de l'éducation, Université de Montréal, 1975 145 p.

Harvey, R.P. "A "People's College" for Truro: the founding of a normal school". Nova Scotia Hist. Quart. (Special Supplement 1975.) 67-84.

Milburn, D. "Paradox farm: or a problems approach to teacher education." Jour. Educ. 21 (Spring 1975) 33-39.

Newton, E.E. "Teacher education beyond the academic ghetto." History and Social Science Teacher 10, 3 (1975) 39-45.

Pratt, D. "A competency-based program for training teachers of history." Teacher Educ. 8 (Spring 1975) 79-91.

Reid, R.M. "Accessibility characteristics in individualized teacher education programs: acquisition of basic skills." Ph.D. thesis, Univ. of Toronto, 1975.

Shore, B.M. and E. Strauss. "What happens to graduate education graduates?" McGill Jour. Educ. 10 (1975) 165-174.

Tiberius, R.G. "An interactive approach to education for independence in fourth year medical students." Ph.D. thesis, Univ. of Toronto, 1975.

1976   Barthe, M. Un coup de barre vers le milieu réel! Educ. Québec 6, 8 (1976) 44-46.

Burton, T. "Subtractive modes in teacher education." Teacher Educ. 9 (Spring 1976) 13-25.

Dalziel, G.G. "Training teachers for the North: the early development of teacher training in North Bay, Ontario, 1905-1920." M.A. thesis, Univ. of Toronto, 1976.

Fraser, J.A.H. and F.T. Vitro. "Effects of empathy-training on student teachers." Teacher Educ. 9 (Spring 1976) 59-65.

Friesen, J.W. "Teacher preparation and intercultural education." Jour. Educ. Thought 10 (December 1976) 179-187.

Nadeau, G.G. "Unité de recherche et développement en éducation." Revue des Sciences de l'éducation, 2, 2 (1976) 107-135.

Russell, T.L. "On the provision made for development of views of science and teaching by science teacher education." Ph.D. thesis, Univ. of Toronto, 1976.

1977   Allen, F.I. and M.F. Wideen. "Establishing objectives in teacher education." Teacher Educ. 11 (Oct. 1977) 50-57.

Brehaut, W. and Gill, M. "Ontario elementary school teachers evaluate their teacher preparation programs." Orbit 8 (April 1977) 5-7.

Burns, M. "Prediction of success in teacher training." McGill Jour. Educ. 12 (Fall 1977) 279-286.

Elie, M.-T. "Etude de l'administration scolaire à l'Université de Montréal, la période de 1960-1977." Revue Information (Fédération des Principaux du Québec) 16 (janvier 1977) 25-29.

Kampf, R. "Teacher education in Ontario -- the status quo." Orbit 8 (April 1977) 3-4.

Koch, E.L. and G.J.A. de Leeuw. "Developing self-directing teachers." Teacher Educ. 11 (Oct. 1977) 60-77.

Morin, L. "La formation des maîtres au Québec depuis dix ans ou ... "l'universitarisation" de l'impuissance continue." Prospectives 13, 3 (1977) 135-145.

Ross, C.J. and L.D. Stewart. "Graduates' assessment of industrial arts education programs." Alta. Jour. Educ. Research 23 (June 1977) 109-117.

Shapiro, P.P. "Evaluation of student teachers." Teacher Educ. 11 (Oct. 1977) 40-48.

Wilson, K.A. "Issues in the training of teachers." Teacher Educ. 11 (Oct. 1977) 24-37.

1978 Morin, A. et R. Viau. "Profil d'apprentissage de l'étudiant universitaire." Bull. AMQ 18, 1 (1978) 8-19.

Pekarske, S.L. "The knowledge legitimatization crisis and competency-based teacher education curricula." Jour. Educ. Thought 12 (April 1978) 37-47.

Slentz, K. "Graduate internship for teachers." Teacher Educ. 12 (April 1978) 92-96.

1979 Allen, S. "Guidelines for inservice programs." Teacher Educ. 14 (Apr. 1979) 86-90.

Bunch, G. and R. Sanche. "An overview of special education programs in Canadian universities." Can. Jour. Educ. 4, 1 (1979) 67-78.

Mallea, J. and J. Young. "Teacher education for a multicultural society." Teacher Educ. 14 (April 1979) 28-38.

Manicom, A. "The role of the universities in continuing teacher education." Jour. Ed. (N.S.) 6, 2 (1979) 17-20.

MᶜCutcheon, W.W. "Follow-up a guide for teacher educators." Teacher Educ. 14 (Apr. 1979) 91-96.

Nixon, M. and E. Miklos. "Admission practices and placement patterns in educational administration programs." Can. Admin. 18 (January 1979).

Peck, B.T. and E.G. Archer. "School-based training of teachers: the British experience." Teacher Educ. 14 (Apr. 1979) 79-85.

Pedersen, K.G. and T.G. Fleming. "Irrationality and teacher education." Teacher Educ. 14 (Apr. 1979) 40-49.

Pike, R. "What is 'a teacher'." Teacher Educ. 14 (Apr. 1979) 64-69.

Richert, R. and A.G. McBeath. "Forging the link between the campus and the classroom." Teacher Educ. 14 (Apr. 1979) 72-78.

1980 Allen, S. "An experiment in field-based education; a description of the program at the University of Lethbridge." Educ. Can. 20 (autumn 1980) 11-13.

Bédard, R. and J.S. Daniel. "Permama: innovation is in-service training of teachers." Can. Jour. Univ. Cont. Educ. 7 (Summer 1980) 19-22.

Blowers, E.A., C.R. Yewchuk and L.R. Wilgosh. "Practica partnerships: three models." Ed. Can. 20, 3 (1980) 4-10.

Campbell, D. "The internship in teacher education." Teacher Educ. (Apr. 1980) 70-78.

Lang, H., W. Cornish and L. Trew. "Partners in training; how it works and why - a description of the University of Regina's special internship seminar for student teachers and cooperating teachers." Educ. Can. 20 (autumn 1980) 14-21.

Massey, M. "Teacher training in Canada: the state of the art." Can. Mod. Lang. Rev. 37, 1 (1980) 25-29.

MᶜCutcheon, W.W. "Three projects in teacher training: How are future 'good' Teachers recognized?" Teacher Educ. 16 (Apr. 1980) 91-96.

Olson, A.T. and D.E. Gillingham. "Systematic desensitization of mathematics anxiety among preservice elementary teachers." Alta. Jour. Educ. Rev. 26 (June 1980) 120-127.

Renihan, P.J. "Preparing teachers for the middle school." Teacher Educ. 16 (Apr. 1980) 80-86.

Ryan, D.W. and E.S. Hickcox. Redefining teacher evaluation: an analysis of practice, policies and teacher attitudes. Toronto: OISE Press, 1980. 120 p.

Tom, A.R. "Teaching as a moral craft: a metaphor for teaching and teacher education." Curriculum Inquiry 10 (Fall 1980) 317-323.

Towler, J. "Are teachers trained environmental education?" Educ. Can. 20, 3 (1980) 32-37.

Twa, R.J. and M. Greene. "Prediction of success in student teaching as a criterion for selection in teacher education programs." Alta. Jour. Educ. Rev. 26 (March 1980) 1-13.

Wilgosh, L.R., C.R. Yewchuk and E.A. Blowers. "Practica partnerships; three models." Educ. Can. 20 (autumn 1980) 4-10.

THEOLOGY/THÉOLOGIE

1969 McLeish, J.B. et al. Theological education for the 70's. Toronto: Anglican Church of Canada, 1969. 47 p.

1970 Baum, G. "Où va la théologie?" Maintenant 93 (février 1970) 40-43.

1972 Stanley, G.F.G. "The big bishop, Alexander MacDonnel of Kingston." Historic Kingston 20 (1972) 90-105.

1974 Dussault, M. "L'Eglise de Montréal et son séminaire: les prêtres de demain." Relations 34 (mars 1974) 85-87.

Moir, J.S. Enduring witness: a history of the Presbyterian Church in Canada. Toronto: Presbyterian Publications, 1974. 309 p.

Schwartz, E. "Clergy education and the 1925 church union." M.A. thesis, Univ. of Alberta, 1974.

1975 Lucier, P. "La Théologie et l'université: les vrais enjeux du débat sur les prêtres laicisés et l'enseignement de la théologie." Relations 409 (november 1975) 298-307.

Ross, B. "James Eustace Purdie: the story of Pentecostal theological education." Jour. Can. Church Hist. Society 17 (December 1975) 94-103.

1977 Langevin, G. "Pourquoi la Théologie doit rester à l'université." Science et Esprit 29, 3 (1977) 241-249.

VETERINARY MEDICINE/MEDECINE VETERINAIRE

1972 Saleemi, A.H. "Continuing education for veterinarians: an attitudinal study of the preprofessional." M.Sc. thesis, Univ. of Guelph, 1972.

1975 Howell, D.G. Report of a study of the establishment of a school of veterinary medicine in the Atlantic region. Fredericton: Maritime Provinces Higher Education Commission, 1975.

1977 Nielson, N. et al. "A study of veterinary manpower in Canada." Can. Vet. Jour. 18 (Jan. 1977) 2-16.

VOCATIONAL GUIDANCE/ORIENTATION PROFESSIONNELLE

1967 Parmenter, M.D. Your further education, Toronto: Crest Publishing, 1967. 102 p.

1969 Cosgrove, G.P. and W.W. Dick. Career Planning. Toronto: Psychological Services Department York University, 1969. 109 p.

1971 Bedal, C.L. "Ontario school guidance challenged." School Guidance Worker 27 (Nov./Dec. 1971) 53-57.

Clarke, S.C.T. "Guidance in the year 2000." School Guidance Worker 27 (Nov.-Dec. 1971) 47-50.

Currey, D. "A reaction to 'Research study #19 - Guidance' from the university viewpoint." School Guidance Worker 27 (Nov./Dec. 1971) 12-15.

Davies, N. "Facts, facts, who's got the facts?" School Guidance Worker 27 (Nov./Dec. 1971) 30-36.

Davies, N. "Vocational guidance - an educational topsy." School Guidance Worker, 27 (Nov.-Dec. 1971) 12-20.

Davies, N., D. Cook, and M. Peck, eds. Spectrum. Toronto: Guidance Centre, College of Education, Univ. of Toronto, 1971. 96 p.

Gaymer, R. "Career counselling - teaching the art of career planning." School Guidance Worker 27 (Nov.-Dec. 1971) 51-56.

Knicely, B., P. Griffin et al. "Is there any place you'd rather be? Reactions by some Ontario school counsellors to the 'Draft report' and 'Research study #19 - Guidance'." School Guidance Worker 27 (Nov./Dec. 1971) 6-12.

Marsh, L. "The new look in post-secondary educational resources: some guide lines for counsellors." School Guidance Worker 27 (Nov.-Dec. 1971) 41-46.

Paterson, J.G. and H. Voth. "Another point of view on 'Research study #19 - Guidance'." School Guidance Worker 27 (Nov./Dec. 1971) 39-43.

Pinder, E.G. "Counsellor's knowledge of the business environment - a must." School Guidance Worker, 27 (Nov./Dec. 1971) 26-29.

Seeley, M. "A college principal's view of 'Research study #19' and the 'Draft Report'." School Guidance Worker 27 (Nov./Dec. 1971) 37-9.

Shields, B.A. "Androgyny is here: on counselling girls now." School Guidance Worker 27 (Nov./Dec. 1971) 28-33.

Turgeon, P. "The guidance report of the Commission on Post-Secondary Education in Ontario: a call for dialogue among counsellors, and counsellor educators." School Guidance Worker 27 (Nov./Dec. 1971) 45-48.

1977   Peavy, R. and M.-A. Linteau. "L'orientation d'aide mutuelle dans le counseling pour adultes." Can. Counsellor 11 (July 1977) 158-165.

1978   Leard, H. M. and A. Hum. "The personality characteristics of counsellors-in-training which correlate with ratings of effectiveness and grades." Can. Counsellor (13 (Oct. 1978) 28-32.

F.   GRADUATE STUDIES/ETUDES POST-UNIVERSITAIRES

1966   U.B.C. Committee on Graduate Studies, I. McTaggart-Cowan chairman. A review of graduate study at the University of British Columbia. Vancouver: UBC, 1966. p. 100

1971   Hogg, B.C. "The scale of the Ph.D. emplyment problem and a partial solution." Science Forum IV (August 1971) 7-8.

1972   Anisef, P. and C. Jansen. "Experiences of those presently in gradu-ate school." vol. VII of York Graduate Study. Toronto: Institute for Behavioural Research, York University, 1972. p. 41.

Council of Ontario Universities, Advisory Committee on Academic Planning and Ontario Council on Graduate Studies. Perspectives and Plans for Graduate Studies. Toronto: the Council.

1. Library Science 1972
2. Education 1973
3. Economics 1974
4. Geography 1973

5. Chemistry 1973
6. Solid Earth Sciences 1973
7. Sociology 1973
8. Anthropology 1974
9. Political Science 1974
10. Physical Education, Kinesiology and Related Areas 1974
11. Engineering 1974

    A. Chemical Engineering
    B. Electrical Engineering
    C. Metallurgical & Materials Engineering
    D. Mechanical Engineering
    E. Industrial Engineering and Systems
    F. Civil Engineering

12. Religious Studies 1974
13. Planning and Environmental Studies 1974
14. Physics and Astronomy 1975
15. History 1975
16. Biophysics 1975
17. Administration, Business and Management Science 1975
18. Fine Arts 1976
19. Mathematical Sciences 1977
20. Psychology 1979

Dodge, D. and D. Stager. "Economic returns to graduate study in science." Can. Jour. Econ. 5 (May 1972) 182-198.

Gurd, F.M. "La formation postscolaire." Union Méd. 101 (Décembre 1972) 2627-2630.

Kreisel, H. "Graduate programs in English in Canadian universities." English Quart. 5 (Spring-Summer 1972) 95-103.

Payton, L.C. Post-doctoral education in the Ontario universities 1969-70. Toronto: Council of Ontario Universities, 1972.

1973 Farine, A. "The output of Canadian universities as measured by graduate degrees." Alta. Jour. Educ. Research. 19 (June 1973) 119-128.

Storr, R.J. The beginning of the future: a historical approach to graduate education in the arts and sciences. New York: McGraw-Hill, 1973. p. 99.

1974 Daine, P., L. Foster and M. Nixon. "Unresolved problems of the graduate student role." McGill Jour. Educ. 9 (Spring 1974) 61-64.

Safarian, A.E. "A perspective on graduate studies in Canada." Jour. Can. Studies 9 (Feb. 1974) 42-52.

1975 Conacher, J.B. "Graduate studies in history in Canada: the growth of doctoral programmes (Presidential address)." Can. Hist. Assoc. Papers (1975) 1-15.

Lefebvre, L. "Doctorats et carrières: essai sur la relation directeur de thèse-étudiant." M.A. thesis, Université de Montréal, 1975.

1976 Preston, M. "Graduate Education." Proc. AUCC. Vol 1 (1976) 23-30. Also J. Smith, 31-36.

1977 Pass, L. and S. Scherer. "Toward more adequate selection criteria: a case study of graduate counselling admissions." Can. Counsellor 13 (April 1977) 127-130.

1978 von Zur-Muehlen, M. "The Ph.D. dilemma in Canada revisited." Can. Jour. Higher Educ. 8, 2 (1978) 49-92.

1979 Nixon, M. and E. Miklos. "Admission practices and placement patterns in educational administration programs." Can. Admin. 18 (Jan. 1979) 6.

1980 Brazeau, I. "L'interdisciplinarité et les études supérieures." Sociologie et Sociétés 12, 2 (1980) 97-106.

Symons, G. "Equality of opportunity in American and Canadian graduate education: a comparison of gender differences." Alta. Jour. Educ. Res. 26 (June 1980) 96-112.

G. ADULT EDUCATION/EDUCATION DES ADULTES

1969 Smyth, F. "The development of the antigonish movement." Convergence 2, 1 (1969) 61-65.

1970 Bélanger, P. et P. Paquet. "Problématique de l'éducation des adultes dans les CEGEP." Prospectives 6 (avril 1970) 104-121.

Cantin, G. "Etude sur le personnel enseignant du service d'éducation des adultes de Montréal." Thèse de maîtrise, Univ. de Montréal, 1970.

Cassirer H.C. "Adult education in the era of modern technology." Convergence 3, 2 (1970) 37-48.

Draper, J. Survey and analysis of adult education and community development certificate, diploma, undergraduate and graduate programs offered by institutions of higher education in Canada." Toronto: Dept. of Adult Education, Ontario Institute for Studies in Education, 1970.

Institut Canadien d'Education des Adultes. Eléments d'une politique
en éducation des adultes. Montréal: L'Institut, 1970. P. 47 (premier partie) et 21 (deuxième).

Kidd, J.R. "Methodology for comparative studies in adult education."
Convergence 3, 2 (1970) 12-25.

Schwartz, B. "Réflexion prospectives sur l'éducation permanente."
Prospectives. 6 (avril 1970) 91-103.

University of Toronto, Presidential Advisory Committee on Extension,
S.J. Colman, Chairman. Report of the Presidential Advisory Committee
on Extension. Toronto: Univ. of Toronto, 1970. P. 62.

1971 Daoust, G. "L'éducation permanente et l'Université de Montréal:
orientation particulière." Univ. Aff./Aff. univ. 12 (nov. 1971) 5-6.

"Education permanente et technologie, le projet multi-média, dossier
spécial." Relations 357 (février 1971) 35-43.

Gendron, L. "Le service de l'extension de l'enseignement de l'Ecole
Polytechnique." Ing. 57 (août 1971) 3-6.

Gill, A. "L'éducation permanente/Continuing education. What is it?
Who is doing what? Where is it going?; a roundup." Univ. Aff./Aff.
univ. 12 (Nov. 1971) 1-3.

Gill, A. "New Brunswick; one university's experience in extending
education." Univ. Aff./Aff. univ. 12 (Nov. 1971) 8.

Kidd, J.R. "Post-secondary tertiary, short cycle and recurrent education." Convergence 4, 3 (1971) 10-16.

McLeish, J.A.B. "New directions in professional education." Orbit 9
(October 1971) 22-24.

O'Connor, R.E. "Adults, education, and the university: more to be
said." Univ. Aff./Aff. univ. 12 (Nov. 1971) ·20.

Shaw, J.A. "What are the tasks of university extension." Univ. Aff./
univ. 12 (Nov. 1971) 6-7.

Simon, P. "L'ingénieur en face de l'éducation permanente." Ing. 57
(août 1971) 13-16.

Touchette, C., J. Lamontagne et S. Henry. L'exercice des fonctions
de l'éducateur d'adultes du Québec: rapport préliminaire. Montréal:
Faculté des Sciences de l'Education, Université de Montréal, 1971.
p. 162 et annexes.

1972   Anisef, P. and C. Jansen. "Atkinson and York Graduates", vol. III of York Graduate Study. Toronto: Institute for Behavioural Research, York University, 1972. p. 41.

Knoll, H. "Adult education with or without universities." Convergence 5, 1 (1972) 71-87.

Sheath, H. "Integrating correspondence study with resident study at the university level." Convergence 5, 2 (1972) 15-20.

Thornron, J.E. ed. "Adult Education in British Columbia." Jour. Educ. 18 (Special Issue, Winter 1972) 1-129.

1973   Bordeleau, J., et G. Gélineau. L'université buissonnière. Montréal: Les Presses de l'Université de Montréal, 1973. p. 156.

Campbell, D. "Taking the tide at the flood; a look at the status of continuing education in Canada." Education Canada 13 (September 1973) 23-27.

"Canadian Reactions to the Faure Report/Réactions canadiennes au rapport Faure." Unesco Occasional Paper (Canadian Commission for Unesco)/Unesco Pages documentaires 12 (December/décembre 1973) 1-8.

Dupré, J.S. et al. Federalism and policy development, the case of adult occupational training in Ontario. Toronto: U. of T. Press, 1973. 264 p.

Gass, J.R. "L'éducation récurrente: une solution à la crise de l'enseignement." Commerce 75 (novembre 1973) 50-56.

Gill, A. "Canadian reactions to Faure report." Univ. Aff./Aff. univ. 14 (July 1973) 14.

Grégoire, R. "Un pas nouveau dans le développement de la formation à distance." Prospectives 9 (fév. 1973) 5-7.

Keane, P. "Joseph Howe and adult education." Acadiensis 3 (Autumn 1973) 35-50.

Murphy, P.J. "Factors affecting an adult's attendance at a community college in the evening." Man. Jour. Educ. 8 (June 1973) 66-72.

Touchette, C.R. "Evolution des objectifs et des programmes en éducation des adultes à l'Université de Montréal (1876-1950)". Ph.D. thesis, Univ. of Toronto, 1973.

Vézina, C. "Plaidoyer pour une coordination de l'éducation des adultes." Prospectives 9 (février 1973) 24-30.

1974 Barbeau, M. "Orientation des universités canadiennes en matière d'éducation permanente." Revue AUPELF 12 (printemps 1974) 42-50.

Belanger, P. "Recherche en éducation des adultes à Quebec." Convergence 7, 2 (1974) 39-46.

Daoust, G. "L'école québécoise va-t-elle récupérer le projet de l'éducation permanente?" Prospectives 10 (oct. 1974) 234-239.

Daoust, G. et P. Bélanger, L'université dans une société éducative, de l'éducation des adultes à l'éducation permanente. Montréal: Les Presses de l'Université de Montréal, 1974. 240 p.

De Marco, F.A. Report on extension and continuing education. Windsor: University of Windsor, 1974. 154 p.

Dion, L. et G. Daoust. "L'université dans une société éducative, Colloque de l'A.C.D.T.A.U.L.F." Revue AUPELF 12 (printemps 1974) 79-84.

"Fer de lance: un projet conjoint de l'Université de Sherbrooke, du Collège de Sherbrooke et de la C.S.R. de l'Estrie." Educ. Q. (janvier 1974) 15-16.

Ferland, M. "L'Education des adultes dans les universités du Canada: bilan et perspectives." Can. Jour. Cont. Educ. 1 (dec. 1974) 12-23.

Fortin, A. "Education des adultes? Education permanente? Bilan d'une expérience à l'Université de Montréal." Revue AUPELF 12 (printemps 1974) 58-67.

Fossien, R.F. "Moses M. Coady and adult education in the Maritimes." M.A. thesis, Univ. of Alberta, 1974.

Gleason, M. "Harbor Grace, Cow Head, Nain - the extension service reaches Ont." Univ. Aff./Aff. univ. 15 (May 1974) 2-4.

"La formation continue dans les universités membres de l'AUPELF." Revue AUPELF 12 (printemps 1974) 97-142.

Ozman, K. "The case for senior students." Univ. Aff./Aff. univ. 15 (March 1974) 6.

Pépin, M. "La formation permanente: position de la C.S.N." Revue AUPELF 12 (printemps 1974) 187-189.

Royce, J. "Foundation for continuing education for women." Queen's Univ. Alumni Rev. 48 (May-June 1974) 6-7, 19.

Selman, G. "Concerning the history of adult education in Canada." Can. Jour. Univ. Cont. Educ. 1 (Dec. 1974) 24-35.

"Université de Montréal: objectifs et fonctionnement du service d'éducation permanente." Revue AUPELF 12 (printemps 1974) 149-53.

Waldron, M. "Continuing education in Ontario universities: the non-credit sector." Can. Jour. Univ. Cont. Educ. 1 (Dec. 1974) 45-76.

Wetmore, W. and G. Dickinson. "An economic approach to the education of general interest adult education." Can. Jour. Univ. Cont. Educ. 1 (Dec. 1974) 1-11.

Whale, W. "The university and lifelong learning." Can. Jour. Univ. Cont. Educ. 1 (Dec. 1974) 36-44.

1975 Faris, R. The passionate educators: voluntary associations and the struggle for control of adult educational broadcasting in Canada, 1919-1952. Toronto: Peter Martin, 1975. 202 p.

Flaherty, M.J. "Continuing education should be voluntary." Can. Nurse 71 (July 1975) 19-21.

Keane, P. "A study on early problems and policies in adult education: the Halifax Mechanics' Institute." Histoire Sociale/Social History 8 (November 1975) 255-274.

Polvin, D. "An analysis of the androggical approach to the didactics of distance education." Can. Jour. Univ. Cont. Educ. 2 (May 1975) 27-36.

Selman, G. "Canadian adult educators on Canadian adult education." Can. Jour. Univ. Cont. Educ. 2 (May 1975) 5-15.

Skelhorne, J.M. The adult learner in the university: does anyone care? Toronto: Ontario Institute of Studies in Education, 1975.

1976 Barbeau, M. "Regard sur l'évolution de l'éducation permanente dans les universités du Québec." Can. Jour. Higher Educ. 6, 3 (1976) 73-77.

Bendor, S. "Continuing education." AUCC Proc. Vol. I (Nov. 1976) 61-66.

Blaney, J. and N. Gamm. "Faculty perceptions of credit and non-credit continuing education programs." Can. Jour. Univ. Cont. Educ. 3 (Autumn 1976) 43-56.

Carrier, H. "Une ère nouvelle de l'éducation: la formation permanente." Relations 36 (Sept. 1976) 240-246.

Collège du Vieux-Montréal, Direction des services pédagogiques. "L'education permanente: un projet pour un cégep." Cégepropos 41 (avril 1976) 29-43.

Cook, G.L. "Alfred Fitzpatrick and the Foundation of Frontier College (1899-1922). Canada 3 (June 1976) 15-39.

Khabd, M.B.M. Le troisième âge à l'université. Digest social 28 (automne 1976) 52-55, 70-71.

Roberts, H. "Perceptions of the scope of the extension function in a Canadian university." Can. Jour. Univ. Cont. Educ. 3 (Autumn 1976) 28-41.

Ruest, M. "Les conditions d'une éducation permanente." Relations 36 (Sept. 1976) 246-248.

Scissons, E. "Contemporary continuing education research in perspective." Can. Jour. Univ. Cont. Educ. 3 (Autumn 1976) 14-27.

1977 Association of Universities and Colleges of Canada. The role of the university with respect to enrolments and career opportunities, admission policies, continuing education and community colleges. Prepared by the Task Force for the study. Ottawa, 1977. 110 p. (AUCC policy studies, Study no. 1)

Campbell, D.D. Adult education as a field of study and practice: strategies for development. Vancouver: Centre for Continuing Education, Univ. of British Columbia, 1977. 230 p.

Campbell, D. "The Symons Report: implications for university continuing education." Can. Jour. Univ. Cont. Educ. 4 (Summer 1977) 6-10.

Desautels, J. "Les continuing education units (CEU): situation au Canada et perspectives." Can. Jour. Univ. Cont. Educ. 4 (Summer 1977) 11-15.

Murray, J. "Research into university continuing education in Canada: a viewpoint." Can. Jour. Univ. Cont. Educ. 4 (Summer 1977) 16-20.

Orton, L. "Completion and nonstart rates in correspondence education." Can. Jour. Univ. Cont. Educ. 4 (Summer 1977) 21-26.

Sacouman, R. "Underdevelopment and the structural origins of Antigonish Movement Co-operatives in Eastern Nova Scotia." Acadiensis 7 (Autumn 1977) 66-85.

1978 British Columbia, Ministry of Education Distance Education Planning Group. Report on a delivery system for distance education in British Columbia. Vancouver: the Ministry, 1978. 123 p.

Farrel, G. "Off-campus instructions through distance education methods." Can. Jour. Univ. Cont. Educ. 4 (Winter 1978) 17-21.

Keane, P. "Library policies and early Canadian adult education." Humanities Assoc. Rev. 29 (Winter 1978) 1-20.

Kidd, J.R. and G. Selman ed. Coming of age: Canadian adult education in the 1980's. Toronto: Can. Adult. Educ. Assoc., 1978. 410 p.

Marcotte, G. "The opinion leader's role in continuing education communication systems." Can. Jour. Univ. Cont. Educ. 5 (Summer 1978) 30-34.

Pike, R. "Declining teacher demand for part-time undergraduate studies in Ontario." Can. Jour. Univ. Cont. Educ. 4 (Winter 1978) 28-31.

Riverin-Simard, D. "L'evaluation educationnelle à la Télé-Université." Rev. Can. ens. sup. 8, 2 (1978) 9-26.

Shute, J. "Toward a world view of continuing education." Can. Jour. Univ. Cont. Educ. 5 (Summer 1978) 19-22.

Timmons, H.P. "Adult education services: 1945-76." Jour. Educ. (N.S.) Sixth series. 6, 1 (1978-1979) 12-22.

Verner, C. "Some reflections on graduate professional education in adult education." Can. Jour. Higher Educ. 8, 2 (1978) 39-48.

1979 Daniel, J.S. and W.A.S. Smiths opening open universities: the Canadian experience." Can. Jour. Higher Educ. 9, 2 (1979) 18-34.

Gooler, D.D." "Evaluating distance education programs." Can. Jour. Univ. Cont. Educ. 6 (Summer 1979) 43-55.

Hoegg, J.L. "Marketing: an integral component of program planning." Can. Jour. Univ. Cont. Educ. 5 (Winter 1979) 14-19.

Holmberg, B. "Practice in distance education: a conceptual framework." Can. Jour. Univ. Cont. Educ. 6 (Summer 1979) 18-30.

Jones, D.R. and N.S. Ernst. "Needs assessment for continuing professional education." Can. Jour. Univ. Cont. Educ. 5 (Winter 1979) 27-29.

Lefebvre, J. "L'université en queste." Education Quebec 9, 4 (1979) 4.

Leslie, J.D. "The University of Waterloo model for distance education." Can. Jour. Univ. Cont. Educ. 6 (Summer 1979) 33-41.

Pederson, K.G. and T. Fleming. "Continuing education divisions and the crisis of success." Can. Jour. Univ. Cont. Educ. 5 (Winter 1979) 5-11.

Riverin-Simard, D. et J.-M. Dion. "Vers un modèle du développement vocationnel de l'adult." Rev. Can. d'Ens. Sup. 9, 3 (1979) 1-18.

Wedemeyer, C.A. "Criteria for constructing a distance education system." Can. Jour. Univ. Cont. Educ. 6 (Summer 1979) 9-15.

1980 Baum, G. "The relevance of the Antigonish Movement today." Jour. Can. Studies. 15 (Spring 1980) 110-17.

Blikinsop, P. "A history of adult education on the prairies, learning to live in agrarian Saskatchewan 1870-1944." Ph.D. thesis, Univ. of Toronto 1980.

Boshur, R. "Theories and models in adult education: a plea for pure research." Can. Jour. Univ. Cont. Educ. 7 (Summer 1980) 12-18.

Bowigeault, G. "L'éducation permanente, l'enseignement et la recherche: les universités canadiennes du langue française." Revue de l'AUPELF. 18 (juin 1980) 95-103.

Cassie, J.R.B. and P. Noble. "A regional perspective on continuing education, the advantages of getting together." Education Canada 20 (Summer 1980) 35-39.

Duguid, S. "Post-secondary education in a prison: theory and praxis." Can. Jour. Higher Educ. X 1 (1980) 29-35.

Leclerc, G. "Les défis de l'éducation permanente pour les universiés du Québec des années 80." revue de l'AUPELF.

Muir, W.R. "The usefulness of open university materials in North American continuing education." Can. Jour. Univ. Cont. Educ. 6 (Winter 1980) 32-35.

Pineau, G. "L'éducation permanente et l'institutionnalisation universitaire: l'example du Québec." Revue de l'AUPELF 18 (juin 1980) 73-82.

1981 Hall, J.W. and E.G. Palola. "Curricula for adult learners." Can. Jour. Univ. Cont. Educ. 7 (Winter 1981) 36-40.

Heap, R. "Un chapitre dans l'histoire de l'éducation des adultes au Québec: les écoles du soir, 1889-1892." Rev. Hist. 34, 4 (1981) 597-625.

Heinlein, R.L. and E.S. Byers. "Assessment of support service needs of adult students." Can. Jour. Univ. Cont. Educ. 7 (Winter 1981) 25-30.

Pedersen, K.G. and T. Fleming. "The academic organization and continuing education." Can. Jour. Univ. Cont. Educ. 7 (Winter 1981) 4-10.

Taylor, W.H. "Computers in continuing education administration." Can. Jour. Univ. Cont. Educ. 7 (Winter 1981) 31-40.

H. ADMISSIONS: INSCRIPTION

1970 Joly, J.-M. "Le service d'admission au collège et à l'université (SACU)." Prospectives 6 (juin 1970) 150-154.

1971 The School Guidance Worker 26, 4 (Mar./Apr. 1971). Whole issue devoted to "Views of SACU", 50 p.

Sterne, H.W. "Selection for admission." Forum 2 (July 1971) 17-27.

1972 Black, D.B. "Admissions and accountability." Forum 2 (May 1972) 5-14.

Pettipiere, H.W. "The Quebec application system." Forum 3 (November 1972) 21-24.

1973 Boronkay, F. and F. Bradley. "Proportion analysis - an alternative approach to university admission." Forum 3 (May 1973) 15-20.

Nyberg, V.R. and R.G. Baril. "SACU test variables as predictors of university GPA." Alta. Jour. Educ. Research 4 (December 1973) 303-308.

Wisenthal, M. "Enrolment fluctuations and patterns for the future." AUCC Proc. (1973) 114-121.

1974 Campbell, D. "Public suspects quotas are set." Univ. Aff./Aff. univ. 15 (December 1974) 8-9.

Canadian Education Association. Requirements for secondary school leaving certificates and for admission to university and teacher training. Toronto: C.E.A., 1974. p. 32.

Cooke, R.H. and D.C. Harper. "College-university transfer: evolving a province-wide solution." CAUT Bull. ACPU. 23 (December 1974) 21-22.

Jardine, D.K. "Transferability: a matter of integrity." CAUT Bull. ACPU 23 (December 1974) 15-16.

1976 Canada, Department of the Secretary of State, Education Support Branch. Some characteristics of post-secondary students in Canada. Ottawa: The Dept., 1976. 179 p.

1977 The Association of Universities and Colleges of Canada. The role of the university with respect to enrolments and career opportunities, admission policies, continuing education and community colleges. Prepared by the Task Force for the study. Ottawa, Ont., 1977. 110 p. (AUCC policy studies, Study no. 1)

Woodcock, L. "Restrictions on visa students are increasing." Univ. Aff./Aff. univ. 18 (January 1977) 2-5.

1978 Dennison, J.D. "University transfer program in the community college." Can. Jour. Higher Educ. 8, 2 (1978) 27-38.

1979 Shepherd, R.M.H. "Testing and university admission: proposals." The School Guidance Worker 34, 4 (1979) 14-17.

1980 Ayers, J. "The relationship of first year university grades of non-high school graduates with the tests of general educational development." Can. Jour. Higher Educ. 10, 1 (1980) 75-82.

I. EVALUATION AND GRADING/EVALUATION ET CLASSEMENT

1970 Gingras, Paul-Emile. Vers l'excellence par l'accréditation. Centre d'animation, de développement et de recherche en éducation, juillet, 1970. P. 88.

Hone, A. et al. "Une technique réaliste de l'évaluation de l'étudiant applicable aux grands groupes." Prospectives 6 (avril 1970) 122-125.

1971 Fleming, W.G. "Evaluation of student success", in Post-Secondary and Adult Education. Vol. IV of Ontario's Educative Society. Toronto: U. of T. Press, 1971. p. 319-334.

1972 Inhaber, H. "Do we really need all these degrees?" Univ. Aff./Aff. univ. 13 (Sept. 1972) 9.

1973 Farine, A. "La responsabilité comptable en matière d'éducation." Act. écon. 1 (janv. mars 1973) 134-139.

Guérin, G.C. "Elaboration d'un modèle de prévision des effectifs étudiants au niveau universitaire." Ph.D. thesis, Université de Montréal, 1973.

1975 Scallon, Gérard. "L'évaluation des étudiants et les principales conceptions de la mesure et de l'evaluation." Prospectives 10 (Oct. 1974) 263-269.

Nadeau, G. "Nouveau sytème d'évaluation de l'enseignement par objectifs." Univ. Aff./Aff. univ. 15 (July 1974) 6-8. See also M. Gleason, "How Moncton's New Evaluating System is Waiting", 16 (Jan. 1975) 5.

1976 Despres-Pominville, M. "La problématique de l'évaluation." Bulletin d'administration scolaire 4 (2:1976) 8-14.

Leibu, Y. "La qualité de l'enseignement universitaire: essai d'approche systématique." Can. Jour. Higher Educ./Rev. Can. d'Ens. Sup. 6 (3:1976) 1-11.

Ligonde, P. "Polyvalence et interdisciplinarité: pour une formation générale universitaire en sciences de l'homme. L'Orientation professionnelle/Vocational Guidance 12 (été 1976) 77-92.

Marino, C. "Flexible learning." Improving College and University Teaching 24 (Summer 1976) 160-161.

1977 "Course evaluations: effective student representation demands a knowledge of classroom atmosphere and attitudes." The Student Advocate 1 (January 1977) 4-5.

1979 Canadian Journal of Higher Education 9 (1:1979) devoted entirely to articles on the evaluation of instruction in Canadian universities.

G.L. Geis. "Evaluation: purposes and levels." 1-4.
J. Parent. "Le rôle d'un service d'une pédagogie universitaire dans l'evaluation des cours." 5-9.
P.A. Cranton. "The McGill Faculty and course evaluation system." 11-16.
C. Pascal & E. Davey. "The politics of evaluating teaching." 17-21.
W.H. Dowdeswell & H.M. Good. "Course evaluation for academic management: a case study in biology." 23-44.
C. Fureday. "Improving lectures in higher education." 45-54.

Wyman, B., and G.De Metra. "Who controls program quality? College Canada 5 (Oct. 80) 4-6.

J. INSTRUCTIONAL AIDS/AIDES DIDACTIQUES

1969 Cloutier, J. "L'audio-visuel au service de l'enseignement universitaire." Rev. l'AUPELF. 7 (printemps 1969) 25-29.

1970 Abols, G. "OCUFA television study." OCUFA Newsletter. 4 (Sept. 1970) 17-18.

Trotter, B. Television and technology in university teaching. Toronto: Committee of Presidents of Universities of Ontario, 1970. p. 84.

"OCUFA recommended ETV contract and guidelines." OCUFA Newsletter. Special issue. (Nov. 1970) 7 p.

Shaw, J.A. "So you really want to know what's new in AV systems?" Can. Univ. and Coll. 5 (Aug. 1970) 22 and 27.

Shaw, J.A. "The only innovation is how we use our resources to improve teaching." Can. Univ. and Coll. 5 (Oct. 1970) p. 23.

Young, W. "Summary of the commission on new learning media." AUCC Proc. (1970) 49-50.

1971 Herald, E.S. "Student attitudes toward the use of televised lectures in introductory sociology at the University of Manitoba." Man. Jour. Educ. 6 (June 1971) 39-47.

Judge, D. "This report challenges conventional views of AV in education." Can. Univ. and Coll. (March-April 1971) 34-35.

Shaw, J.A. "Putting more control in the hands of the AV users." Can. Univ. and Coll. 6 (July-August 1971) 38.

"Tuning in to a new AV link between student and teacher." Can. Univ. and Coll. 6 (March-April 1971) 31-33.

1972 Doyle, W.G. "Multimediated instruction in the health sciences." Jour. Educ. (N.S.) 22 (Summer 1972) 36-43.

Gordon, D.R. "Exploring the new literacy." Univ. Aff./Aff. univ. 13 (Sept. 1972) 2-3.

McLean, N. The utilization of electric technology in post-secondary education in Britain and West Germany. Toronto: Queen's Printer, 1972. p. 193.

Wakarchuk, A. "CAI: an innovation slow to diffuse." Man. Jour. Educ. 7 (June 1972) 55-64.

Brown, M.P. "Ontario university computers to be linked in network." Canadian Datasystems 4 (March 1972) 48-50.

Canada, Statistics Canada, Education Division. Instructional media in universities of the Atlantic provinces 1972. Ottawa: Information Canada, 1973. p. 37.

1973 Gillet, M. "Hard, soft, or medium." McGill Jour. Educ. 8 (Fall 1973) 129-144.

Knowles, A. "The fourth revolution - a challenge for Canadian universities." Univ. Aff./Aff. univ. 14 (Feb. 1973) 6.

Moore, G.A.B. "Education communications and technology in the teaching-learning enterprise." National Research Council of Canada. Associate Committee on Instructional Technology. Newsletter/Conseil national de recherches du Canada. Comité associé de technologie pédagogique. Bulletin. 2 (April 1973) 11-13.

Saettler, P. "Theory and research in instructional technology." McGill Jour. Educ. 8 (fall 1973) 157-64.

Prémont, P. "Une analyse de l'attitude des étudiants de l'Université Laval à l'égard de l'enseignement par la télévision en circuit fermé." M.A. thesis, Université Laval, 1973.

Shore, B. "Computer, teacher and learner: some technological implications." McGill Jour. Educ. 28 (Fall 1973) 150-156.

1974 Kalman, C.S. and D. Kaufman. "Language Loyola CAI 'T' (Language pour enseignement automatisé)." Con. du techn. péd. Bull. 3 (mars 1974) 29-30.

Kalman, C.S. and D. Kaufman. "Loyola CAI Language." Instr. Techn. Newsletter 3 (Mar. 1974) 25-28.

Labrousse, F. "L'enseignement assisté par ordinateur au service de l'informatique du Ministère de l'éducation du Québec." Techn. péd. Bulletin 3 (mars 1974) 14-17.

Labrousse, F. "Computer-assisted instruction in the data-processing service of the Quebec Department of Education 'T'." Instr. Techn. Newsletter. 3 (Mar. 1974) 17-20.

Whitworth, F.E. "Intégration des nouveaux moyens de communication dans les processus d'enseignement 'T'." Instr. Technol. Newsletter 3 (mars 1974) 22-25.

Whitworth, F.E. "On Integrating the Newer Media Into Learning Situations." Instr. Technol. Newsletter 3 (March 1974) 20-22.

Cloutier, J. "L'audio-visuel à l'Université." Prospectives 2 (1:1975) 24-39.

K. CANADIAN STUDIES/ETUDES CANADIENNES

1970 "Canada Council launches new program of Canadian studies." Univ. Aff./Aff. univ. 11 (Dec. 1970) 3.

Lentner, H.H. "Canada and the U.S. there's a profound difference." Can. Jour. Hist. & Soc. Sci. 6 (November-December 1970) 9-19.

Michaud, Lucien. "Summary of the commission on Canadain studies in Canadian universities." AUCC Proc. (1970) 54-55.

Smith, D.B. "The Canada Studies Foundation." Can. Jour. Hist. & Soc. Sci. 6 (November-December 1970) 30-33.

1971 Kidd, J.R. "Canadian studies at the Ontario Institute for Studies in Education." ACSUS Newsletter [U.S.] 1 (Autumn 1971) 36-41.

Mathews, R.D. "U.S. expansionism, Canadian literature, and Canadian intellectual history." Jour. Can. Studies 6 (November 1971) 30-42.

Mulcahy, D.G. "An emerging curriculum force in Canadian studies." Jour. Can. Hist. & Soc. Sci. 7 (Fall 1971) 9-18.

1972 Clarkson, S. "Lament for a non-subject: reflections on teaching Canadian-American relations." International Jour. 27 (Spring 1972) 265-275.

Miles, E.J. "Canadian studies in the United States: challenge and frustrations." International Jour. 27 (Spring 1972) 250-264.

Slater, D.W. "Canadian Studies and Canadian faculty at Canadian universities." Univ. Aff./Aff. univ. 13 (February 1972) 6-7.

Tucker, A. "Canadian studies - problem and prospects." Can. Forum 51 (October/November 1972) 50-51.

1973 Dyck, Rand. "The Canadian North/Canadian studies at Laurentian University." Laurentian Univ. Review 5 (Sept. 1973) 3-9.

Gutteridge, D. "Teaching the Canadian Mythology: a poet's view." Jour. Can. Studies 8 (February 1973) 28-32.

Page, J.E. Canadian studies in community colleges. Toronto: O.I.S.E., n.d. (1973) p. 175.

Waterman, A.M.C. "The Canadian identity and Canadian universities." Univ. Aff./Aff. univ. (Feb. 1973) 2-3.

1975 Symons, T.H.B. Se connaître; le rapport de la Commission sur les Études Canadiennes. vol. 1 et 2. Ottawa: AUCC, 1975. 366 p. Publié aussi en anglais sous le litre To know ourselves.

1976 Drummond, I. "Canadian studies at Edinburgh: model or mistake?" CAUT BULL. ACPU 24 (September 1976) 9.

"Reflections on the Symons' Report." Jour. Can. Studies 11 (November 1976) 50-68.

Woodcock, L. "Conference on publishing examines lack of popular culture." Univ. Aff./Aff. univ. 17 (December 1976) 12.

Wojciechowski, J. "Universities and Canadian culture." Rev. Univ. Ottawa 46 (avril-juin 1976) 169-179.

1977 Applebaum, L. "The reasonable balance: the arts and Canadian studies." Jour. Can. Studies 12 (Summer 1977) 100-102.

Gibson, J.A. "Canadian studies in Edinburgh - on the way to projecting Canada abroad." CAUT Bul. ACPU 26 (Sept. 1977) 4.

"U. of T. task force reports on state of activities related to Canada." Univ. Aff./Aff. univ. 18 (Dec. 1977) 12.

1980 Cameron, B. "Problems in the study of Canadian literature." English Q. 12 (Spring 1980) 59-65.

4. Research and Scholarship/Recherche

A. GENERAL/GÉNÉRALITÉS

1968 Medical Research Council of Canada. Canadian medical research survey and outlook: a report. Ottawa: Queen's Printer, 1968. 416 p.

1970 Michaud, L. "Summary of the commission on possibilities of Canada-wide rationalization in major university research areas." AUCC Proc. (1970) 62-63.

Whalley, G. "Scholarship, research and the pursuit of truth." Trans. RSC. 1970, 299-322.

1971 Gill, A. "Lamontagne committee is critical of university research effort." Univ. Aff./Aff. univ. 12 (Mar. 1971) 20-21.

Hettich, W. "Federal science policy and social science research in Canadian universities." Can. Public Admin. 14 (Spring 1971) 112-28.

1972 Anderson, D.O. "The double standard of R and D." Can. Jour. Public Health 63 (Jul.-Aug. 1972) 317-326.

Armstrong, R.P. "Revising the dissertation and publishing the book." Schol. Pub. 4 (Oct. 1972) 41-50.

Bélanger, P.W., Rocher, G. et l'équipe ASOPE. "Une recherche qui vient à point." Educ. et Soc. 3 (Déc. 1972) 12-13.

Bonneau, L.-P. "La rationalisation de la recherche." AUCC Proc. (1972) 73-76.

Corry, J.A. "Rationalization of university research." AUCC Proc. (1972) 77-82.

Charles, B. "Au risque d'enfoncer quelques portes ouvertes: recherches, université et Tiers Monde." Maintenant 116 (mai 1972) 22-25.

Deutsch, J.J. "University attitudes: where does research stand now?" Medical Research Council. Newsletter 2 (Apr. 1972) 1-4.

"Is this what you are looking for ???" A review of the Bonneau-Corry report. OCUFA Newsletter 6 (Dec. 1972) 1-2+

Letourneux, J. "Peut-on planifier la recherche fondamentale à l'université?" Maintenant 115 (avril 1972) 33-34.

Monette, J. "Une expérience multidisciplinaire." Educ. et Soc. 3 (Sept. 1972) 14-15.

"Quest for the Optimum/Poursuivre l'optimum." [interview] Univ. Aff./ Aff. univ. 13 (Nov. 1972) 2-7.

Rocher, G. "La recherche, l'enseignement, les études supérieures et les humanités." AUCC Proc. (1972) 104-113.

Smith, A.H. The production of scientific knowledge in Ontario's universities: an overview of problems. Toronto: Queen's Printer, 1972. Pp. 173.

Spinks, J.W.T. "Stringing educational pearls." AUCC Proc. (1972) 82-91.

Uffen, R.J. "The political science of research policy." AUCC Proc. (1972) 91-104.

Wassef, W.Y. "University research: growth maintenance for attrition?" Univ. Windsor Rev. 7 (Spring 1972) 21-33.

Wiseman, I. "Silent university support aids our war machine." This Magazine 6, 1 (1972) 147-153.

1973 Baby, A. "Une meilleure rationalisation peut tuer la spontanéité." Univ. Aff./Aff. univ. 14 (sept. 1973) 1-2.

Couillard, P. "Le rapport Bonneau-Corry: équilibre entre le laisser-aller et le dirigisme trop rigide." CAUT Bull. ACPU. 21 (avril 1973) 6-7.

Jackson, R.W. "A new model of the university: not one thing, but many." Science Forum 6 (Aug. 1973) 9-13.

Minassian, C. "Problème des subventions de recherche: une expérience canadienne." Revue AUPELF 11 (printemps-automne 1973) 90-92.

Polanyi, J.C. "Rationalizing research in the universities: the Bonneau-Corry report." CAUT Bull. ACPU. 21 (Apr. 1973) 10-13.

"Quest for the optimum - a brief commentary/Poursuivre l'optimum - court commentaire." Medical Research Council. Newsletter 3 (Jan. 1973) 6-7.

"Reactions to the Bonneau-Corry report." Univ. Aff./Aff. univ. 14 (Apr. 1973) 6-7.

Sheehan, B.S. "Federal funds and university research." Can. Jour. Pol. Sci. 6 (Mar. 1973) 121-130.

Sheehan, B.S. "Simulation modelling in institutional research." McGill Jour. Educ. 8 (Fall 1973) 192-97.

"Survey of Canadian university practice with respect to faculty offprints and university publications." CACUL Newsletter 5 (Sept. 1973) 7-11.

Wyman, M. "Rationalization of research: will it become irrational?" CAUT Bull. ACPU 21 (Apr. 1973) 8-9.

Yates, K. "Research planning by bureacracies: lessons from others." Science Forum 6 (Feb. 1973) 6-9.

1974 Gilson, J.C. "Canadian Association of University Research Administrators." AUCC Proc. (Nov. 1974) 28-31.

1976 Connell, G.E. "The nature and level of university research." AUCC Proc. 2 (Nov. 1976) 69-73.

Lemieux, R.M. Doctoral fellows - what happens? Ottawa: Canada Council, 1976. 83 p.

1977 Clark, T.C. "The future of research funding." Can. Research 10 (Jul./Aug. 1977) 10-13.

Katz, B. "Copyright or copy wrong?" CAUT Bul. ACPU 25, 6 91977) 15-16.

Priestley, F.E.L. and H. Kerpneck. "Publication and academic reward." Scholarly Publishing 8 (Apr. 1977) 233-238.

Savage, D.C. "Who owns your book, film or videotape? CAUT and copyright." CAUT Bul. ACPU 25, (1977) 13-15.

Thiir, L.M. "Financement de la recherche universitaire." Rev. Can. d'Ens. Sup. 7, 1 (1977) 43-46.

What Canada is doing for Third World research. Science Forum 10, 4 (1977) 18-20.

Wynne-Edwards, H.R. "Towards a Canadian Association for Science: the evolving role of SCITEC." Canadian Research 10 (Jul./Aug. 1977) 7-8.

1978 Association of Universities and Colleges of Canada. Copyright and patents in Canadian universities. Compiled by Beverlee Stevenson. Ottawa: AUCC, 1978. 1 vol. (looseleaf)

Buchanan, J. "Research and development in Canada." Proc. R.S.C. (1978) 337-341.

Ostry, B. The cultural connection. Toronto: McClelland & Stewart, 1978. 192 p.

1979 Michaud, D. Council of University Presidents Conference on excellence, June 6, 1979: some references. Ottawa: AUCC, 1979. 43p.

Research and Development/La recherche et le developpement: papers presented at a meeting of the Council of University Presidents, 14 March 1979. Ottawa: Association of Universities and Colleges of Canada, 1979. 45p.

Rushton, J.P. and S. Meltzer. "Research productivity, university revenue, and scholarly impact of 31 Canadian universities." Can. Jour. Higher Educ. 9, 3 (1979) 74-81.

The pursuit of excellence in teaching and research and the maintenance and improvement of the quality of professorial staff in the
future/La poursuite de l'excellence dans l'enseignement et dans la
recherche et le maintien et l'amelioration de la qualité du corps
professoral dans l'avenir; papers presented at a meeting of the
Council of University Presidents at the Université de Sherbrooke, 6
June, 1979. Ottawa: AUCC, 1980. 78p.

Research and development/La recherche et le developpement; papers
presented at a meeting of the Council of University Presidents,
Skyline Hotel, Ottawa, 14 March, 1979. Ottawa: AUCC, 1980. 45p.

Wolfe, S. "The nature of scientific research." Queen's Quart. 86
(Summer 1979) 195-214.

B. HISTORICAL DEVELOPMENT/DÉVELOPPEMENT HISTORIQUE

1958 Goodspeed, D.J. A history of the Defence Research Board of Canada.
Ottawa: Queen's Printer, 1958. 259 p.

1965 Eggleston, W. Canada's nuclear story. Toronto: Clarke Irwin, 1965.
368 p.

1966 Thomson, D.W. Men and meridians: the history of surveying and map-
ping in Canada. Ottawa: Queen's Printer, 1966, 1967. 2 vols.

1975 Zaslow, M. Reading the rocks: the story of the Geological Survey of
Canada 1842-1972. Toronto: Macmillan, 1975. 599 p.

1977 Johnstone, K. The aquatic explorers: a history of the Fisheries
Research Board of Canada. Toronto: Univ. of Toronto Press, 1977.
342 p.

1978 Eggleston, W. National research in Canada: the N.R.C. - 1916-1966.
Toronto: Clarke Irwin, 1978. 470 p.

C. IN THE SCIENCES/SCIENCES

1970 Brochu, M. "Le 4e congrès international de la Fondation française
d'Etudes nordiques." Act. Econ. 45 (jan.-mars 1970) 803-818.

1971 Caron, F. "Troisième conférence nordique canadienne, Poste-de-la-
Baleine, 26-29 mai." Cah. Géog. 15 (avril 1971) 137-138.

1972 Babbitt, J.D. "The Senators and scientific information." Can. R.
and D. 5 (Jul./Aug. 1972) 37-8.

Betts, D.D. et al. "Research in physics at the University of Alberta." Physics in Canada. 28 (Mar. 1972) 30-33.

Hamelin, L.-E. "Le Centre d'études nordiques de l'Université Laval." Univ. Aff./Aff. univ. 13 (Jun.-Jul. 1972) 10.

Hartle, D.G. "Medical research viewed as a public investment." Excerpts from an Address to the Conference of MRC Scholars. Medical Research Council. Newsletter. 2 (Jan. 1972) 5-8.

Smith, A.H. The production of scientific knowledge in Ontario's universities: an overview of problems. Toronto: Queen's Printer, 1972. 173 p.

Towell, M.E. "What does society want of us? A summation of the Conference of MRC Scholars." Medical Research Council. Newsletter 2 (Jan. 1972) 2-4.

Tremblay, G.Y. "Le scientifique exige..." Conseil de recherches médicales. Actualités. 2 (Jan. 1972) 8-10.

1973   Babbitt, J.D. "Tunnelled views? The rise of the dilettante science advisor." Can. R. and D. 6 (May/June 1973) 32.

Garigue, P. "La politique scientifique: nécessité practicologie des sciences." Science Forum 6 (avril 1973) 22-24.

Kirkaldy, J.S. "A science policy for Canada?" OCUFA Newsletter 7 (Dec. 1973) 3.

"NRC grants and scholarship - a link between university and industry/ Les subventions et les bourses du CNRC, lien entre les universités et l'industrie." Science Dimension 5 (Oct. 1973) 16-23.

Paquet, J.-G. "Nos universités doivent planifier la recherche en génie." Science Forum 6 (août 1973) 26-8.

"Quebec universities express concern about research institute (INRS)." Univ. Aff./Aff. univ. 14 (Apr. 1973) 9.

Schroeder-Gudehus, B. "Foreign degrees and autonomy in science: what is the relationship?" Science Forum 6 (Aug. 1973) 14-7.

1974   Baroux, J. "SITEST pour sauver le français scientifique." Univ. Aff./Aff. univ. 15 (fév. 1974) 2, 3.

Carruthers, J. "The first three years of the science ministry: what has been achieved?" Science Forum 7 (Oct. 74) 8-11.

Douglas, V.I. "SCITEC: what has been done in its first four years?" Science Forum 7 (Apr. 1974) 32-35.

Wilson, A.H. "Science policies, laws and regulations." Can. Research 7 (Jan.-Feb. 1974) 27-31.

1976 MacRae, D. and H. Hogg. "The Canadian telescope in Chile." Physics in Canada 32 (April 1976) 23-31.

1977 Clark, T.C. "The future of research funding." Canadian Research 10 (Jul./Aug. 1977) 10-13.

Locke, J.L. "Report on construction of the Canada-France-Hawaii telescope." Jour. Royal Astronomical Soc. Canada 71 (Feb. 1977) 9-20.

Suzuki, D.T. "Jobless Ph.D's, the public, and the media." Science Forum 10 (June 1977) 11.

1978 Goetze-Martin, L. "Developing models of predictability for the environment: Montreal fish toxicology lab is in the forefront." Can. Research 11 (May 1978) 17-20.

Kucharczyk, J. "Tell the government how much your 1978 test-tube really costs." CAUT Bull. ACPU. 25 (Feb. 1978) 6, 19.

McFetridge, D.G. "On the economics of science policy." Canadian Research 11 (Jan.-Feb. 1978) 14-16.

Shore, V. "Scientists and humane societies work together." Univ. Aff./ Aff. univ. 19 (Feb. 1978) 5-6.

1979 "The Atlantic Regional Laboratory - a quarter century of research." Science Dimension 9, 5 (1979) 12-19.

Gordon, J.K. ed. Canada's role in science and technology for development: proceedings of a symposium held at the Ontario Science Centre, Toronto 10-13 May, 1979. Ottawa: International Development Research Centre, 1979. 136 p.

Gridgeman, N.T. Biological science at the National Research Council of Canada: the early years to 1952. Waterloo: Waterloo, Wilfrid Laurier Univ. Press, 1979. 153 p.

Hertzberg, G. "The importance and needs of Canadian research in science." Proc. R.S.C. (1978) 311-316.

1980 Clark, T.C. "Federal governments and university science research: a comparison of the practices in the United States and Canada, 1970-1979." Can. Public. Policy 6 (Spring 1980) 342-351.

Dialogue with NRC's Gerhard Herzberg: "All the technical progress that we have experienced owes its existence to basic research." Can. Research 13 (Nov. 1980) 18-23.

Dialogue with Patrick McTaggart-Cowan: "It's time we stopped playing ostrich about what is going on in Canada in the sciences and realize we are in deep trouble of our own making." Can. Research 13 (Oct 1980) 10-14, 49.

"Egalitarianism is the real enemy of excellence in science and technology; dialague with Omand Solandt." Canadian Research 13(1,1980) 18-27.

"Ethics of animal experimentation. Principes régissant l'expériment-ation sur les animaux." MRCC Newsletter/CRMC Actualités 10 (Jul 80) 4-8.

Hutchison, G. "Science eye in Ottawa." Canadian Research 13 (May 1980) 82, 65.

Imlach, A. "Alberta to finance a boom in medical research." Can. Med. Assoc. Jour. 123 (20 September 1980) 550-552.

Labreche, J. "NRC: where science fiction often comes true." Can. Geog. Jour. 100, 4 (1980) 24-33.

Lamelin, A. A la recherche d'un Québec scientifique." Educ. Québec 9 (juin 1979) 11-17.

"Provincial research institutions complete Canadian R & D picture." Canadian Research 13(June-Jul 80) 9, & 11.

"Sometimes you have to tell the guys: 'Gentlemen, the long term has arrived'; dialogue with ARC's Gilles Cloutier." Canadian Research 13(June-Jul 80) 14-22.

1981   "The clinician - scientist in Canada." Medical Research Council Newsletter 11 (Jan. 1981) 1-10.

D.   IN THE HUMANITIES AND SOCIAL SCIENCES/
     HUMANITÉS ET LES SCIENCES SOCIALES

1971   Hettich, W. "Federal science policy and social science research in Canadian universities." Can. Public Admin. 14 (Spring 1971) 112-128.

1972   Hersch, J. "Cultural pluralism/Le pluralisme culturel." Unesco Occasional Paper/Pages documentaires 7 (June/Juin 1972) 1-8.

Johnson, R. "La perspective et l'apport des sciences sociales dans la médecine de la fin du XXe siècle." Union Méd. 101 (juillet 1972) 1331-32.

Social Science Research Council of Canada. The social sciences and science policy: the response of the Social Science Research Council of Canada to a Science Policy for Canada, report of the Senate Special Committee on Science Policy V. 2: Targets and Strategies for the Seventies. Ottawa: Information Canada, 1972. 21 p.

1973 Drummond, I. "Bonneau, Corry, and the social sciences: is planning necessary?" CAUT Bull. ACPU. 21 (Apr. 1973) 14+

Greenglass, E. and M. Stewart. "The under-representation of women in social psychological research." Ont. Psych. 5 (1973) 21-29.

Inglis, G. et al. "Nationalism in Canadian science: brief to the AUCC Committee on the Rationalisation of University Research, presented by the Canadian Sociology and Anthropology Association." Minerva 11 (Jan. 1973) 113-20.

1974 Conger, D.S. "Looking for new ways to solve social problems [letter]." Science Forum 7 (Apr. 1974) [ix]

Klinck, C.F. "Bookmen and scholars", in Aspects of nineteenth century Ontario. Edited by F. Armstrong. Toronto: U. of T. Press, 1974. P. 327-333.

1976 Chaisson, A. "Le centre d'etudes acadiennes de l'Université de Moncton et son folklore." Laurentian Univ. Rev. 8 (Feb. 1976) 115-121.

Clarkson, S. "Socking it to the scholars: the First National Conference of the Social Science Research Council of Canada." Queen's Quart. 83 (Winter 1976) 547-555.

Hiller, H. "The contribution of S.D. Clark to the sociology of Canadian religion." Studies in Religion 6, 4 (1976-77) 415-427.

Rowat, D. "The decline of free research in the social sciences." Can. Jour. Pol. Sci. 9 (Dec. 1976) 537-47.

Social Science Research Council of Canada. Canadian international links in the Social Sciences and Humanities, by Jan. J. Loubser ... Ottawa, Council for the Academic Relations Division, Dept. of External Affairs, 1976. 162 p.

1977 Coburn, K. In pursuit of Coleridge. Toronto: Clarke, Irwin, 1977. 202 p.

1978 Mackey, W.F. "Organizing research on bilingualism: the ICRB story."
      McGill Jour. Educ. 13 (Spring 1978) 116-127.

1979 Marijn, C.   "Archeological research in Quebec: an historical
      overview." Man in the Northeast 18 (Fall 1979) 3-13.

1980 Irving, A. "Social science research in the university: an examina-
      tion of the views of Harry Cassidy and Harold Innis." Can. Jour.
      Higher Educ. 10, 1 (1980) 95-110.

      Woodcock, G. "When the past becomes history: the half-century in
      non-fiction prose." Univ. Tor. Q. 50, 1 (1980) 90-101.

E.   IN EDUCATION/L'ENSEIGNEMENT

1970 Aubin, G. "La recherche en pédagogie." Prospectives 6 (fév. 1970)
      16-30.

      Gagné, F. et M. Chabot. "PERPE, une conception neuve du perfection-
      nement pédagogique." Prospectives 6 (juin 1970) 160-189.

1971 Fleming, W.G. "University research", in Post-secondary and adult
      education. Vol. IV of Ontario's Educative Society. Toronto: U. of
      Toronto Press, 1971. p. 335-47.

      Pascal, C.E. "Instructional options, option preferences and course
      outcomes." Alta. Jour. Educ. Res. 17 (mar. 1971) 1-11.

      Pedersen, E.D., T.A. Faucher and K.J. Dowd. Status and prospects of
      educational research in Québec. Québec: Dept. of Education, 1971.
      2 v.

      Radcliffe, D. "Comparative education and 'developed' countries."
      Lakehead Univ. Rev. 4 (Fall 1971) 109-18.

      Struger, G. et J. Martel. "L'Auto-instruction guidée: une expéri-
      ence d'apprentissage au niveau universitaire." Stoa I (1971) 15-26.

1972 Goldshmid, B. and M.L. Goldshmid. Modular instruction in higher edu-
      cation: a review. Montréal: Centre for Learning and Development,
      McGill University, 1972. 48 p.

      Lamontagne, M. "Needed: a new approach to research in education."
      Educ. Canada 12 (Mar. 1972) 35-43.

1973 Paton, J.M. Concern and competence in Canadian education. Essays
      ed. by D.A. MacIver. Toronto: Guidance Centre, Faculty of Education,
      Univ. of Toronto, 1973. 151 p.

1974 Association of Universities and Colleges of Canada. Inventory of research into higher education in Canada/Inventaire des recherches sur l'enseignement supérieur au Canada, 1974 - . Compiled by J.F. Houwing and A.M. Kristjanson. Ottawa: Assoc. of Universities and Colleges of Canada, 1975 -   . Annual.

1976 "Graduate theses, monographs and projects in education in the social sciences at Canadian universities (1970-1976)" McGill Jour. Educ. 11 (Fall 1976) 217-224.

1977 Wilson, D.J. "Historiographical perspectives on Canadian educational history: a review essay." Jour. Educ. Thought 11 (Apr. 1977) 49-63.

1978 Ad Hoc Joint Education Committee on Copyright. The effects of the proposed new copyright act for Canada on educational purposes. Toronto: Canadian Education Association, 1978. 11p.

      Arlen, M. "Quantity and impact of scholarly journal publication in Canadian faculties of education." Can. Jour. Educ. 3, 1 (1978) 1-18.

1979 Holmes, J. ed. Proceedings of a colloquium on data needs on higher education for the eighties/Procés-verbal du colloque sur les besoins en données statistiques pour les années 80. Ottawa: Statistics Canada, 1979. 93 l.

      Sheffield, E.F. Policy-oriented research on national issues in higher education: a discussion paper for the colloquium on data needs for higher education in the eighties. Ottawa: Statistics Canada, 1979. 146 l.

1980 Inventory of research into higher education in Canada/Inventaire des recherches sur l'enseignement supérieur au Canada, 1980. Edited by J.F. Houwing and A.M. Kristjanson. Ottawa: Association of Universities and Colleges of Canada, 1980. 85p.

1981 "OISE's Department of Sociology in Education." Orbit. 12, 2 (1981) 3-7.

F. LIBRARIES/BIBLIOTHEQUES

1961 Weilbrenner, B. "The Public Archives of Canada, 1871-1958." Journal of the Society of Archivists 2 (April 1961) 101-113.

1967 Ridge, A.D. "The McGill University Archives." Archives: Journal of the British Records Association 8 (April 1967) 16-23.

1969 Archer, J.H. "A study of archival institutions in Canada." Ph.D. thesis, Queen's Univ., 1969.

Taylor, H. "Archives in Britain and Canada: impression of an immigrant." Canadian Archivist 1, 7 (1969) 22-33.

Varennes, R. de. "L'ordinateur dans le monde des bibliothèques." Rev. AUPELF 7 (été 1969) 66-77.

1970 Blackburn, R.H. "Photocoping in a university library." Scholarly Publishing 2 (Oct. 1970) 49-58.

Boucher, R. "Le collège-bibliothèque, une solution cadre." Prospectives 6 (Nov. 1970) 341-48.

Clauser, M. "Les archives universitaires et le rapport Deschênes." Archives; Revue de l'Association des Archivistes du Québec. 70 (jan./juin 1970) 74-77.

1971 Baird, D.A. "Simon Fraser university library." Can. Library Jour. 28 (May-June 1971) 190-192.

Burgis, G.C. "A systems concept of organization and control for large university libraries." Can. Library Jour. 28 (Jan.-Feb. 1971) 24-29.

Canadian Library Association. "Brief to the Commission on Post-Secondary education in Ontario." Can. Library Jour. 28 (Jul.-Aug. 1971) 310.

1971 Greene, R. "Library co-operation and the rationalization of curricula." Can. Library Jour. 28 (May-Jun. 1971) 206-208.

Ironside, D.J. "Some thoughts on uses of data banks." Can. Library Jour. 28 (Jan.-Feb. 1971) 30-35.

Kates, Peat, Marwick & Co. Libraries and information storage and retrieval systems. Toronto: Queen's Printer, 1971. 134 p. (Study prepared for the Commission on Post-Secondary Education in Ontario)

Lessard, C. "Les archives de l'Université du Québec à Trois-Rivières." Archives; Revue de l'Association des Archivistes du Québec. 71 (janvier/juin 1971) 32-54.

Minnick, J.A. "Approaching the librarian." Scholarly Publishing 2 (Jan. 1971) 179-188.

Omelusik, N.E. "Ex uno plures- the libraries of the University of British Columbia." Can. Library Jour. 28 (May-Jun. 1971) 186-88.

1972 Bassnett, P.J. "Library research in Canada." Can. Library Jour. 29 (Jul.-Aug. 1972) 307-9.

Bourque, J. "The Public Archives of Canada, 1872-1972." Can. Lib. Jour. 29 (Jul.-Aug. 1972) 330-333.

Connolly, P. "An attempt to design a low cost alternative to the standard academic library." Lib. Assoc. Alta. Bull. 3, 4 (1972) 7-12.

"Need scientific or technical information? NSL has the answer/La BSN peut répondre à vos besoins scientifiques et techniques." Science Dimension 4 (Aug. 1972) 24-31.

Pannu, G.S. "Research in librarianship and the Canadian Library Association." Can. Library Jour. (Jul.-Aug. 1972) 300-06.

Rothstein, S. "From reaction to interaction: the development of the North-American university library." Can. Library Jour. 29 (Mar.-Apr. 1972) 111-15.

Stacey, C.P. "The Public Archives of Canada at the end of its first century." Hist. Papers (1972) 11-22.

Taillemite, E. "Une visite aux archives canadiennes." La Gazette des Archives 77 (1972) 107-121.

Warner, R.M. "Archival training in the United States and Canada." Am. Archivist 35 (Jul.-Oct. 1972) 347-58.

1973 Donnelly, F.D. The National Library of Canada. Ottawa: Canadian Library Association, 1973. 281 p.

Smith, W.I. "The Public Archives of Canada." Records Management Quart. 7 (Jan. 1973) 23-25, 30.

Stierwalt, R. "A cooperative library system for the Ontario universities." CACUL newsletter 5 (Sept. 1973) 3-6.

Wilson, I.E. "Shortt and Doughty: the cultural role of the Public Archives of Canada, 1904-1935." Can. Archivist 2, 4 (1973) 4-25.

1974 Beckman, M. "Library networks in the '70's: university libraries." Can. Library Jour. 31 (Jun. 1974) 197-200.

Bishop, O.B. "Developments relating to health sciences libraries in Canada with emphasis on Ontario. 1958-1973." Agora 7 (1974) 28-32.

Cameron, W.J. and G. Piternick. "Research in Canadian librarianship and the Canadian Library Association." Can. Library Jour. 31 (Dec. 1974) 570-574.

Lamonde, Y. "Les archives de l'Institut canadien de Montréal, 1844-1900." Revue Hist. 28 (juin 1974) 77-93.

McDonough, I. "Libraries and the learning society: a Ministry conference." Ont. Library Rev. 58 (Mar. 1974) 4-10.

Worth, W.H. "From autonomy to system: a provincial perspective." Lib. Assoc. Alta. Bull. 5, 2 (1974) 56-65.

1975 Piternick, A. and D. McInnes. "Sharing resources: outside use of academic libraries in British Columbia." Can. Library Jour. 32 (Aug. 1975) 299-304.

Wiseman, A. "Community use of university libraries." Can. Library Jour. 32 (Oct. 1975) 373-376.

1976 Wilson, I.E. "Canadian University Archives." Archivaria 3 (Winter 1976-1977) 17-27.

1977 Annual report (of) Canadian Association of College and University Libraries. Feliciter 23, 11 (1977) 11.

"Libraries 'expert examiners' under cultural property act." Feliciter 23 (Sept. 1977) 3.

Orton, L. and J. Wiseman. "Library service to part-time students: a survey at Queen's and Trent universities." Can. Library Jour. 34 (Feb. 1977) 23-27.

Wilwood, R.J. "Book budget allocations." Can. Library Jour. 34 (June 1977) 213-219.

1978 Brown, J.E. "Information users versus information systems." Can. Library Jour. 35(Dec78) 433-436.

Mount, J. "Faculty status at Laurentian - two years later." Can. Library Jour. 35(Dec' 78) 427-431.

"Final version of brief submitted to National Librarian." Feliciter 24 (Feb. 1978) 4.

Rothwell, H. "Centre for Research in Librarianship Canadian non-print media project." Can. Library Jour. 35(Dec '78) 454-455.

Thomas, L.F. "Tri-University Libraries." Can. Library Jour. 35 (Feb. 1978) 27-33. A cooperative library program at U.B.C., Victoria and Simon Fraser universities.

Wees, I. "The National Library of Canada: the first quarter-century." Can. Lib. Jour. 35 (June 1978) 153-163.

1979   Auster, E. and S.B. Lawton.   "The negotiation process in on-line bibliographic retrieval." Can. Jour. Information Science 4 (May 1979) 86-98.

Brown, N. "Academic libraries: an operational model for participation." Can. Library Jour. 36(Aug. 1979) 201-207.

Piterneck, A.B. "The challenge to bibliographical control." Can. Library Jour. 36 (Dec '79) 343-346.

"Study proposes B.C. library network." Feliciter 26 (Ap. 1980) 1,3.

1980   Mount, J. and J. Turple. "University library service for off campus students." Can. Library Jour. 37 (Feb. 1980) 47-50.

Ross, I. "Library-archive relations: the question of education." Can. Library Jour. 37 (February 1980) 39-44.

Sylvestre, G. "National Library report: what it is - what it is not." Can. Lit. Jour. 37 (June 1980) 137-140.

G. MUSEUMS AND ART GALLERIES/GALERIES D'ART ET MUSÉES

1932   Miers, H.A. and S.F. Markham. A Report on the Museums of Canada to the Carnegie Corporation of New York. Edinburgh: Constable, 1932. 63 p.

1933   Miers, H.A. and S.F. Markham. Directory of museums and art galleries in Canada. London: Museum Association, 1933. 92 p.

1972   Gresco, J. "Towards the college as muse ... the teacher and the museum as partners in stimulation." BC Perspectives 2 (Oct. 1972) 25-35.

1973   Key, A.F. Beyond four walls: the origins and development of Canadian museums. Toronto: McClelland & Stewart, 1973. 384 p.

1976   Boulizon, G. Les musées du Québec. Tome I Montréal et l'ouest du Québec; Tome II La vieille Capitale et l'est du Québec. Montréal: Fides. T.I 205 p., T.II 205 p.

Hawthorn, A. "UBC's new Museum of Anthropology." Can. Geog. Jour. 93 (Oct./Nov. 1976) 52-57.

1977   Stevenson, L.S. "Natural history museum services to the university." Can. Museum Assoc. Gaz. (Spring 1977) 12-16.

Edwards, R.Y. "Tomorrow's museum." Can. Museum Assoc. Gaz. (Winter 1977) 6-11.

1978   Finley, G. "The museum and the historian: toward a new partnership."
        Can. Museum Assoc. Gaz. (Spring 1978) 6-10.

        Segger, M. "Standards and criteria for the training of Canadian
        museum workers: towards some definitions of the problem." Can.
        Museum Assoc. Gaz. (Summer 1978) 20-25.

1979   Collinson, H. A university collects. Edmonton: Univ. of Alberta
        Press, 1979. 52 p.

        Ettlinger, J.   "The Dawson Room - a practical centre for the book
        arts." Can. Library. Jour. 36 (Feb./Apr. 1979) 43-48.

        Sangster, D. "The ROM: Canada's lively, largest museum." Can. Geo.
        Jour. 98, 2 (1979) 12-31.

H. LEARNED AND PROFESSIONAL SOCIETIES/
    SOCIÉTÉS SAVANTES ET PROFESSIONNELLES

1952   Gullett, D.W. "Notes on the development of the Canadian Dental Asso-
        ciation." Jour. Can. Dent. Assoc. 18 (1952) 303-309.

1956   Graham, D. "Canadian Physiotherapy Association 1939-1949.   Can.
        Physiotherapy Jour. 8 (Mar. 1956) 15-22, 36-39.

1965   Blackstock, C.R. "The Canadian Association for Health, Physical Edu-
        cation and Recreation", in Physical Education in Canada. Edited by
        M.L. Van Vliet. Scarborough: Prentice Hall, 1965. p. 276-291.

1968   Lower, A.R.M. "Adam Shortt, founder [of the Kingston Historical
        Society]. Historic Kingston XVII, 3-15.

1969   Greathed, E.D. "Antecedents and origins of the Canadian Institute of
        International Affairs", in Empire and Nations: essays in honour of
        F.H. Soward. Ed. by H.L. Dyck and H.P. Krosby. Toronto: Univ. of
        Toronto Press, 1969. p. 91-115.

1970   Dolman, C.E. "St. Elmo's and St. Anthony's Fires." Proc. R.S.C.
        (1970) 31-51. [Presidential Address]

1971   Wright, M.J. "The psychological organizations of Canada." Can. Psych.
        12 (Jul. 1971) 420-31.

1972   Babbitt, J.D. "The senators and the scientific societies." Can. R.
        and D. 5 (Nov./Dec. 1972) 21-2+

        Fleming, W.G. Educational contributions of associations. Toronto:
        U. of T. Press, 1972. 463 p. (Ontario's Educational Society VII)

Lambi, I.N. "Fifty years of the Canadian Historical Association: what next?" Can. Hist. Assoc. Papers (1972) 1-10.

West, A.S. National engineering, scientific and technological societies of Canada. Ottawa: Science Council of Canada, 1972. 131 p. (Background Study No. 25 for the Science Council of Canada)

1973 Carrière, G. "Les quarante ans de la Société canadienne d'histoire de l'Eglise catholique." Rev. Univ. Ottawa 43 (oct.-déc. 1973) 485-93.

Jackson, R.W. "What then should be SCITEC's function in all of this?" Science Forum 6 (Apr. 1973) 9-12.

Killan, G. "Preserving Ontario's heritage: a history of the Ontario Historical Society." Ph.D. thesis, McMaster Univ., 1973.

Lang, M. and E. Upton, eds. The dietetic profession in Canada. Toronto: Canadian Dietetic Assoc., 1973. 98 p.

Maskow, M. "The future of C.H.E.A." Can. Home Econ. Jour. 23 (Oct. 1973) 3-9.

Michaud, L. "Nouvelles orientations de l'AUPELF." Univ. Aff./Aff. univ. 14 (mar. 1973) 8.

Schlosser, E.F. "The meeting of Canadian Byzantinists at Queen's University." New Rev. 13 (Sept. 1973) 58-60.

Wallace, J.D. "Your national associations and you." Can. Family Physician 19 (July 1973) 63-70.

Wilson, J.T. "The Royal Society: now a revitalized national academy." Science Forum 6 (Oct. 1973) 3-6.

Wilson, J.T. "The scientific societies: what are they - and what should they become?" Science Forum 6 (Apr. 1973) 7-9.

1974 Douglas, V.I. "SCITEC: what has been done in its first four years?" Science Forum 7 (Apr. 1974) 32-33.

1975 Cormier, C. "Origines de la Société Historique Acadienne." Cah. Soc. Hist. Acadienne 6 (déc. 1975) 169-80.

Fortier, C. "The Royal Society of Canada as a federation of three national academies: a challenging future." Mém. S.R.C. (1975) 3-13.

1976 Evans, A.M. and C.A.V. Barker. Century one: a history of the Ontario Veterinary Association. Guelph: The authors, 1976. 516 p.

1978   de Chantal, R. "Le jardin de l'academie." Mém. S.R.C. (1978) 195-204.

        Kerwin, L. "The role of the Royal Society in the future of Canadian science." Proc. R.S.C. (1978) 329-336.

1979   Lebel, M. "Apport de la Societé royale du Canada à la vie intellectuelle du pays dans le domaine des humanités et des sciences sociales (1982-1978)." Mém. S.R.C. (1979) 3-16.

        Misener, A. "The Canadian Association of Physicists - an historical review." Physics in Canada 35 (September 1979) 115-118.

1981   Daley R. and P. Defour. "Creating a "Modern Minerva": John William Dawson and the Royal Society of Canada." Journal for the History of Canadian Science, Technology and Medicine 1 (January 1981) 3-13.

I.   LEARNED AND PROFESSIONAL JOURNALS/REVUES PROFESSIONNELLES

1969   Bowen, C. "The university press in the computer era." Scholarly Publishing 1 (Oct. 1969) 55-60.

        Jeanneret, M. "Editorial: universities as publishers." Scholarly Publishing 1 (Oct. 1969) 3-4.

1971   Strachan, R. "A Canadian experiment." Scholarly Publishing 2 (1971) 173-177. [McGill-Queen's Univ. Press]

        Johnson, F.H. "The first Canadian journal of education and historical review." McGill Jour. Educ. 6 (Fall 1971) 170-76.

1972   Webber, H.R. "University presses and the powers that be." Scholarly Publishing 4 (Oct. 1972) 13-18.

1973   "Séminaire international des presses d'université de langue française." Rev. AUPELF 21 (printemps-automne 1973) 23-31.

1974   "Antennes des sciences au Canada: les journaux canadiens de la recherche". Science Dimension 6 (1974) 15-19

        Woodcock, L. "The university presses." Univ. Aff./Aff. univ. 15 (Sept. 1974) 2-4.

1975   Association of Canadian University Presses. Values in publishing: observations on the final report of the enquiry into the support of scholarly publication by the Social Science Research Council of Canada and the Humanities Research Council of Canada. Toronto, 1975. 38 p.

Bohne, H. "The crisis of scholarly publishing." Jour. Can. Studies 10 (May 1975) 9-15.

Breton, R. "The review and the growth of sociology and anthropology in Canada." Can. Rev. Soc. Anthrop. 12 (Feb. 1975) 1-5.

"Communicating research results - The Canadian journals of research." Science Dimension 6 (4) 14-18.

Neill, R.F. Final report of the enquiry into the support of scholarly publication by the Social Science Research Council of Canada and the Humanities Research Council of Canada. Ottawa, Ont., S.S.R.C., 1975. 37 p.

1976 Rotbrock, J. "A room of its own: the University of Alberta Press." New Trail 31, 3 (Spring 1976) 2-3.

1978 Mills, A. "The Canadian Forum and socialism, 1920-1934." Jour. Can. Studies 3 (Winter 1978-79) 11-27.

1979 Davin, D. "Editor and author in a university press." Scholarly Publishing 10 (Jan. 1979) 121-127.

Halpenny, F.G. "Canadian scholarly publishing: a tour d'horizon 1979." Can. Library Jour. 36(Oct. 79) 279-286.

Hornbeck, P. "Scholarly publishing faces the crunch." CAUT Bull. ACPU 26 (Oct. 79) 23-24.

Rosenbluth, G. "Publishing economics." Can. Jour. Econ. 12 (Nov. 1979) 551-574.

1980 Keith, W.J. and Shek, B.-Z. "A half-century of UTQ." Univ. Tor. Q. 50, 1 (1980) 146-154.

Roland, C.G. "Ontario medical periodicals as mirrors of change." Ont. Hist. 72 (Mar. 1980) 3-15.

5.   The Student and Student Services/
      L'Etudiant et les services aux étudiants

A.   GENERAL/GÉNÉRALITÉS

1967 Hacks, R.E. "The liberatated generation: an explanation of the roots of student protest." Jour. Social Issues 23 (1967) 52-75.

1968 Dunton, A.D. "The student today." Carleton Alumni News 17, 1 (1968) 5-8.

1970   Boucher, P. "Le monde étudiant à toute allure." <u>Prospectives</u> 6 (sept. 1970) 212-219.

Dansereau, P. "Finding new ways to communicate with students." <u>Science Forum</u> 3 (Oct. 1970) 24-26.

Gagnon, J.-A. "An analysis of student life developments in Quebec: implications for other Canadian universities." <u>Jour. Council Student Services</u> 5 (Autumn-Winter 1970) 7-21.

Hendley, B. "What ails universities?" <u>McGill Jour. Educ.</u> 2 (Fall 1970) 196-204.

Lazure, J. "Les jeunes québécois encore à l'âge métaphysique." <u>Prospectives</u> 6 (fév. 1970) 31-45.

McLeish, J.B. <u>Student attitudes and college environments</u>. Cambridge: Cambridge Institute of Education, 1970. 251 p.

O'Brien, J.W. "Emerging trends in student life: implications for student services." <u>Jour. Council Student Services</u> 5 (Autumn-Winter 1970) 2-6.

Reimer, L. "Summary of the commission on AUCC services for students". <u>AUCC Proc.</u> 1970, 38-39.

Rogers, D. "Hostility to science: a science student view." <u>Science Forum</u> 3 (Aug. 1970) 3-6.

Turcotte, R. "P.B.I. sur le développement des services aux étudiants." <u>Prospectives</u> 6 (sept. 1970) 226-235.

1971   Bell, R.E. "Too much college." <u>McGill Jour. Educ.</u> 6 (Spring 1971) 15-22.

Desgroseillers, P. "Le CEGEP milieu de vie et le rôle des services aux étudiants." <u>Prospectives</u> 7 (sept. 1971) 211-214.

Dupont, R.M. "Valeurs de travail d'étudiants en droit, en génie et en psychologie." Thèse de doctorat, Univ. de Montréal, 1971.

Engel, D. et al. <u>The campus as the campus centre, a manual</u>. Toronto: Students Administrative Council, Univ. of Toronto, 1971. 88 p.

Fleming, W.G. "Student activities and attributes in post-secondary and adult education", in <u>Ontario's Educative Society, Vol. 4</u>. Toronto: Univ. of Toronto Press, 1971. p. 371-406.

George, P.M. "An experiment in participatory democracy." <u>McGill Jour. Educ.</u> 6 (Fall 1971) 187-194.

1972   Beaudry, A.   "Le pouvoir étudiant aux enfers."   Relations 370 (avril 1972) 118-21.

Kraus, A.S. et al.   "Non-medical use of drugs by students and alumni of Queen's University."   Can. Jour. Public Health 63 (Jul./Aug. 1972) 296-303.

Simoneau, R.   "Les étudiants, les dirigeants et l'université: doctrines étudiantes et doctrines universitaires."   Recherches soc.   13 (sept.-déc. 1972) 343-364.

1973   Allaire, J. et J.M. Toulouse.   "Profil psychologique des étudiants canadiens francais du M.B.A.:   conséquences pour une politique de sélection."   Relations Ind.   28 (1973) 476-496.

Barrett, F.M. and M. Fitz-Earle.   "Student opinion on legalized abortion at the University of Toronto."   Can. Jour. Public Health 64 (May/ June 1973) 294-299.

Camp, D.   "The public image of the university."   AUCC Proc.   1973, 92-94.

Denyer, J.   "Student expectations and needs."   AUCC Proc.   1973, 124-130.

Filion, G.   "Ce que le public pense des étudiants."   AUCC Proc. 1973, 95-97.

Lacroix, R. et M. Proulx.   Une évaluation partielle des pertes ou des gains des provinces résultant de la mobilité des étudiants et diplômés universitaires.   Montréal: Centre   de   Recherches   en Développement Economique, 1973.   55 p.

Rivard, C.   "Etude transversale des valeurs de travail chez des étudiants en psychologie et des psychologues."   Thèse de doctorat, Univ. de Montréal, 1973.

Woodcock, L.   "New union exorcising ghost of CUS."   Univ. Aff./Aff. univ.   14 (Oct. 1973) 2.

1974   Bordeleau, Y.   "Les motivations au travail, la conception des objectifs des entreprises et la relation entre ces deux variables chez un groupe d'étudiants   canadiens-français   en   commerce."   Thèse   de doctorat, Univ. de Montréal, 1974.

Cleason, T.P. and P. Dumas.   "Perspectives sociales des étudiants de l'Université de Moncton."   Rev. Univ. Moncton 7 (jan. 1974) 43-48.

Ouellet, G. "Relations entre les valeurs de travail et de loisir d'étudiants de niveaux collégial et universitaire." Thèse de doctorat, Univ. de Montréal, 1974.

Perron, J. "Les valeurs en éducation: vers un portrait psycho-social de l'étudiant Québécois." Can. Counsellor 8 (Jan. 1974) 23-36.

"Toronto has a new code of behaviour." Univ. Aff./Aff. univ. 15 (Feb. 1974) 7.

1975 Matthews, A.W. "The role, organization and support of university athletic programs." AUCC Proc. (Nov. 1975) 32-40.

McLeod, E.M. A study of child care services at Canadian Universities. Ottawa: Assoc. of Universities and Colleges of Canada, 1975. 44 p.

1976 Clifton, R.A. "The socialization of graduate students in the social and natural sciences." Ph.D. thesis, Univ. of Toronto, 1976.

Dorin, J. "Je pensais que l'Université c'était la place où tu pouvais créer beaucoup par toi-même. Education Québec 6 (1976) 29-31.

Laurence, M. "Senior citizens in degree credit courses." Can. Jour. Univ. Continuing Educ. 3 (Autumn 1976) 2-13.

1977 Jeanrenaud, C. et D. Bishop. "La différenciation de la forme comme fonction du névrotisme chez l'étudiant universitaire." Rev. can. des sciences du comportement 9 (jan. 1977) 49-58.

Lefebvre-Bergeron, L. et P. Doyon. "L'étudiant est-il adulte?" Prospectives 13 (fév. 1977) 54-58.

Morin, A. et R. Viau. "Le profil d'apprentissage de l'étudiant universitaire." Pédagogiques 2 (avril 1977) 21-25.

Morse, S.S. "Being a Canadian: aspects of national identity among a sample of university students in Saskatchewan." Can. Jour. Behav. Science 9 (July 1977) 265-273.

Woodcock, L. "Part-time students make great strides at U. of T." Univ. Aff./Aff. univ. 18 (Nov. 1977) 4-5.

1978 Gillet, M. "The majority minority: women in Canadian universities." Can. International Educ. 7 (June 1978) 42-50.

Gold, J.H. "University students, mental health and development." Can. Psych. Assoc. Jour. 23 (August 1978) 303-308.

Leduc, C. "Les orientations des femmes à l'Université de Montréal en 1949-50 et en 1974-75." Can. International Educ. 7 (jun. 1978) 51-58.

Sullivan, N. "Coordinated policy on foreign students essential." Univ. Aff./Aff. univ. 19 (Jan. 1978) 2-3.

Wilson, L. and B. Lipinski. "A longitudinal study of mature students in credit programs." Can. Jour. Univ. Continuing Educ. 4 (Winter 1978) 22-27.

Woodward, C.A. "Diogenes in the Tower of Babel: The generation gap and the role of the university." Jour. Educ. Thought 12 (Dec. 1978) 190-196.

Zur-Meuhlen, M. von. Foreign students in Canada and Canadian students abroad. Ottawa: Statistics Canada, 1978. 156 p.

1979 Wong. T. "The contest to become top banana: Chinese students at Canadian universities." Can. Ethnic Studies 11, 2 (1979) 63-69.

1980 Karagianis, L.D. and W.C. Nesbit. "Special education: public policy in Canada." Education Canada 20 (Summer 1980) 4-10.

Sheffield, E.F. "Student mobility no simple matter." Univ. Aff./Aff. univ. 21, 7 (1980) 8-9.

B. POLITICAL AND SOCIAL INVOLVEMENT/
ENGAGEMENT POLITIQUE ET SOCIAL

1970 Gilmor, R.P. and W.G. Scott. "University government and student organizations". Jour. Council Student Services 5 (Spring 1970) 23-30.

1971 Kaufmann, O. "La contestation estudiantine et son incidence sur la structure dès programmes de formation." Act. Econ. 47 (avril-juin 1971) 135-147.

1972 Bennett, A. "The growth of militancy among university students in Quebec: a short history." This Magazine is About Schools 6 (Spring 1972) 39-48.

Quarter, J. The student movement of the 60's: a social-psychological analysis. Toronto: Ontario Institute for Studies in Education, 1972. 138 p.

1973 Axelrod, P. "Patterns of student politics." Univ. Aff./Aff. univ. 14 (Oct. 1973) 4-5.

Ghaem-Maghami, F. "Political climates, political knowledge and political preferences of university students." Alta. Jour. Educ. Res. 19 (Mar. 1973) 22-29.

Gingras, J.R. "La révolution étudiante." Act. Nat. 54 (1973) 296-306.

Reed, T. and J. Reid. Student power and the Canadian campus. Toronto: Peter Martin, 1973. 226 p.

Stern, S. "Jewish youth and Canadian concerns." Can. Jewish Outlook 11 (Apr.-May 1973) 17-18.

1975 Gingras, J.B. "La révolution étudiante: le conflit des générations." Act. Nat. 56 (mai 1975) 734-757.

1977 Richard, J.-Y. "La participation en milieu universitaire: un rêve habitable." Prospectives 13, 1 (1975) 37-45.

1978 Allaire, G. "L'influence du milieu étudiant québecois sur l'action de l'Eglise Catholique." Act. Nat. (mai 1978) 737-744.

1979 Frieson, O. "Student activism in retrospect." Can. Admin. 18 (Feb. 1979).

"More info needed to document sexual harassment." Student Advocate 4 (Sept '79) 2.

1980 Sévigny, R. "Les contestations étudiantes à l'université: quelque éléments d'analyse." Sociologie et sociétés. 12, 2 (1980) 143-168.

C. FINANCIAL AID/AIDE FINANCIÈRE

1970 "Alberta study tackles problem of student fees and income." Univ. Aff./Aff. univ. 11 (May 1970) 4.

Canada Dept. of the Secretary of State. Education Support Branch. Federal and provincial student aid in Canada 1966-67 and 1967-68/Aide féderale et provincial accordée aux étudiants au Canada 1966-67 et 1967-68. Ottawa: 1970. 125 p.

Primeau, W.J. "Public financial aid to undergraduates in Canadian universities for the year 1970-71." Univ. Aff./Aff. univ. 11 (July 1970) 1-6.

Fisher, F.A. "Financial accessiblity to higher education in Canada." CAUT Bull. ACPU 18 (Summer 1970) 92-106.

1971 D'Auray, G.P. "Student aid plan becomes university financing scheme."
      Univ. Aff./Aff. univ. 12 (May 1971) 9-10, 19-24.

      Farine, A. "Fonds d'autofinancement des frais de scolarité." CAUT
      Bull. ACPU 19 (Spring 1971) 13-18.

      Fleming, W.G. "Student assistance", in Ontario's educative society,
      V. 4: post-secondary and adult education. Toronto: Univ. of Toronto
      Press, 1971. p. 407-28.

      Stager, D. and G. Cook. "Student aid: a proposal and its implica-
      tions." Can. Tax Jour. Nov.-Dec. 1971, 558-564.

1973 Porter, M., J. Porter and B. Blishen. Does money matter? prospects
      for higher education. Toronto: Institute for Behavioural Research,
      York Univ., 1973. 318 p.

      Boucher, J. Aide financière aux étudiants et problèmes financiers
      des étudiants. AUCC Proc. 1973, 110-113.

1977 "The current Canada Student Loans Plan: 'the opportunity to reach ...
      educational potential'." The Student Advocate 2 (Oct. 1977) 4.

1980 Association of Student Awards Personnel of British Columbia. Student
      assistance in the eighties. Vancouver, B.C.: A.S.A.P., 1980. 15
      leaves. (A brief submitted to the Federal-Provincial Task Force on
      Student Assistance)

      D. HOUSING/LOGEMENT

1970 Judge, D. "The give and take of housing budgets; but you'd have a
      hard time convincing this Students' Union Commission." Can. Univ. &
      Coll. 5 (Aug. 1970) 18-21.

      Robb, G. "Living and learning new attitudes challenge today's pat-
      terns of campus life." Can. Univ. & Col. 5 (Aug. 1970) 15-17.

      Robb, G. "University living: a new idea." McMaster News 40, 3
      (1970) 2-6.

1972 Jansen, C. Housing, transportation and social participation at York.
      Toronto: Institute for Behavioural Research, York University, 1972.
      2 v.

1973 Abbott, L. "Residences resurrected." McGill News 54, 2 (1973) 6-9.

      Guttman, M.A. and J.A. Southworth. "The impact of liberalized resi-
      dence hall regulations." McGill Jour. Educ. 7 (Spring 1973) 99-105.

Rannels, G. and J. Southen. "Trends in university residences." Univ. Aff./Aff. univ. 14 (Nov. 1973) 12-13.

1978 Association of Universities and Colleges of Canada. The Canadian directory to foundations and granting agencies. Edited by Allan Arlett. 4th ed. Ottawa: AUCC, 1978. 1 vol. (looseleaf)

1979 Adequate and accessible student aid needed more then ever." (Editorial) Student Advocate 4 (Sept '79) 6.

1979 National Union of Students (Canada) Student memorandum on national student aid. Ottawa: NUS' 1979. 13 leaves. Brief presented to the Canada Student Loans Plenary Group, The Council of Ministers of Education (Canada) and the Secretary of State.

1980 Association of Student Awards Personnel of British Columbia. Student assistance in the eighties. Vancouver, B.C.: A.S.A.P., 1980. 15 leaves. A brief submitted to the Federal-Provincial Task Force on Student Assistance.

Association des Universitiés et col;èges de Canada. Mémoire présenté au groupe d'etuae fédéral-provincial sur l'aide aux étudiants. Ottawa: AUCC, 1980. 10 feuilles.

Association des Universités et Collèges du Canada. Comité spécial de l'aide aux étudiants. Mémoire présenté au Groupe d'Étude Fédéral-Provincial sur l'aide aux Edudiants, juillet 1980. Ottawa: AUCC, 1980. 17p.

Association of Universities and Colleges of Canada. Ad Hoc Committee on Student Assistance. Brief presented to the Federal-Provincial Task Torce on Student Asistance, July 1980. O. Hawa: AUCC, 1980. 16p.

Campbell, D.R. Student aid in Manitoba. Winnipeg, Man.: U. of Manitoba, 1980. 24 leaves. Draft brief to the Federal-Provincial Task Force on Student Assistance.

National Union of Students (Canada) Student loans: making a mockery of equal opportunity. Ottawa: NUS, 1980. 39p. Submission to the Federal-provincial Task Force on Student Assistance.

Ontario Federation of Students. Swimming against the current: a brief to the Federal-Provincial Task Force on Student Assistance. Toronto: OFS, 1980. 43p.

E. COUNSELLING AND GUIDANCE/ORIENTATION

1969 Hudson, R.I. "The university counselling service: an alternative model." Jour. Council Student Services 4 (Spring 1969) 6-13.

1970 Talley, W.M. "Some concerns about group experiences." Jour. Council Student Services 5 (Autumn-winter 1970) 22-26.

1972 Hickling-Johnston, Ltd. Guidance. Toronto: Queen's Printer, 1972. 229 p. (Study prepared for Commission on Post-Secondary Education in Ontario)

Hudson, R.I. "Canadian university counselling services." Univ. Aff./ Aff. univ. 13 (Feb. 1972) 12-13.

1977 Haywood, L. "Adult counselling services in post-secondary educational institutions." Can. Jour. Univ. Continuing Educ. 4 (Summer 1977)

Meuser, P. and C.E. McInnis. "Differentiation of university freshmen in arts and science on the general occupational themes of the Strong-Campbell Interest Inventory." Can. Counsellor 11 (July 1977) 166-172.

1978 Miller, G. "Client ratings of a university counselling service and respondent anonymity." Can. Counsellor 12 (Apr. 1978) 184-89.

Thompson, A.P., et al. "Delivery of counselling and psychological services in a faculty of education. Can. Counsellor 12 (Apr. 1978) 190-93.

1979 Poirier, P.-P. et al. "Adjustment and self-esteem of users and non-users of a university counselling service." Can. Counsellor 13 (April 1979) 140-146.

F. PLACEMENT

1969 Goodman, F.V.S. "The supply and demand for graduates of post-secondary school institutions in the next decade." Jour. Council Student Services 4 (Autumn 1969) 20-26.

1971 "Les diplômés universitaires à la recherche d'emplois." Univ. Aff./ Aff. univ. 12 (fév. 1971) 1.

"The employment of university graduates." Univ. Aff./Aff. univ. 12 (Feb. 1971) 2-3, 9-10, 20-22.

Kushner, J. and I. Masse. "Special report: summary of studies on job opportunities." Science Forum 4 (Oct. 1971) 24-25.

Martel, J.-P. "Engager un étudiant en pharmacie constitue un bon placement." Pharmacien 55 (mars 1971) 32.

1973 Canada, Department of Manpower and Immigration. Career outlook, university and community college: arts and science, 1972-73. Ottawa: Information Canada, 1973. 41 p.

Canada, Department of Manpower and Immigration. Career outlook, university and community college: environmental sciences and studies, 1972-1973. Ottawa: Information Canada, 1973. 34 p.

Canada, Department of Manpower and Immigration. Career outlook, university and community college: fine arts and communications, 1972-1973. Ottawa: Information Canada, 1973. 41 p

Canada, Department of Manpower and Immigration. Career outlook, university and community college: health and health services, 1972-1973. Ottawa: Information Canada, 1973. 31 p.

1974 Boulay, G. "A la recherche du travail: un bureau universitaire de l'emploi." Educ. Q. 4 (août 1974) 5-8.

Yarmey, A.D. "Appreciation of university education in relation to employment expectations." Can. Psych. 15 (April 1974) 165-177.

1975 Harvey, E.B. and A. Kazanjian. Education and employment of arts and science graduates: the class of 1972. Toronto: Ontario Institute for Studies in Education, 1975. 195 p.

Shore, B.M. and E. Strauss. "What happens to graduate education graduates?" McGill Jour. Educ. 10 (Fall 1975) 169-174.

1976 Farine, A. et P.-P. Proulx. "La correspondance entre la formation et l'emploi chez un échantillon des sortants de l'université." Orientation professionnelle 12 (été 1976) 49-61.

1977 Woodcock, L. "Employment picture rekindles the manpower vs free choice controversy." Univ. aff./Aff. univ. 18 (Oct. 1977) 6-7.

1978 Rousseau, J. "L'implantation de la profession de travailleur social." Recherches Soc. 9, 2(1978) 171-189.

1979 Navarau L. and R.W. Walker. "Longtitudinal changes in vocational interests of Canadian military college cadets." Can. Counsellor 13 (April 1979) 136-139.

1980 Selleck, L. The university graduate and the marked place. Toronto: Council of Ontario Universities, 1980. 58.

G. EXTERNAL ORGANIZATIONS/ORGANISATIONS EXTÉRIEURES

1970 Hamilton, I. The children's crusade: the story of the Company of Young Canadians. Toronto: Peter Martin, 1970. 312 p.

1975 Patterson, M.E. et al. "Canadian University Service Overseas: an experience in education." Can. & International Educ. 4 (Dec. 1975) 24-32.

6. The Professor and Conditions of Work/
    Le Professeur et les conditions de travail

A. GENERAL/GÉNÉRALITÉS

1970 Wilson, H.T. "Continentalism and higher education." Can. Rev.
      American Studies 1 (Fall 1970) 89-97.

1971 Gingras, P.-E. "AIES-ACQ: profil des enseignants." Prospectives
      7, 3 (June 1971) 141-147.

      Hawkins, C. "A storm in a teAQUPE." McGill Jour. Educ. 6 (Spring
      1971) 84-89.

      Kaplan, J.G. "Professor-power and some of its consequences." CAUT
      Bull. ACPU 19 (Summer 1971) 25-35.

      Ravary, V. "La mobilié des cadres supérieurs en éducation." Pros-
      pectives 7 (sep. 1971) 197-199.

1972 Brayne, R.C. and C.C. Wood. "Faculty consensus: is it necessary?"
      Man. Jour. Educ. 7 (June 1972) 31-41.

      Drummond, I. "A black future for the professoriate." CAUT Bull.
      ACPU 21 (Dec. 1972) 12-16.

      Griffiths, N. "National affiliations of faculty: dispassionate dis-
      cussion difficult." Univ. Aff./Aff. univ. 13 (Dec. 1972) 5.

      "Non-Canadian faculty: response of the Moir Committee." Univ. Aff./
      Aff. univ. 13 (Dec. 1972) 5.

      Page, R. "Canada Canadian studies, and the identity that is." Univ.
      Aff./Aff. univ. 13 (Dec. 1972) 2-3.

      Rintala, M. and Z. Dreijmanis. "The academic labor market: with
      special reference to political science." Jour. Educ. Thought 6 (Aug.
      1972) 105-114.

      Thorhallsson, J., L.A. Bubba and H. Thorhallsson. "The classic cari-
      cature - a thing of the past." Univ. Aff./Aff. univ. 13 (Oct. 1972)
      5-6.

1973 Bélanger, L. "Le rôle d'un service du personnel dans l'administration
      scolaire plus humaine." Relations Ind. 28 (1973) 720-734.

      Boiven, N. "The academic woman and the Canadian university." Univ.
      Aff./Aff. univ. 14 (July 1973) 2-3.

Canadian Association of University Teachers. "Guideline concerning faculty workload." CAUT Bull. ACPU 21 (Mar. 1973) 23-24; "Directives concernant la charge de travail confiée aux professeurs." 25-26.

Canadian Association of University Teachers. "Guidelines concerning the patent policies of universities." CAUT Bull. ACPU 21 (Jan. 1973) 27-28.

Daly, J. "Academic liberalism and the Canadian identity question." Univ. Aff./Aff. univ. 14 (May 1973) 6-7.

Margeson, J. "Hidden forces transform activist U.S. professors into quiet Canadians." OCUFA Newsletter 6, 4 (Apr. 1973) 11-

Savage, D.C. "Professional societies and trade unions: the Canadian experience in higher education." CAUT Bull. ACPU 21 (Mar. 1973) 4-11.

Thomson, D. "Studying Canada from the outside." Univ. Aff./Aff. univ. 14 (Jan. 1973) 10.

1974   Carroll, W. "The response of the Canadian academic community to the Chilean crisis." CAUT Bull. ACPU 23 (Oct. 1974) 1-2.

"A faculty member suggests policies for Canadianization." Univ. Aff. /Aff. univ. 15 (Sept. 1974) 20-21.

Frappier, G. "Congés sabbatique et autre congés dans les universités canadiennes." CAUT Bull. ACPU 23 (oct. 1974) 12-19.

Holmes, J. "Deomography affects employment, promotion." Univ. Aff. /Aff. univ. 15 (Mar. 1974) 2-3.

1975   Cook, R. "The professor and the prophet of unrest." Trans. R.S.C. 1975 Academy II 227-250.

1976   Baker, M. "Academic queen bees." Atlantis. 1 (Spring 1976) 83-93.

Vickers, J. and J. Adams. But can you type?: Canadian universities and the status of women. Toronto: Clarke Irwin, 1976. 142 p.

1977   Ambert, A.M. "Academic women on the fringe?" Society/Société 1 (Jan. 1977) 6-8, 11-13.

Ambert, A.M. and D. Smith. "Do women professors want more women colleagues?" Society/Société 1 (Jan. 1977) 6-

Priestley, F.E.L. and H. Kerpneck. "Publication and academic reward." Scholarly Publishing 8 (Apr. 1977) 233-238.

Scarfe, J. and E.F. Sheffield. "Notes on the Canadian professoriate." Higher Educ. [Amsterdam] 6 (Aug. 1977) 337-58.

1978 Holmes, J. The age structure and anticipated retirement and replacement demand for full-time faculty by province and university. Ottawa: Statistics Canada, 1978. 50 p.

Holmes, J. Structure par âge, retraites prévues et demande de remplacement dans le corps professoral à plein temps selon la province et l'université. Ottawa: Statistique Canada, 1978. 50 p.

1979 Association of Universities and Colleges of Canada. Sabbatical leave policies at Canadian universities/Politiques des universités canadiennes à l'égard du congé sabbatique. Ottawa: A.U.C.C. 1979. 177p.

Bélanger, C.H. "Managerial and disciplinary constraints applied to faculty staffing." Can. Jour. Higher Educ. 9, 2 (1979) 51-62.

1979 Holmes, J. Potential academic rank distributio of ful-time faculty at Canadian universities 1975/76-1984/85. Prepared by J. Holmes and M. von Zur-Muehlen for presentation at the colloquium "Data Needs for the Eighties," March 26, 1979, Ottawa. 77 leaves.

Macdonald, H.I. "The changes, role of the professor and administrator", in Issues in higher education. Edited by A. Gregor and K. Wilson. Winnipeg: Univ. of Manitoba, 1979. p. 55-66 (Monographs in Education I)

Vickers, J.M. "The changing roles of professors and university administrators", in Issues in higher education. Edited by A. Gregor and K. Wilson. Winnipeg: Univ. of Manitoba, 1979. p. 67-76 (Monographs in Education I)

Small, J.M. "Academic careers in a time of recession." Can. Jour. Higher Educ. 9 (3) 63-7.

von Zur-Muehlen, M. "The age structure of Canadian university teachers and its implications." Interchange 10, 3 (1979-80) 38-52.

1980 McDaniel, S.A. "The greying of the academy." Can. Forum 60, 699 (1980). 25-27.

Moffat, L.K. Room at the bottom job mobility opportunities for Ontario academics in the mid-seventies. Toronto: Ministry of Colleges and Universities, 1980. 251 p.

von Zur-Muehlen, M. and J.-A. Belliveau. Three decades of full-time Canadian university teachers: a statistical portrait. Prepared for the tenth anniversary meeting of the Canadian Society for the Study of Higher Education. June 5-7, 1980. Ottawa: the authors, 1980. 295 p.

B. PROFESSOR AS TEACHER/LE PROFESSEUR COMME ENSEIGNANT

1970   Randhawa, B.S. and H.W. Savage. "Student criteria for evaluating college instructor effectiveness." Man. Jour. Educ. 6 (Nov. 1970) 35-44.

Taylor, P.A., E. de Corte and K. Swinnew. "Standards for judging instructional effectiveness." Man. Jour. Educ. 6 (Nov. 1970) 5-13.

1971   Penner, P.G. "The teacher in a landscape of a changing curriculum." English Quart., 4 (Winter 1971) 5-16.

1972   Knapper, C. "Improving teacher effectiveness." CAUT Bull. ACPU 21 (Oct. 1972) 9-11.

Knapper, C., B. McFarlane and J. Scanlon. "Student evaluation: an aspect of teaching effectiveness; report of the Professional Orientation Committee to CAUT Council." CAUT Bull. ACPU 21 (Dec. 1972) 26-29.

1973   Hedley, R.L. and C.C. Wood. "Improving university teaching." Univ. Aff./Aff. univ. 14 (Ap. 1973) 2-3.

Murray, H.G. A guide to teaching evaluation: a study commissioned ... by the Ontario Confederation of University Faculty Associations. Toronto: OCUFA, 1973. 56 p.

Sheffield, E.F. "Approaches (mostly elsewhere) to the improvement of teaching in higher education." Improving Coll. & Univ. Teaching (Winter 1973) 5-9.

1974   Bolgan, A.C. "Program for instructional development: do we really need it?" OCUFA Newsletter 7 (Jan. 1974) 2-3.

Daoust, G. et P. Bélanger. "Les pratiques universitaires de perfectionnement des maîtres et le rapport université-milieu." Prospectives 10 (2) (août 1974) 81-85.

Park, J., W. Matheson, and J. McLeish. "Classroom dynamics: both sides of the mirror." Improving College and University Teaching 22 (Spring 1974) 113-14, 116.

Proulx, R. "Teacher classification - a case of ill-inspired rationalization." CAUT Bull. ACPU 23 (Dec. 1974) 24-25, 28.

Sheffield, E.F. (ed) Teaching in the universities: no one way. Montréal: McGill-Queen's Univ. Press, 1974. 264 p.

1975 Foster, S.F. "Teaching improvement at the university level - some views and some prospects." Jour. Educ. (U.B.C.) 21 (Spring 1975) 63-71.

1976 Birch, D. "Evaluation of performances in the universities." AUCC Proc. (1976) 51-57.

Knapper, C. "Evaluation of performances in the universities." AUCC Proc. (1976) 43-49.

Leibu, Y. "La finalité de l'enseignement universitaire: essai d'approche systématique." Rev. can. ens. sup. 6 (1976) 1-11.

1977 Martin, J. and S. Auerbach. "Differential outcome effects in teacher training research as a result of functional versus structural behavioral recording." Alta. Jour. Educ. Res. 23 (June 1977) 128-137.

C. ACADEMIC FREEDOM/LIBERTÉS UNIVERSITAIRES

1970 Berland, A. "Academic freedom and tenure/Liberté universitarie et permanence de l'emploi: Simon Fraser University dispute." CAUT Bull. ACPU 19 (Autumn 1970) 65-85.

Canadian Association of University Teachers. Committee on Academic Freedom and Tenure. "Academic freedom and tenure/Liberté universitaire et permanence de l'emploi, Mount Allison University." CAUT Bull. ACPU 19 (Autumn 1970) 51-58.

Deane, P. "Tenure: a fortress where professors ignore students, the winds of change and even the need to work." Globe Magazine Dec. 19, 1970, 2-4. See also Globe and Mail, Dec. 23, 1970, 7.

Dunlop, J.B. "Academic freedom and tenure committee chairman's report." CAUT Bull. ACPU 18 (Summer 1970) 25-32.

Monahan, E.J. "Academic freedom and tenure and the C.A.U.T. - the first twenty years." CAUT Bull. ACPU 18 (Summer 1970) 80-91.

Polka, B. "Freedom and responsibility in the university." OCUFA Newsletter 3 (Jan. 1970) 1-3.

1971   "Academic freedom and tenure/Liberté universitaire et permanence de
       l'emploi, Université d'Ottawa." CAUT Bull. ACPU 19 (Spring 1971)
       39-69.

       "Arbitration at SFU: The Popkin case." CAUT Bull. ACPU 19 (Winter
       1971) 3-29.

       Berland, A. "The role of the university president in dismissal proce-
       dures." CAUT Bull. ACPU 19 (Summer 1971) 13-16.

       Brazeau, J.   "Academic freedom and tenure/Liberté universitaire et
       permanence de l'emploi, Université du Québec constituante de
       Montréal." CAUT Bull. ACPU 19 (Winter 1971) 75-98.

       Dunlop, J.B. "Guidelines on appointment and tenure: the CAUT's or
       the AUCC's?" CAUT Bull. ACPU 19 (Summer 1971) 3-11.

       Lapointe, M. "Tenure in institutions of higher education in Canada;
       survey/Permanence de l'emploi dans les institutions d'enseignement
       supérieur au Canada; étude." CAUT Bull. ACPU 19 (Winter 1971) 39-73.

       Smith, J.P. "What matters in academic freedom." Stoa 1 (1971) 5-13.

1972   Brewster, K. "Should universities retain tenure." CAUT Bull. ACPU
       21 (Dec. 1972) 4-7.

       "Primer on tenure." CAUT Bull. ACPU 20 (Spring 1972) 23-31.

       Malloch, A.E. "Committee on academic freedom and tenure." CAUT Bull.
       ACPU 21 (Oct. 1972) 6-8.

       "Tenure - the government and British Columbia universities." Univ.
       Aff./Aff. univ. 13 (Apr. 1972) 4-5.

       Wyman, M.   "Tenure granting procedures: how good are they?" Univ.
       Aff./Aff. univ. 13 (Sept. 1972) 3-4.

1973   Hutcheon, P.D. "Academic freedom: an evolving concept?" Jour. Educ.
       Thought 7 (Apr. 1973) 25-35.

       Wyman, M.   "Tenure, tenure procedures and sabbatical year." Queen's
       Quart. 80 (Spring 1973) 12-21.

1974   Hunt, R.A.   "Academic freedom and the curriculum: a problem and a
       proposal." CAUT Bull. ACPU 22 (Apr. 1974) 4-5, 9.

1975   Hanly, C.M. "Problems of academic freedom in Canada", in Universities
       in the Western World. Edited by P. Seabury. New York: Free Press,
       1975. P. 157-75.

1976   "Admit 1 university teacher to an uninterrupted career with a finan-
cially secure university, valid for a lifetime: a special report."
CAUT Bull. ACPU 24 (Sept. 1976) 16-22, 25.

"Unfair dismissal at Lakehead." CAUT Bull. ACPU 24 (Sept. 1976)
30-33.

1978   Horn, M. "Academics and Canadian social and economic policy in the
depression and war years." Jour. Can. Studies 13, 4 (Winter 1978-
79) 3-10.

Thompson, M. "Seniority in the university." CAUT Bull. ACPU 25
(Feb. 1978) 12-13.

1979   "Academic freedom and tenure; a CAUT special report." CAUT Bull.
ACPU 26 (Sept '79) 15-24.

1980   Horn, M. "Free speech within the law: the letter of the sixty-eight
Toronto professors, 1931." Ontario Hist. 72 (March 1980) 27-48.

Smith, J.P. "Academic freedom and institutional autonomy", in
Critical issues facing Ontario universities: papers presented at a
seminar April 17, 1980. Toronto: Higher Education Group, Ontario
Institute for Studies in Education, 1980. p. 9-35.

D. SALARY AND BENEFITS/SALAIRES ET AVANTAGES

1967   Smith, M. "CAUT policy statement on sabbatical leave/Declaration de
principes sur les régimes de congé sabbatique." CAUT Bull. ACPU 16
(Oct. 1967) 102-108.

1970   Bird, R.M. "Tax reform and the university professor." OCUFA Newsletter 3 (Jan. 1970) 4-5.

Canadian Association of University Teachers. "Brief on taxation."
CAUT Bull. ACPU 19 (Autumn 1970) 31-50.

Hanly, C.M. "Salary action at the provincial level." OCUFA Newsletter
3 (Jan. 1970) 10-13.

Hanly, C.M. "Salary policy." OCUFA Newsletter 4 (Sept. 1970) 5-7.

1972   Winch, D.M. "Council approves joint committee report on pensions."
OCUFA Newsletter 6 (Dec. 1972) 3.

Woods, S. "Tenure: do professors need lifetime job security?" Univ.
Aff./Aff. univ. 13 (Apr. 1972) 5-6.

1973 Harrington, W.E. "Report on a survey of librarians' vacation, study
      leave and other conditions of work." CACUL Newsletter 4 (Apr. 1973)
      694-699.

      Hebdon, C. "Some financial aspects of planning for retirement."
      OCUFA Newsletter 6 (Feb. 1973) 3.

      Trotter, B., D.L. McQueen and B.L. Hansen. "The ten-o'clock scholar?
      what a professor does for his pay." CAUT Bull. ACPU 21 (Jan. 1973)
      4-10.

1974 Tracz, G.S. Research into academic manpower and salary issues: a
      select bibliography. Toronto: Ontario Institute for Studies in Edu-
      cation, 1974. 35 p.

1977 Schrank, W.E. "Sex discrimination in faculty salaries." Can. Jour.
      Econ. 10 (Aug. 1977) 411-433.

      Sida, D. "Faculty economic benefits: some observations." CAUT Bull.
      ACPU 25 (Apr. 1977) 11-12.

1978 Smith, L.B. and N. Choudhry. "Academic salaries in economics and the
      returns to academic productivity: a case study." Can. Jour. Econ.
      11 (Aug. 1978) 603-613.

1979 Balzarini, D. "The economic state of the academic profession." CAUT
      Bull. ACPU. 26 (Oct '79) 36-35.

      Tausig, C. "Women academics: little change in status over past
      decade." Univ. aff./Aff. univ. 20, 9 (1979) 2-3.

      E. COLLECTIVE BARGAINING/NÉGOCIATIONS COLLECTIVES

1972 Adell, B. Collective bargaining for university faculty in Canada.
      Kingston: Industrial Relations Centre, Queen's University, 1972. 95
      p.

      Monahan, A. "Collective bargaining – the issue for the 70s." Univ.
      Aff./Aff. univ. 13 (Nov. 1972) 10.

      Proulx, P.-P. "La syndicalisation et ses effets en milieu universi-
      taire." Univ. Aff./Aff. univ. 13 (fév. 1972) 2-3.

1973 Brazeau, J. "Syndicalisation chez les professeurs: quelques causes
      et certaines conséquences." Univ. Aff./Aff. univ. 14 (Nov. 1973)
      5-6.

Chung, J.H. "Le syndicalisme des professeurs d'université: quelques réflexions." Relations Ind. 28 (1973) 325-341.

Friedmann, K.A. "Collective bargaining in Calgary?" CAUT Bull. ACPU 21 (Mar. 1973) 14-15.

Pommez, M.-C. The formation of bargaining units: the problems of exclusion and inclusion; a few problems arising from legislation and the labour code. Ottawa: Can. Assoc. of University Teachers, 1973. 16 p.

Pommez, M.-C. "La syndicalisation des professeurs d'université: suggestions et mises en garde." CAUT Bull. ACPU 21 (Apr. 1973) 18-23.

Pommez, M.-C. "Tour d'horizon - les syndicats des professeurs." Univ. Aff./Aff. univ. 14 (Sept. 1973) 5.

Savage, D.C. "Professional societies and trade unions: the Canadian experience in higher education." CAUT Bull. ACPU 21 (Mar. 1973) 4-5.

1974 "Academic collective bargaining: some models." OCUFA Newsletter 8 (Sept. 1974) 4-5, 8.

Bairstow, F. "Some implications of unionization of faculty." Univ. Aff./Aff. univ. 15 (Oct. 1974) 9-10.

Bélanger, G. "La syndicalisation des professeurs d'université." Relations Ind. 29 (1974) 857-864.

Bigelow, C. "The affiliation question: the CAUT or another central union?" CAUT Bull. ACPU 23 (Sept. 1974) 18.

Debicki, M. "Vademecum of a campus unionizer." CAUT Bull. ACPU 23 (Sept. 1974) 14-17.

George, D.V. "Collective bargaining - the management rights issue." Univ. Aff./Aff. univ. 15 (Nov. 1974) 8-9.

"Guidelines on collective bargaining/Directions en matière de négociation collective." CAUT Bull. ACPU 23 (Sept. 1974) 19.

Pommez, M.-C. "Le syndicalisme dans les universités: francophones vs anglophones." CAUT Bull. ACPU 23 (Sept. 1974) 12-14.

Pommez, M.-C. "What is a union?" CAUT Bull. ACPU 23 (Oct. 1974) 21-22.

Rachar, R. "Collective bargaining in Ontario Colleges of Applied Arts and Technology: an employee view point." CAUT Bull. ACPU 23 (Dec. 1974) 23-24.

Sanguinetti, S., and D. Kelgard. "Collective bargaining in B.C. community colleges - the first steps." CAUT Bull. ACPU 23 (Dec. 1974) 13-14.

Savage, D.C. "Collective bargaining: the state of the nation." CAUT Bull. ACPU 23 (Sept. 1974) 10-12.

Serediak, M.S. and M.V. Roberts. "Collective bargaining in Alberta colleges." CAUT Bull. ACPU 23 (Dec. 1974) 17-20.

Ward, E. "Librarians and unions: the St. Mary's experience." Can. Lib. Jour. 31 (June 1974) 238-240.

1975 Beatty, D.M. "La négociation collective pour les professeurs d'université: le pour et le contre." Relations Ind. 30 (1975) 707-723.

Boivin, J. "La négociation collective chez les professeurs d'université." Relations Ind. 30 (1975) 674-702.

Carter, D. "Collective bargaining in Canadian colleges and universities: some unresolved dilemmas." Relations Ind. 30 (1975) 662-673.

Schroeder, J. "The bargaining unit for the academic librarian." Can. Lib. Jour. 32 (Dec. 1975) 463-473.

1975 Woods, H.D. "Collective bargaining and academic freedom: are they compatible?" Relations Ind. 30 (1975) 643-657.

1976 Dorais, L. "The future of the community of scholars." AUCC Proc. 1 (1976) 37-41.

Savage, D. "Exigency and the Carleton collective agreement." CAUT Bull. ACPU 24 (Sept. 1976) 23.

1977 Bowen, D. "On being locked out of C.A.U.T." CAUT Bull. ACPU 25 (Apr. 1977) 10.

Cinman, I. "Government lauches attach on basic faculty rights." CAUT Bul. ACPU 25, 5 (1977) 1.

"Copyright." (draft model clauses on copyright for collective agreements) CAUT Bul. ACPU 25, 6 (1977) 12-13.

Côté, F. "Première convention collective pour les professeurs de Laval." Univ. Aff./Aff. univ. 18 (Feb. 1977) 5, 7.

"Faculty collective bargaining at Canadian post-secondary institutions/Négociations collectives des professeurs des institutions postsecondaires au Canada." Univ. Aff./Aff. univ. 8 (May 1977) 15.

Sullivan, N. "Governments legislate against faculty unionization."
Univ. aff./Aff. univ. 18 (Nov. 1977) 2.

Sullivan, N. "Mediation ends in agreement at Laval." Univ. Aff./
Aff. univ. 18 (Feb. 1977) 4.

Le syndicalisme universitaire et l'État: un collectif d'universitaires. Montréal: Editions Hurtubise, 1977. 208 p.

1978 Black, E. "Affiliation with the C.L.C. - the logical culmination of
the unionization of university faculty." CAUT Bull. ACPU 25 (Feb.
1978) 10-11.

Coté, A. "Laval University: one year after the strike." CAUT Bull.
ACPU 25 (Feb. 1978) 15.

Eadie, T. "Librarians and collective bargaining." CAUT Bull. ACPU
25 (Feb. 1978) 13-14, 19.

Lowe, R. "Government policy vs. bargaining rights." CAUT Bull. ACPU
25 (Feb. 1978) 11, 17, 21.

Mount, J. "Faculty status at Laurentian - two years later." Can.
Lib. Jour. 35 (Dec. 1978) 427-431.

Penner, R. "Collective bargaining: the next ten years." CAUT Bull.
ACPU 25 (Feb. 1978) 9.

Savage, D.C. "Collective bargaining: where are we now?" CAUT Bull.
ACPU 25 (Feb. 1978) 7-8.

Smith, J.E. "Non-certified agreements: the Toronto approach." CAUT
Bull. ACPU 25 (Feb. 1978) 16.

Thompson, M. "Seniority in the university." CAUT Bull. ACPU 25
(Feb. 1978) 12-13.

1979 Black, E. "Social relations and collective bargaining in the university; Brandon: a case study." CAUT Bull. ACPU 26 (Dec '79) 15-18.

Chaison, G.N. "The certification campaign at the University of New
Brunswick." CAUT Bull. ACPU 26 (Oct '79) 17-20.

Landry, S. "Impacts of university professors' unionization on roles
and role perceptions of a group of selected participants: the case of
the University of Ottawa." Ph.D. thesis, Univ. of Toronto, 1979.

Sim, V. "Dispute at Acadia comes to a close." CAUT Bull. ACPU 26
(Oct '79) 7-8.

1980 Association des universités et collèges du Canada. Bureau d'information sur la négociation collective. Index des sentences arbitrales en matière de droits pour les professeurs des universités Canadiennes: 1976-1980. Ottawa: AUCC, 1980. 55p.

Association of Universities and Colleges of Canada/Association des universités et collèges du Canada. Index to interest arbitration awards for Canadian university faculty/Index des sentences arbitrales en matière d'interets pour les professeurs des universités Canadiennes 1972-1980. Ottawa: AUCC, 1980. 5 leaves

Association of Universities and Colleges of Canada. Collective Bargaining Information Office. Index to rights arbitration awards for Canadian university faculty: 1976-1980. Ottawa: AUCC, 1980. 54p.

II -- NON-DEGREE GRANTING INSTITUTIONS
ETABLISSEMENTS QUI NE CONFERENT PAS DE GRADE

---

1. GENERAL/GÉNÉRALITÉS

1970 Anden, A. "A national body for community colleges, but vive les différences." Can. Univ. & Coll. 5 (Nov. 1970) 15-16.

1971 Campbell, G. "Balancing control and independence in college government." Can. Univ. & Coll. 6 (Jan.-Feb. 1971) 30-33.

Campbell, G. "Canadian community colleges: progress and problems." Convergence 4, 3 (1971) 78-85.

Campbell, G. The community college in Canada: an annotated bibliography. Calgary: Univ. of Calgary, 1971. 80 p.

Campbell, G. Community colleges in Canada. Toronto: Ryerson McGraw-Hill, 1971. 346 p.

Oureshi, M. "Academic status, salaries and fringe benefits in community college libraries of Canada." Can. Library Jour. 28 (Jan.-Feb. 1971) 41-45.

Pardoen, A. "Techniques policières au CEGEP." Educ. Q. I (23 juin 1971) 4-6.

Stamp, R.M. "Technical education, the national policy and federal-provincial relations in Canadian education, 1899-1919." Can. Hist. Rev. 52 (1971) 404-423.

Stinson, A. "Striving to meet the challenges of community needs." Can. Univ. & Coll. 6 (May–June 1971) 44–48, 57.

Whitelaw, J.H. "From CEGEP to university: problems of articulation in Quebec." Can. Univ. & Coll. 6 (Mar.-Apr. 1971) 52–55.

1972 Aubin, G. "Le collège des années 80: les besoins éducatifs." Prospectives 8 (déc. 1972) 395–400.

Dennison, J. and A. Tunner. The impact of community colleges: report #1, bibliography. Rev. edition. Vancouver: B.C. Research, 1972. 152 p.

Foucher, R. "La satisfaction des étudiants: une composante importante de l'apprentissage." Prospectives 8 (mars 1972) 67–87.

Gagné, F. "Perceptions étudiantes concernant l'utilisation des techniques audio-visuelles au niveau collégial." Prospectives 8 (mai 1972) 183–93.

Marcotte, P., et L. Pineau. "Une proposition d'accréditation d'activités parascolaires." Prospectives 8 (sept. 1972) 291–301.

1973 Canada. Statistics Canada. Education, Science and Culture Division. Education in Canada: a statistical review for the period 1960–61 to 1970–71. Ottawa: Information Canada, 1973. 613 p.

Gingras, P.-E. "Place aux sciences humaines." Prospectives 9 (avril 1973) 104–107.

Konrad, A.G. "Staff development in Western Canadian colleges." Stoa 3 (1973) 47–52.

1974 Angers, P. "Le projet éducatif de l'étudiant et les objectifs des programmes", Prospectives 10 (fév. 1974) 8–23.

Konrad, A.G., ed. Clientele and community: the student in the Canadian junior college. Toronto: Assoc. of Can. Community Colleges, 1974. 158 p.

Konrad, A.G. La clientèle du collège communautaire. Toronto: L'Association des collèges communautaires du Canada, 1974. 183 p.

1975 Garry, C. Administrative and curricular changes in a Canadian community college. Montreal: Can. Sociology & Anthropology Assoc. 1975. 61 p.

1976 Dufresne, J. "Le temps perdu à la recherche." Prospectives 12 (avril 1976) 115–119.

Konrad, A.G. "College trustees examine their role." Can. Admin. 16 (Nov. 1976) 5-

Marshall, J. "Library technician programs." Can. Library Jour. 33 (June 1976) 273-289.

1977 Angel, M.R. and G.R. Brown. "Survey of library technician programs in Canada. Can. Library Jour. 34 (Feb. 1977) 41-55.

des Grossilliers, P. "A la recherche d'une philosophie de l'education pour le niveau collegial: eduquer ou instruire les CEGEPians." Journal of the ACCC/Journal de l'ACCC 1 (Spring 1977) 77-93.

Giroux, R.F. The instructional revolution: implications for educational leaders. Jour. A.C.C.C./Jour. A.C.C.C. 1 (Spring 1977) 1-14.

Konrad, A.G. "Clientele and community: issues in Canadian post-secondary education." Jour. Assoc. Can. Community Coll. 1 (Spring 1977) 32-47.

Konrad, A.G. "Profile of community college trustees." Can. Jour. Educ. 2 (1977) 65-77.

Konrad, A.G. "College trustees view their selection." Alta. Jour. Educ. Res. 23 (1977) 138-150.

McRoberts, S. "New federal-provincial funding arrangements announced for education." College Canada 2, 7 (1977) 5-6.

Simard, M. "La 'pedagogie de situation' comme modele pedogogique de la formation et du perfectionnement des professeurs des collèges communautaires." Jour. ACCC 1 (Spring 1977) 64-76.

Thompson, S.D. "Career mobility; a community college nursing program." Jour. Assoc. Can. Community Coll. 1 (Fall 1977) 11-28.

1978 Dennison, J.D. University transfer program in the community college." Can. Jour. Higher Educ. 8, 2 (1978) 27-38.

Gartley, W. "Co-op education aids in student placement." College Canada 4 (Jan. 1979) 24.

1979 Demicell, J.A. "The problem of student diversity in community colleges." English Q. 12 (Fall 1979) 67-71.

Dennison, J. "Penitentiary education in Canada - the role for community colleges." Jour. A.C.C.C. 3 (Summer 1979) 12-23.

Gallagher, P. "Examining organizational mlyths: an administration's approach to institutional renewal." Jour. A.C.C.C. 3 (Autumn 1979) 83-99.

Gordon, R. "Organizational growth and development and the national association." Jour. A.C.C.C. 3 (Autumn 1979) 13-27.

Konrad, A. and J. Small. "Institutional renewal: a planning mechanism for the 1980's." Jour. A.C.C.C. 3 (Autumn 1979) 1-11.

Laurent, I. "L'animation un souffle de vie dans l'administration d'un collège." Jour. A.C.C.C. 3 (Autumn 1979) 101-112.

Nelson, S. "Literacy and the aims of community colleges." Jour. A.C.C.C. 3 (Autumn 1979) 115-140.

"Student services in Canadian community colleges: the current state of the art." JOur. A.C.C.C. 3 (Spring 1979) entire issue.

Tolley, G. Community colleges in Canada: report of a visit ... March 1978. Sheffield: Sheffield City Polytechnic, 1979. 28 p.

Weihs, J. "Survey of library technician programs in Canada." Can. Library Jour. 36 (Dec. 1979) 354.362.

Wragg, G. "Division of postsecondary provincial funding between colleges/universities; a letter to the editor." College Canada 4 (June 1979) 3.

1980 "Governance & administration in Canadian community colleges: theory and practice." Jour. A.C.C.C. 4, 1 & 2 (Winter/Spring 1980) entire issue.

Terry, J. "Atlantic Canada's community colleges." College Canada 5, 2 (1980) 18-20.

2. NEWFOUNDLAND/TERRE-NEUVE

1977 Sainty, G. "The community college in Newfoundland/Le collège à Terre-Neuve." College Can. 2 (April 1977) 6-7.

3. PRINCE EDWARD ISLAND/ILE-DU-PRINCE-EDOUARD

1978 "Holland College develops marine training program." College Canada 3 (Sept. 1978) 4.

MacDonald, H. "PEI's Holland College Institute provides leadership training." College Canada 3 (Nov. 1977) 12-13.

1980   Bennett, G.   "Ten years later."   College Canada   5 (Jan. 80) 11.

4.   NOVA SCOTIA/NOUVELLE-ECOSSE

1976   MacNeil, K.   "College of Cape Breton, an educational innovator."
       College Canada   1 (Nov. 1976) 1, 10.

       MacNeil, K.   "Le Collège du Cap Breton."   College Canada   1 (Nov.
       1976) 1, 7.

1977   Jala, T.   "Far East comes down east at College of Cape Breton."
       College Canada   2 (May 1977) 3, 14-15.

1979   MacDonald, S.   "Centre for International Studies started by College
       of Cape Breton."   College Canada   4 (Feb. 1979) 17.

5.   NEW BRUNSWICK/NOUVEAU-BRUNSWICK

1974   Costello, E.P.   "A report on the Saint John Mechanics Institute,
       1838-1890."   M.A. thesis, Univ. of New Brunswick, 1974.

1977   New Brunswick Community College unveils mobile hospitality training
       unit."   College Canada   2 (Feb. 1977) 10.

1979   Murphy, T.   "Woodstock's community college."   Atlantic Advocate
       (September 1979) 50-53.

6.   QUEBEC/QUÉBEC

1970   Bellavance, A.   "La fonction du directeur des services pédagogiques
       de CEGEP dans la province de Québec." M.A. thesis, Univ. de Montréal,
       1970.

       Côté, M.   "L'image de la philosophie chez les étudiants du CEGEP."
       M.A. thesis, Univ. de Montréal, 1970.

       Gagné, F.   "La recherche pédagogique au niveau collégial."   Act. Péd.
       15 (juin 1970) 39-61.

       Thibault, M.   "Etudiants et professeurs: combien sont-ils dans les
       institutions privées et les CEGEP?"   Prospectives. 6 (fév. 1970) 8-15.

1971   Crépeau, J.-C. "PERPE: Une évaluation scientifique de l'enseignement
       collégial."   Educ. Q.   13 (mars 1971) 4-8.

       Pelletier, D.   "Le rapport Roquet: un complément au rapport Parent."
       Educ. Q.   I (26 mai 1971) 22-24.

Watson, C. Innovations in higher education: a Canadian case study.
Paris, OECD, 1971. 453 p.

1972 Denis, A. and J. Lipkin. "Quebec's CEGEPS: promise and reality."
McGill Jour. Educ. 7 (Fall 1972) 119-34.

Escande, C. "L'entrée au C.E.G.E.P.: étude sociologique sur l'orientation des étudiants. Thèse de doctorat, Univ. de Québec à Montréal,
1972.

Gallagher, P. "Power and participation in educational reform."
McGill Jour. Educ. 7 (Fall 1972) 149-65.

Henchey, N. Quebec education: the unfinished revolution." McGill
Jour. Educ. 7 (Fall 1972) 95-118.

LeBlanc, A.E. "La coopération entre les collèges anglophones."
Prospectives 8 (déc. 1972) 365-71.

Maheu, R. "La clientèle de niveau collégial par régions." Prospectives 8 (déc. 1972) 380-393.

1973 Le CEGEP 5 ans après, succès ou échec. Montréal-Nord, Les Grandes
Editions du Québec, 1973. 96 p.

Denis, A. et J. Lipkin. "Le CEGEP: promesse et réalité." Prospectives 9 (fév. 1973) 14-23.

Gadbois, L. "A propos d'une relance des sortants de l'enseignement
collégial (1970-1971)." Prospectives 9 (sépt. 1973) 208-219.

Pelletier-Baillargeon, H. "L'exode vers les collèges privés; l'échec
de la participation scolaire." Maintenant 123 (fév. 1973) 10-13.

Rivet, D. "Perception par les professeurs de CEGEP des habiletés
pédagogiques nécessaires à l'enseignement des techniques infirmières." M.A. thesis, Univ. de Montréal, 1973.

1974 Aubin, G. "Recherche prévisionnelle sur l'enseignement collégial au
Québec." Prospectives 10 (juin 1974) 213-23.

Aubin, G. et M. Girard. Recherche prévisionnelle sur l'enseignement
collégial au Québec. Montréal, CADRE, 1974. 102 p.

Diamant, R. "Relations entre élémentaire, secondaire, collégial et
universitaire." Prospectives 10 (Oct. 1974) 226-229.

Farine, A. "Demographic and social accounting: a follow-up on the
withdrawals from Quebec colleges." Can. Admin. 13 (Jan. 1974) 19-22.

Gagnon, M. "Disparue depuis Gutenberg, la formation pédagogique de l'universitaire réapparaît." Prospectives 10 (avr. 1974) 133-140.

Lebel, M. "Succès ou faillite du CEGEP." Mém. SRC 1974. 147-178.

Lipkin, J.P. "The 'academic tilt' in Quebec post-secondary education." Can. & International Educ. 3 (June 1974) 53-60.

Muller-Hehn, A. "Analyse historique des objectifs pédagogiques de l'enseignement du français dans les cours communs au CEGEP." M.A. thesis, Univ. de Montréal, 1974.

Paré, L. "De l'enseignement collégial à la coopération avec l'Afrique." Educ. Q. 4 (mars 1974) 27-31.

1975 Angers, P. "Le Collège": un rapport audacieux et réfléchi; le rapport Nadeau. Relations 35 (déc. 1975) 327-332.

Crescenty, J.-C. "Définition d'un enseignement professionnel pour faire du CEGEP une unité plus cohérente." M.A. thesis, Univ. de Montréal, 1975.

Le Roux, J. & D. Campeau. "Un nouveau mode d'intervention éducative auprès des adultes au niveau collégial: la formation sur mesure." Prospectives 11 (déc. 1975) 293-302.

Lucier, P. "Le Collège": des visées prospectives à déployer; le rapport Nadeau. Relations 35 (déc. 1975) 333-338.

Longtin, J. & J.-P. Masse. "Une approche systémique de l'enseignement au niveau collégial; L'enseignement télévisé modulaire." Prospectives 11 (fév. 1975) 15-22.

1976 Greenberg, A. et al. "Au CEGEP Vanier: kaléidoscope un nouveau cadre d'apprentissage." Prospectives 12 (avril 1976) 75-81.

Laberge, P.-E. et R. Raymond. "Au cégep de Rimouski: l'étude des sciences humaines dans un programme de techniques infirmières." Prospectives 12 (avril 1976) 95-99.

Monette, G. "Au CEGEP du Veux Montréal: l'expérience du multi." Prospectives 12 (avril 1976) 83-87.

Morand, J.-M. "Au cégep de Limoilou: accréditation d'activités d'apprentissage hors cours. Prospectives 12 (avril 1976) 110-114.

1977 Des Groseillers, P. "A la recherche d'une philosophie de l'éducation pour le niveau collégial: éduquer ou instruire les CEGEPiens?" Jour. Assoc. Coll. Communautaires Can. 1 (printemps 1977) 77-93.

Nemiroff, G. "The new school of Dawson College: a humanistic alternative." College Canada 2 (May 1977) 2, 6-7, 16.

Simard, M. "'La pédagogie de situation' comme modèle pédagogique de la formation et du perfectionnement des professeurs des collèges communautaires." Jour. Assoc. Coll. communautaires Canada. 1 (printemps 1977) 64-76.

Stubbs, P. "Anglophone CEGEP - mosaic or maelstrom?" College Canada 2 (May 1977) 4.

1978 Kazi, S. "CEGEPs are thriving after ten years." College Canada 3 (Mar. 1978) 2-3.

Pantazis, F. "Library technicians in Ontario academic libraries." Can. Library Jour. 35 (April 1978) 77-91.

1979 Gingras, P.-E. "C.A.D.R.E.-l'institutionnelle." Jour. A.C.C.C. 3 (Autumn 1979) 61-81.

1981 Sénéchal, M. "Le Cégep milieu de vie." Prospectives 17 (fév. 1981) 44-46.

7. ONTARIO

1970 Commission on Post-Secondary Education in Ontario. Post-secondary education in Ontario: a statement of issues. Toronto: The Commission, 1970. 20 p.

Kelly, D.A.G. "A study of the student population at an Ontario college of applied arts and technology between 1967-69 with an analysis of factors relating to academic success." Ed.D. thesis, Univ. of Toronto, 1970.

1971 Canadian Library Association. "Brief to the Commission on Post-Secondary education in Ontario." Can. Library Jour. 28 (July-Aug. 1971) 310.

"George Brown's modular system: room to grow in a crowded city." Can. Univ. & Coll. 6 (July-Aug. 1971) 20-21, 32.

Jacobs, D.E. The Community college and their communities: a report of the Community Colleges Committee, Ontario Association for Continuing Education. Toronto: The Association, 1971. 56 p.

Ontario Dept. of Education. School Planning and Building Research Section. Colleges of applied arts and technology: planning for change. Toronto: The Dept., 1971. 32 p.

Skolnik, M.L. and G.S. Tracz. Technology, education and employment – a study of interactions. Part II: A micro-model of the production and use of technicians. Toronto: OISE, 1971. 200 p.

Watson, C. Innovations in higher education: a Canadian case study. Paris: OECD, 1971. 453 p.

1972 D'Costa, R.B. Post-secondary educational opportunities for the Ontario Francophone population. Toronto: Queen's Printer, 1972. 109 p.

Environics Research Group. Post-secondary educational opportunity for the Ontario Indian population. Toronto: Queen's Printer, 1972. 238 p.

Sterling Institute Canada Ltd. Manpower retraining programs in Ontario. Toronto: Queen's Printer, 1972. 195 p.

"Storefront campus." School Progress 41 (Feb. 1972) 24-25.

Systems Research Group. The Ontario Colleges of Applied Arts and Technology. Toronto: Queen's Printer, 1972. 149 p. (Study prepared for the Commission on Post-secondary Education in Ontario.)

1973 Dupre, J.S. et al. Federalism and policy development: the case of adult occupational training in Ontario. Toronto: U. of T. Press, 1973. 264 p.

1974 Ontario. Ministry of Colleges and Universities. Annual survey of 1971 graduates of the Colleges of Applied Art & Technology. Toronto: The Ministry, 1974. 19 p.

1975 Blackwood, T. "Teaching reading at the community college. English Quart. 8 (Fall 1975) 21-28.

1976 Colvin, J.A. "Centralism: threat to colleges." College Canada 1 (Oct. 1976) 4-5.

Colvin, J.A. "More local autonomy College president urges." College Canada 1 (Nov. 1976) 4-5.

Desroches, J.J. "The concepts of and determinants of job satisfaction: an exploratory study in the colleges of applied arts and technology in Ontario." Ph.D. thesis, Univ. of Toronto, 1976.

Dutchak, P.E. College with a purpose: Kemptville. Belleville, Ont.: Mike Publishing, 1976. 176 p.

1977 Christianson, P. "St. Lawrence Learning Centre: a model for the future." College Canada 2 (May 1977) 10, 13, 15.

Franklyn, G. "Academic, social and value orientations at a community college in Ontario." Jour. Assoc. Can. Community Coll. 1 (Spring 1977) 15-31.

Graham, J. "Centennial College: a decade of growth." College Canada 2 (Nov. 1977) 1.

Park, M. "Ontario CAATs: the first 10 years." College Canada 2 (Nov. 1977) 1, 5.

Wheeler, G.W.B. Centennial College: the early years. Scarborough, Ont.: Centennial College, 1977. 128 p.

1978 Desroches, J. "Authority conflict in relation to the job satisfaction of Ontario CAAT's instructors." Can. Jour. Higher Educ. 8, 1 (1978) 33-46.

Isabelle, L. "Bilingual education in the CAATS/Education des franco-ontariens dans le système collegial en Ontario." College Canada 3 (Feb/fév 1977) 9-10.

Jones, C. "Ontario MCU promotes apprenticeship training." College Canada 3 (Jan. 1978) 5.

Jones, C. "La remise en valeur de l'apprentissage." College Canada 3 (janv. 1978) 6.

Preddie, C. "Education for the whole person." College Canada 3 (Mar. 1978) 5.

1979 Buchar, F. "Training forestry filers the modern way at Northern College." College Canada 4 Mar '79) 8-9.

"Cambrian College: serving the Studbury district." College Canada 4 (Mar '79) 12-13.

King, A. "CAPRI: an institutional self-evaluation system." Jour. A.C.C.C. Coll. 3 (Autumn 1979) 141-158.

Picot, J. "Toronto Institute of Medical Technology: meeting the needs of medical technology." College Canada 4 (May 1979) 12-13.

Van Nest, P. and W. Warren. "The implementation of CAPRI at St. Lawrence College." Jour. A.C.C.C. 3 (Autumn 1979) 159-175.

1980 Chouinard, N. "The present physical education programs in the community colleges of Ontario." Can. H.P.E.R. Jour. 47 (Sept.-Oct. 1980) 39-42.

Pascal, C.E. ed. The year of the C.A.A.T. Toronto: Committee of Presidents, Assoc. of Colleges of Applied Arts and Technology of Ontario, 1980. 151 p.

Peszat, L. "The development of health science education programs in Metropolitan Toronto region Colleges of Applied Arts and Technology, 1967-1977: a study of selected factors influencing their development." doctoral thesis, University of Toronto, 1980.

8. MANITOBA

1967 Manitoba Educational Research Council. Report on post-secondary education needs and training in Manitoba. Part 1: the social and economic structure. Winnipeg, 1967. 215 p.

1973 Manitoba Task Force on Post-Secondary Education. Position papers. no. 3. "The community colleges." Winnipeg, 1973. 35 p.

1978 Gregor, A. "University-college relationships: the Manitoba experience." Paper presented at the 1978 Conference of the Society for the Study of Higher Education, London, Ont. 17 leaves (typescript).

9. SASKATCHEWAN

1972 Faris, R. "Community college development in Saskatchewan: a unique approach." Can. Forum 51 (Oct.-Nov. 1972) 60-61.

Saskatchewan. Dept. of Continuing Education. Report of the Minister's Advisory Committee on Community Colleges. Regina, The Department, 1972. 64 p.

1977 Browne, G. "SRCC: college responsiveness with a non-traditional look." College Canada 2 (Apr. 1977) 3.

Browne, G. "Saskatoon Region C.C. spécialité: l'éducation populaire." College Canada 2 (av. 1977) 1, 3.

"L'Education en Saskatchewan: pas de campus comme tel." College Canada 2 (av. 1977) 5.

Faris, D. "The College in Saskatchewan: where community is campus." College Canada 2 (Ap. 1977) 4.

1979 Dyck, E. "The Saskatchewan Technical Institute." College Canada 4 (Jan. 1979) 12-13.

Rothery, A. "New parts marketing program piloted at Kelsey Institute." College Canada 4 (Feb. 1979) 10.

10. ALBERTA

1968 Hanson, E.J. <u>Population analysis and projections college areas in Alberta</u>. Edmonton: Provincial Board of Post Secondary Education, 1968. 112 p.

1970 Berghoffer, D.F. "General education in post-secondary non-university educational institutions in Alberta." M. Ed. thesis, Univ. of Alberta, 1970.

Gordon, P.A. "Student services in Alberta colleges." M.Ed. thesis, Univ. of Calgary, 1970.

Martin, R.H. "Future issues in co-ordinating Alberta post-secondary education." M.Ed. thesis, Univ. of Alberta, 1970.

1971 Watson, C. <u>Innovations in higher education: a Canadian case study</u>. Paris: O.E.C.D. 1971. 453 p.

1972 Committee of Inquiry into non-Canadian influence in Alberta post-secondary education. <u>Report</u>. Edmonton: 1972. 139 p.

1974 Fast, R.G. <u>Red Deer College: the critical years: report of the administrator of Red Deer College</u>. Red Deer, 1974. 52 p.

1977 "Grant MacEwan Community College." <u>College Canada</u> 2 (Sept. 1977) 7.

Red Deer College: serving Central Alberta." <u>College Canada</u> 2 (Oct. 1977) 1.

Well, C.V. "Alberta colleges: a product of their times." <u>College Canada</u> 2 (Sept. 1977) 1, 9.

1978 "Mount Royal College." <u>College Canada</u> 3 (Ap. 1978) 1, 11.

"Old Sun College." <u>College Canada</u> 3 (Ap. 1978) 1, 8.

1979 Wieler, D. "Regional commitment and the community college at Grande Prairie Regional College." <u>College Canada</u> 4 (Mar. 1979) 10-11.

11. BRITISH COLUMBIA/COLOMBIE-BRITANNIQUE

1970 Jansen, D. "How big is enough? Vancouver City College moves on to its new campus." <u>Can. Univ. & Coll.</u> 5 (Sept. 1970) 38-39.

1971 Dennison, J.D. "The colleges of British Columbia: some basic issues." <u>Stoa</u> 1 (1971) 27-33.

Dennison, J.D. and A. Tunner. The impact of community colleges. Vancouver: B.C. Research, 1971-74. 11 vols.

1. Bibliography of community colleges, 1972. 141p.
2. Socio-economic survey, 1972. 63p.
3. Opinion questionnaire, 1972. 141p.
4. Academic background and ability of college students, 1972.
5. Health survey, 1972. 58p.
6. Survey of grade 12 students, 1972.
7. Post-secondary student survey, 1973. 92p.
8. Survey of grade 12 students, 1973. 34p.
9. Community survey - a pilot project, 1973. 62p.
10. Survey of college faculty, 1973.
11. College-university articulation study, 1974.

Dennison, J.D. and G. Jones. A socio-economic study of college students. Vancouver: Academic Board for Higher Education in British Columbia, 1971. 26 p.

1972   Dennison, J.D. and A. Tunner. The impact of community colleges. (rev). Vancouver: B.C. Research, 1972. 141 p.

1974   Royal Commission on Post-secondary Education in the Kootenay Region. Report. Nelson, B.C., 1974. 133 p.

1975   Marsh, L. "Learning community for the Lower Mainland: report of the survey committee on community colleges in the Lower Mainland, British Columbia. Victoria, B.C. Dept. of Education, 1975. 119 p.

1977   Dennison, J.D. "B.C. Colleges Act heralds new era." College Canada 2 (Oct. 1977) 3.

Forsythe, K. "North Island College: its 'community' spans 26,000 square miles." College Canada 2 (Feb. 1977) 4.

Leach, B. "Environmental education at Douglas College." College Canada 2 (May 1977) 4-5.

Marvin, J. "Aboriginal Studies at Northwest C.C.: a unique offering." College Canada 2 (Nov. 1977) 3.

McMullan, P. "Malaspina College: meeting the needs of its community." College Canada 2 (Mar. 1977) 1,15.

1978   "B.C. colleges experience era of rapid growth." College Canada 3 (Feb. 1978) 1-2.

1978   Forsythe, K. "Long distance education a challenge for teacher at North Island College." College Canada 3 (Feb. 1978) 8.

1979 Clark, K. "Retail fashion programme at Capilano College meets needs of Vancouver clothing industry." College Canada 4 (May 1979) 10, 14.

Clark, K. "Unique health education centre established by Douglas College." College Canada 4 (Feb. 1979) 14, 23.

Dennison, J.D. "The community college in comparative and historical perspective: the development of the college concept in British Columbia." Can. Jour. Higher Educ. 9 (3) 19-28.

Fisher, G. "Institutional evaluation at Camosum." Jour. A.C.C.C. 3 (Autumn 1979) 41-60.

Forsythe, K. "North Island College: an idea creating its reality." Jour. A.C.C.C. 3 (Summer 1979) 01-88.

Fraser, B. "Educational program planning in British Columbia: the context for institutional renewal." Jour. A.C.C.C. 3 (Autumn 1979) 29-39.

McMullan, P. "Malaspina College plays major training role in West Coast forest industry." College Canada 4 (April 1979) 12-13.

Lightning Source UK Ltd.
Milton Keynes UK
UKHW010002210722
406167UK00001B/211